THE WAR FOR RIGHTEOUSNESS

THE WAR FOR RIGHTEOUSNESS

Progressive Christianity, the Great War,
and the Rise of the Messianic Nation

RICHARD M. GAMBLE

ISI BOOKS
Wilmington, Del.

Library of Congress Cataloging-in-Publication Data:

Gamble, Richard M.

   The war for righteousness : progressive Christianity, the great war, and the rise of the Messianic nation / Richard Gamble. — Wilmington, Del. : ISI Books, 2003.

   p. ; cm.

   includes bibliographical references and index.

   ISBN: 1-932236-14-7
   1-932236-16-3 (pbk.)

1. Progress — Religious aspects — Christianity. 2. Christianity and politics. 3. Messianism, Political. 4. Nationalism. 5. War — Religious aspects — Christianity. 6. World War, 1914–1918. I. Title.

BR115.P77 G36 2003   2003109726
261.7—dc22   0310

Published by: ISI Books
                     Intercollegiate Studies Institute
                     P.O. Box 4431
                     Wilmington, DE 19807-0431

Interior design by Kara Beer

To my mother and father

Were I not a wandering citizen whose city is the world,
I would not weep for all that fell before the flags were furled;
I would not let one murmur mar the trumpets volleying forth
How God grew weary of the kings, and the cold hell in the north.
But we whose hearts are homing birds have heavier thoughts of home,
Though the great eagles burn with gold on Paris or on Rome,
Who stand beside our dead and stare, like seers at an eclipse,
At the riddle of the island tale and the twilight of the ships.

For these were simple men that loved with hands and feet and eyes,
Whose souls were humbled to the hills and narrowed to the skies,
The hundred little lands within one little land that lie,
Where Severn seeks the sunset isles or Sussex scales the sky.

And what is theirs, though banners blow on Warsaw risen again,
Or ancient laughter walks in gold through vineyards of Lorraine,
Their dead are marked on English stones, their lives on English trees,
How little is the prize they win, how mean a coin for these—
How small a shriveled laurel-leaf lies crumpled here and curled:
They died to save their country and they only saved the world.

—G. K. Chesterton, "The English Graves"

TABLE OF CONTENTS

Acknowledgments

More than custom and good manners prompts me to thank the people who have contributed to the research, writing, and publication of this book. It is a privilege to acknowledge my debt to those who have shaped and guided this volume over many years of labor.

From the earliest stages, John G. Sproat of the University of South Carolina provided generous and fair-minded mentoring. From his practical wisdom, he taught me never to separate style from content, and the degree to which I have lived up to that standard is due entirely to his example. Clyde Wilson, also of the University of South Carolina, has been a trusted friend whose integrity as a teacher and courage as a scholar continue to inspire me in my calling. I am also grateful to Martin Marty of the University of Chicago Divinity School for his repeated affirmation of my work at critical points in its development. Without his careful reading and penetrating suggestions, this book would not have its present form and structure. My thanks are due as well to Kendrick A. Clements, Marcia Synnott, Kevin Lewis, Elizabeth Fox-Genovese, Claes Ryn, and George Carey, all of whom read this book in various versions. Errors of fact and limitations of perception and judgment remain my own.

Financial support for this project came from the H. B. Earhart Foundation and from the Center for Study of Public Choice, George Mason University. Public Choice provided office space, a stretch of uninterrupted time, and a lively academic community in which to revise and rewrite the entire manuscript. The center's Jennifer Roback Morse, now of the Hoover Institution, twice helped a young historian stay committed to the academic life at a time when career opportunities seemed few and grim.

To Michael Federici of Mercyhurst College I offer profound thanks for many years of honest friendship, exemplary integrity, and intellectual motivation. Brooke and Mari Cadwallader and Cecilia Harrison, my kind hosts in France, have shown me warm hospitality on several excursions to the battlefields of Verdun. They have introduced my students and me to the strange beauty and haunting tragedy of the Western Front as no one else could have. Their irrepressible curiosity has stimulated my own fascination with the Western Front and deepened my abiding respect for the soldiers who fought there. This book's publication is due in no small part to their unflagging enthusiasm for the project and to their conviction that I had told a story that needed to be known.

ISI Books has been a privilege to work with from the moment of our first contact. The editors and staff at ISI conduct themselves with a professionalism that ought to serve as a model for the world of academic publishing. I am grateful to publisher Jeff Nelson for supporting this project, to editor in chief Jeremy Beer for cultivating me as an author and for skillfully shepherding this book through to completion, and to production editor Nan Halsey for her sharp editorial eye. Her grasp of the smallest nuance and detail reassured me that I was in the care of a very capable editor.

My colleagues at Palm Beach Atlantic University, both faculty and staff, have provided an academic home for me for nearly a decade. Special thanks are due to my fellow teachers in the Honors Program and in the Department of History and Political Science. Foremost among these is Carol Woodfin, who provides ballast and good humor in the unpredictable currents of academia. Students in my course on the American identity helped me ponder the long history of America's messianic self-understanding and to place American involvement in the First World War within the larger context of national experience and aspirations. A special place in my memories will always belong to the students who have accompanied me to the Western Front. They have enabled me to glimpse through fresh eyes the poignancy of the war experience and the degree of sacrifice demanded on both sides. Sam Fielder has trudged with me through miles of forests and trenches and mud. He has taught me something every step of the journey.

Finally, I wish to thank my family for many years of faithful support, love, and patience. If possible, their eager anticipation of this book's appearance has exceeded my own. I hope that the accumulated and accumulating debt of gratitude I owe to my parents is repaid, at least to a small degree, by this book's dedication.

Introduction

Wandering for miles along the narrow roads that thread their way among the modest farms and tiny villages of northeastern France, the modern pilgrim is unprepared for the dazzling spectacle of the American military cemetery of the Meuse-Argonne. Situated in a rural landscape that still bears the scars of the twentieth-century's domineering will to power, the massive cemetery blankets hundreds of perfectly manicured acres donated to the United States by a grateful France in 1918. A chapel stands at one end with a commanding view of tree-lined roads, tranquil gardens, and endless rows of thousands upon thousands of precisely aligned white crosses. Inside the chapel, a book of remembrance records the sentiments of guests, often simply saying, "*Merci pour la France.*" The ceiling and walls bear pious inscriptions promising that these men and their brave deeds will never be forgotten.

On rare sunny days in the otherwise sodden and chilly climate of this remote part of France, the marble crosses gleam with an arresting brilliance. They silently await the Judgment Day in solemn testimony to the American servicemen who died in the grim and bloody action along the Western Front, not far from the horror of Verdun, in the final autumn of the war. Scattered among the crosses are some that simply read, "Here rests in honored glory an American soldier known but to God." But most provide the soldier's name, rank, home state, and date of death. Some were killed as late as the very morning of the Armistice; others died of their wounds months later. No date of birth is given, however, obscuring just how young, how tragically young, most of these soldiers were when they fell. Despite the apparent uniformity and blended anonymity of this voiceless "democracy of the dead," these crosses bear family names from Italy, Poland, Germany, France, the British Isles, Russia, and beyond—Europe's sons returned to fight Europe's war.

The story that follows recovers part of the reason these American soldiers lie buried in France. It is not a story of military tactics, innovative weaponry, or trench life. It is not primarily an account of diplomacy and politics—although diplomats and politicians appear in these pages. Rather, it is a story of ideas, of the deepest ideas regarding purpose and meaning, and the definition of national identity and destiny at a critical moment. It is not a story about the physical landscape of the First World War, but rather about the inner landscape of one prominent group of Americans and what they imagined to be true about their God, their nation, their enemies, and the unfathomable European War of 1914 to1918. It is an attempt to map the geography of a set of ideas, to trace the use of the redemptive imagery of the cross of Christ to wage an uncompromising war for righteousness. It begins and ends with theology, and shows how one group of American pastors, theologians, seminary professors, and college presidents confronted some of the timeless problems of Christian theology in the context of total war.

The self-described "progressives" among America's Protestant clergy at the turn of the twentieth century were well known in church circles and beyond for their advanced thinking on theology, politics, and foreign affairs. As they faced the prospect of a new century, these ministers and academics thought of themselves as broad-minded, humane, and cosmo-politan, in harmony with the very best scientific, political, and theological wisdom of the age. In short, they were among the "right thinking" leaders of their day. These reformers have since been labeled "liberal" or "modernist" by historians, but the word "progressive" suited their character and their times. It was the adjective they chose to describe their vision. They were eager participants in a world marked by material progress and technological efficiency and by an increasing moral rigor and earnestness in domestic and foreign policy. The progressive clergy imagined themselves, their faith, and their nation as poised on the brink of opportunity, on the verge of an unprecedented chance to serve Humanity by spreading America's material, political, and spiritual progress.

But these clergy were also aware of standing between two worlds, as they would have described the sensation, between a receding order of tradition, conservatism, and reaction on the one hand, and an approaching order of reform, liberalism, and reconstruction on the other; between an intellectual obscurantism fraught with barbarism, depravation, and war arrayed against a coming clarity of thought that promised civilization, plenty, and peace. Within their own churches, these progressive ministers strove against theological traditionalism for the sake of a new Christianity, one that would make its peace with the modern world. The names of these clergy may have slipped from modern memory, yet they spoke for their generation's serious and urgent effort to adapt itself to the emerging world that was so quickly replacing the old.

Primarily, these religious progressives interpreted the First World War in light of their social gospel theology. The liberal clergy were not merely lackeys in the Wilson administration's attempts at social control, nor were they caught unaware and unprepared by the outbreak of the war; rather, these forward-looking clergy embraced the war as a chance to achieve their broadly defined social gospel objectives. In the same way that American imperialism at the turn of the century was, as historian William E. Leuchtenburg argued,[1] not a betrayal of domestic reform idealism but rather the expression of the same expansive, interventionist spirit on an international scale, so too the progressive clergy's enthusiasm for American participation in the Great War did not contradict their progressive theology. Their enthusiasm for the war was an acknowledged extension of their theological progressivism. They seized upon the war as an opportunity to reconstruct the churches, America, and the world according to the imperatives of the social gospel. Their peacetime crusade became a wartime crusade.

Judging by how many books and articles appeared during the war bearing such titles as "The War and Religion," and by the degree to which theological interpretations of the war permeated wartime political rhetoric, it is clear that the Great War struck a number of Americans first and foremost as a battle possessing transcendent meaning, as the knowable outworking of God's plan for humanity. The progressive clergy were quick to point out this significance and to advance their interpretation. Throughout the following study, the participants speak for themselves as much as possible. How they expressed themselves—the words and metaphors they habitually chose—reveals much about how they thought. Their language was shared by a large community in the church and beyond, appearing repeatedly in sermons, books, denominational magazines, and also, to a remarkable degree, in the secular press and in political speeches directed to a variety of audiences, all of whom were expected to respond in a predictable way to these sacred images. Their own words help open the interior world of the progressive clergy and reassemble the ideas they used to explain the war to themselves, to the American public, and to the world.

The title for this book comes from an essay by the distinguished twentieth-century British historian Herbert Butterfield. In his essay "The War for Righteousness," Butterfield argued that the horror of modern warfare is not attributable primarily to advanced industrial technology, as we might naturally assume, but rather to modern states' willingness to engage in ideological wars with no room for compromise or limited objectives. The brutal "Wars of Religion" that devastated Europe after the Protestant Reformation, Butterfield argued, were reincarnated in the twentieth century, when once again international contests were invested with transcendent meaning and transformed into absolute struggles between light and darkness. In 1914, he continued, each nation told its people "that our enemy is worse than the rest of human nature and that his wickedness demands utter destruction."[2] The progressive clergy contributed profoundly to this mentality of total war and played a vital role in turning at least their side of the Great War into a "war for righteousness," an ultimate spiritual battle to rid the earth of a pagan nation that impeded the progress of God's righteous kingdom.

SOLDIERS OF THE CROSS

Redemptive imagery and wars for righteousness were by no means new to the American experience in the First World War. By 1914, the American identity and sense of national mission had accumulated and synthesized a range of doctrines, ideals, and metaphors assembled from Roman antiquity, the Old and New Testaments, Enlightenment rationalism, Romantic nationalism, and evolutionary naturalism. This stock of images and language was not always compatible, internally consistent, or coherent, but it was always ready to be drawn upon, reshaped, reused, expanded, and adapted—a treasury of powerful metaphors that helped Americans define themselves, their enemies, their purpose, and their future. With surprising consistency, though to varying degrees over time and with shifting emphases, Americans have been habitually drawn to language that is redemptive, apocalyptic, and expansive. Americans have long experienced and articulated a sense of urgency, of hanging on the precipice of great change, of living in the "fifth act" of history, as poet and philosopher George Berkeley famously wrote about the emerging American empire in the eighteenth century. They have fallen easily into the Manichean habit of dividing the world into darkness and light, Evil and Good, past and future, Satan and Christ. They have seen themselves as a progressive, redemptive force, waging war in the ranks of Christ's army, or have imagined themselves even as Christ Himself, liberating those in bondage and healing the afflicted. From the time of the earliest colonial settlements, for good or ill, the metaphors of the cross of Christ and of the mission of His Church have been deeply embedded in the story of the American people and their relations with the rest of the world.

THE PURITANS' NEW ISRAEL

In many ways, America's millennial enthusiasm is as old as the voyages of Columbus. As historian Jan Willem Schulte Nordholt makes clear, the Spanish empire invested its New World expeditions with messianic hope and with anticipations of the end of history, prophetic fulfillment, the universal dominion of Christ's kingdom, and a return to paradise.[3] These motifs are more typically associated with the United States' Puritan forebears, however, and for good reason. Nevertheless, the infusion of Europe's westward advance with millennial fervency was not exclusively the work of England's most famous refugees. The colonists who ultimately settled British North America in the seventeenth century came from a variety of doctrinal and ecclesiastical backgrounds, often disagreeing sharply about how to please God. But as fellow Christians—Protestant Christians, typically, they shared clear assumptions about the nature and character of God, His way of working in the world, their relationship to the created order, the meaning of life, and their hope for the future. They disagreed about liturgy, translations of Scripture, ecclesiology, and the finer points of eschatology, but from the James River to Cape Cod, from the Atlantic Seaboard to the Appalachian Mountains, they entertained little doubt about God's presence and superintending purposes in the settlement of the New World. They believed in God's "special providence," as it was called, and in miracles, the righteous judgments of the moral law, the need to lead an exemplary life, the certainty of reward and punishment now and in the life to come, and the conviction that events here on earth are bound up inextricably with events in heaven. By these measures, American colonists were not notably different from the European neighbors they left behind.

Among the earliest settlers of the American wilderness, the Puritans of New England were animated by a powerful consciousness of who they were, what they had fled from, and the new world they were laboring to redeem and build for themselves and all mankind in North America. They were a people possessed by an unmistakable sense of mission and of being the objects of a divine covenant with all its attendant blessings and curses. The Puritans were set apart to be, as John Winthrop famously and enduringly labeled them, a "Citty upon a Hill" with the eyes of the world fixed upon them.[4] God entered into a literal new covenant with a new chosen people, called out of bondage in Egypt for a particular task at a special moment in redemptive history, escaping from a modern Pharaoh and his army across a great sea. Their election was confirmed by signs and wonders, by attesting miracles of deliverance and safety and provision. They were unshakably certain of God's calling. They fled from a corrupt Europe and from an England bound in spiritual decline and apostasy. Or, to change the biblical metaphor, they were the Woman of the Book of Revelation (12: 14–17) who fled from the Dragon and escaped into the wilderness.[5]

The new world encountered by this chosen people was envisioned as both wilderness and Promised Land, barren desert and Canaan flowing with milk and honey, a trial to be endured and a captive land to be ransomed and possessed, a Babylon and a New Jerusalem. They found a wilderness to be crossed, transformed, and redeemed, a place populated by brutes of Hell, wild beasts, heathen darkness, barbarism, and modern Amalekites. The wilderness also symbolized the ever-present humbling possibility of spiritual wandering as the penalty of backsliding, of even the elect's propensity to disobedience, sin, and rebellion like the ancient Israelites under Moses. Nevertheless, the settlers came to build a New Israel, a new Mt. Zion, a new city of Jerusalem, a realm of light, safety, peace, purity, and prosperity, of both temporal blessing and abundant anticipation of eternal reward. As historian Sacvan Bercovitch summarizes the perspective of Puritan minister John Cotton, "America . . . was the new promised land, reserved by God for His new chosen people as the site for a new heaven and a new earth."[6]

One of the most striking features of the Puritan sense of mission was its "fusion of secular and sacred history," as Bercovitch emphasizes.[7] Whether or not these settlers intended to build a literal theocracy, they mentally inhabited a Holy Commonwealth; their worldview generally failed to distinguish between the City of Man and the City of God. As historian Ernest Lee Tuveson observes of the Puritans in his masterful *Redeemer Nation,* "they considered themselves in fact as advancing to the next step beyond the Reformation—the actual reign of the spirit of Christ, the amalgamation of the City of the World into the City of God."[8] Confident of their divine appointment, oriented toward their "errand," the Puritans fought to advance the Kingdom of Christ on Earth. Drawing habitually on the language and symbolism of the Old and New Testaments, the Puritans often portrayed themselves as soldiers of God. They were "troops of Christ's army," an invincible force marching under the leadership of their divine Captain, waging battle after battle in a campaign of conquest, expanding

Christ's realm and dominion and tearing down the walls of Babylon. They were engaged in a cosmic struggle being fought on the front lines in North America between Christ's Kingdom and the kingdom of the Antichrist.

The New England Puritans believed the curtain had opened on the last act of history, the fulfillment of all promise and hope and longing in a spectacular grand finale. Their age as a whole was one of expectation, both religious and secular. Back in England, Francis Bacon had recently proclaimed in *The Advancement of Learning* (1605)—and repeated more explicitly in his *Novum Organum* (1620)—the fulfillment of Daniel's prophecy (Daniel 12:4) that "many shall run to and fro, and knowledge shall be increased." The many voyages of the Age of Exploration and the intellectual curiosity of the Scientific Revolution had realized the prophet's vision.[9] Daniel was "clearly intimating," Bacon wrote, "that the thorough passage of the world . . . and the advancement of the sciences, are destined by fate, that is, by Divine Providence, to meet in the same age."[10] Indeed, through the power of knowledge applied to nature, the Fall of man would be reversed, his dominion restored. From the scientific method "there cannot but follow an improvement in man's estate and an enlargement of his power over nature. For man by the Fall fell at the same time from his state of innocency and from his dominion over creation. Both of these losses however can even in this life be in some part repaired; the former by religion and faith, the latter by arts and sciences."[11]

Similarly, Cotton Mather promised that the Puritan calling anticipated "the *Generall Restoration of Mankind from the Curse of the Fall,* and the opening of [the last stage in] that Scheme of *the Divine Proceedings,* which was to bring a blessing upon all the *Nations of the Earth.*"[12] On the shores of New England, God was performing a unique work on behalf of his new covenant people. As Mather rejoiced,

This at last is the spot of *earth,* which the God of heaven *spied out* for the seat of such *evangelical,* and *ecclesiastical,* and very remarkable transactions, as require to be made an history; *here* 'twas that our blessed JESUS intended a *resting place,* must I say? or only an *hiding place* for those *reformed* CHURCHES, which have given him a little accomplishment of his eternal Father's promise unto him; to be, we hope, yet further accomplished, *of having the utmost parts of the earth for his possession?*[13]

Reflecting on this passage and others, literary historian David Lyle Jeffrey concluded that "in a fashion unprecedented in Christian cultural history American Puritan divines applied biblical promises about the coming millennium to America, as if New England had become a heavenly kingdom in the here and now."[14]

Many years later, in *The Scarlet Letter,* Nathaniel Hawthorne captured a parallel attitude in the Reverend Arthur Dimmesdale's Election Day Sermon:

> His subject, it appeared, had been the relation between the Deity and the communities of mankind, with a special reference to the New England which they were here planting in the wilderness. And, as he drew towards the close, a spirit as of prophecy had come upon him, constraining him to its purpose as mightily as the old prophets of Israel were constrained; only with this difference, that, whereas the Jewish seers had denounced judgments and ruin on their country, it was his mission to foretell a high and glorious destiny for the newly gathered people of the Lord.[15]

These "newly gathered people of the Lord" who fled to North America believed they were completing the Protestant Reformation that had begun on the continent of Europe a century before, been momentarily thwarted in Stuart England (a "hopeless retardation," Mather complained[16]), and was soon to be accomplished in the New World. The earliest American settlers sensed that they were performing on a world stage, acting out a drama that would ultimately affect all mankind. World renewal would flow from the work begun in America. Settlement marked the first light of dawn, the mere anticipation of the full light of day, of the coming of the new heavens and the new earth. The Puritans' sense of mission expanded rapidly in the seventeenth century, from that of a remnant people fleeing oppression, to an outpost in the New World of the spreading Reformation, to a continental vision to redeem North America, and finally to "a community of visible saints charged with a world-redemptive mission."[17] Worldwide renovation would begin in America—the Fall reversed, dominion restored, the earth renewed, paradise regained. The Puritans were living out an apocalyptic experience, expecting the imminent fall of Antichrist. The "man of sin" was about to be cast down.[18] These settlers lived on the edge of a great transformation; history raced toward the consummation of the ages.

THE REVOLUTION

In the eighteenth century, the Puritans' descendants adapted and secularized their inherited stock of metaphors. "In effect," writes Bercovitch of the Puritans' ambitious "Yankee heirs," "they incorporated Bible history into the American experience—they substituted a regional for a biblical past, consecrated the American present as a movement from promise to fulfillment, and translated fulfillment from its meaning within a closed system of sacred history into a metaphor of limitless secular improvement."[19] The Puritan errand became secularized as temporal progress, social amelioration, material well-being, and the regeneration of society. This attitude was evident in an emerging political figure like John Adams, who, in 1765, confided to his diary, "I always consider the settlement of America with reverence and wonder, as the opening of a grand scene and design in Providence for the illumination of the ignorant, and the emancipation of the slavish part of mankind all over the earth."[20]

The evocative, volatile, redemptive language of Puritan New England flowed into the following century, ready to be applied to the Revolution and the birth of a nation. The political, constitutional, and economic conflict between Britain and its colonies was often framed by ministers as a new engagement in the ongoing struggle between the New Israel and Egypt or Assyria. Patriots continued to identify America as "Zion," as "Jerusalem," as the "Kingdom of God," and as the Woman fleeing the Dragon. As historian Nathan Hatch observes, "The cosmic interpretation of the conflict—God's elect versus Antichrist—appeared as a significant pattern in the intricate tapestry of ideas used by New England clergymen to explain the war's purpose."[21]

Among the most frequently cited examples of wartime political sermons is Samuel Sherwood's "The Church's Flight into the Wilderness" from early 1776. Evidently, Sherwood was convinced he was witnessing the literal fulfillment of the prophecies of the book of Revelation. He believed the world was fast approaching the universal reign of peace and righteousness as America vanquished Britain, the current embodiment of the Dragon. He prayed

> that the dragon will be wholly consumed and destroyed; that the seat and foundation of all tyranny, persecution and oppression, may be for ever demolished; that the horns, whether civil or ecclesiastical, may be knocked off from the beast, and his head receive a deadly wound, and his jaws be effectively broken; that peace, liberty and righteousness might universally prevail; that salvation and strength might come to Zion; and the kingdom of our God, and the power of his Christ might be established to all the ends of the earth.[22]

At war's end, Ezra Stiles, president of Yale College, vividly pictured victorious America as "God's New Israel" in a sermon preached before Connecticut's General Assembly.[23] He depicted George Washington as none other than Joshua commanding the armies of the Children of Israel and leading them into the Promised Land. In language typical of the revolutionary mind at work, moreover, he spoke of his awareness of the acceleration of time and the compression of events: "We live in an Age of Wonders. We have lived an age in a few years. We have seen more wonders accomplished in eight years than are usually unfolded in a century."[24] With the exuberance of Francis Bacon from nearly two centuries before, he proclaimed that "that prophecy of Daniel is now literally fulfilling—there shall be an universal traveling 'too [sic] and fro, and knowledge shall be increased.' This knowledge will be brought home and treasured up in America: and being here digested and carried to the highest perfection, may reblaze back from America to Europe, Asia and Africa, and illumine the world with TRUTH and LIBERTY." America's universal redemptive role could not have been more clearly expressed. But the original Puritan expectation of spiritual salvation is notably missing, replaced by a gospel of science, the "empire of reason," accelerated progress, the "unfettered mind," emancipation from the past, "unbounded freedom," and humanitarian benevolence.[25] This sort of secularized sermonizing is evidence of what Hatch marks as a "profound shift in emphasis [as] the religious values that traditionally defined the ultimate goal of apocalyptic hope—the conversion of all nations to Christianity—became diluted with, and often subordinated to, the commitment to America as a new seat of liberty."[26]

The predominance of political and earthly values over the spiritual and eternal was evident among other clergymen as well. An earlier sermon preached in the midst of the war by Abraham Keteltas at the First Presbyterian Church of Newburyport, Massachusetts, while not necessarily representative in every way of the thousands preached during the crisis, reveals further doctrinal imperatives in America's political theology, creedal affirmations that would persist right through the First World War and beyond. Keteltas identified the "cause of God" as the "cause of universal righteousness" and then unhesitatingly and seamlessly as the "cause of this much injured country." Keteltas assured his congregation that God's activity in history, his providence and intentions, can be read in the pattern of secular history, can be clearly seen and properly, accurately, confidently interpreted by observation of the rise and fall of nations, making success the mark of God's favor. Bypassing the troubling implications of this reasoning, Keteltas pressed on to articulate an outward-directed, universal mission as the work of a chosen nation, struggling in a righteous cause, and battling apocalyptically on the brink of the "paradise of God":

> We are contending for the rights of mankind, for the welfare of millions now living, and for the happiness of millions yet unborn. If it is the indisputed [sic] duty of mankind, to do good to all as they have opportunity, especially to those who are of the household of faith, if they are bound by the commandment of the supreme law-giver, to love their neighbor as themselves, and do to others as they would that others should do to them; then the war carried on against us, is unjust and unwarrantable, and our cause is not only righteous, but most important: It is God's own cause: It is the grand cause of the whole human race, and what can be more interesting and glorious. If the principles on which the present civil war is carried on by the American colonies, against the British arms, were universally adopted and practiced upon by mankind, they would turn a vale of tears, into a paradise of God: whereas opposite principles, and a conduct, founded upon them, has filled the world with blood and slaughter, with rapine and violence, with cruelty and injustice, with wretchedness, poverty, horror, desolation, and despair: We cannot therefore doubt, that the cause of liberty, united with that of truth & righteousness, is the cause of God.[27]

Consistently, Keteltas identified backsliding Britain with the "cause of the devil" and defined the Revolutionary War as "the cause of heaven against hell" and "against the prince of darkness."[28] In an ecstasy of prophetic vision, Keteltas finally linked the American cause to the atonement on Calvary. In its fight for truth, righteousness, benevolence, liberty, and other limitless ideals, the American cause "is a cause, for which the Son of God came down from his celestial throne, and expired on a cross—it is a cause, for the sake of which, your pious ancestors forsook all the delights and enjoyments of England, that land of wealth and plenty, and came to this once howling wilderness, destitute of houses, cultivated fields, the comforts and conveniences of life. This is a cause, for the prosperity of which, millions of saints are praying, and our gracious High Priest is interceding."[29] These confident definitions of America, the foe, the cause and its significance, so familiar from the Puritans and wrapped in millennial, global, apocalyptic intensity and finality, continued to weave their way through the fabric of the American imagination for generations to come.

The Enlightenment

While the Puritan settlers had clearly desired to spread the gospel as they busily reversed the Fall, by the time of the Revolution it is fair to ask what "converting the world" had come to mean. Was the good news now a proclamation of an enlightened world of political and economic liberty, freedom of conscience and worship, and unlimited scope for unfettered human reason? Regardless of how many Americans anticipated an earthly redemption through the agency of the Revolution, many Enlightenment thinkers fully expected the American cause to usher in a secular, global redemption. The American myth and the definition of its mission were not just the product of its own history and principles, but also of the expectations—often very flattering expectations—thrust upon the new nation by the *philosophes* and other European intellectuals.

French immigrant Hector St. John de Crèvecoeur, author of the celebrated *Letters from an American Farmer* (1782), helped redefine American exceptionalism. Crèvecoeur had fought in Canada in the French and Indian War, labored for a time as a farmer in the Hudson River Valley, and then returned to Europe in 1781.[30] From Europe, he envisioned a new sort of escape from bondage and spiritual enemies. No longer pictured as fleeing from the Puritans' Dragon or Egypt, Crèvecoeur's "new man" fled from the past and its hateful institutions, finding in America "no aristocratical families, no courts, no kings, no bishops, no ecclesiastical dominion"—the Enlightenment hope of emancipation from the tyranny of both prince and priest. America was the land not of the dead past but of the vital future and freedom and material progress. In America, the faith of a Voltaire or Addison in the power of commerce to bring every former foe into amicable relations through the miracle of the marketplace was being realized, along with a Lockean free-market of ideas and beliefs. The egalitarianism of the melting pot's "mixture of blood" had ended Europe's centuries'-old hostilities.[31] The redemptive language in Crèvecoeur's vision of the future is unmistakable. America meant regeneration, newness, resurrection, and the birth of a new man, stripped of the past and ready to start the world over.[32] All the nations of the earth would be blessed by this new hope:

> Here the individuals of all nations are melted into a new race of men, whose labours and posterity will one day cause great changes in the world. Americans are the western pilgrims who are carrying along with them that great mass of arts, sciences, vigour, and industry which began long since in the East; they will finish the great circle.[33]

An even more radical role in the impending world renewal was projected onto the young United States by such Enlightenment figures as Richard Price in England and Condorcet and Turgot in France. For most radical Enlightenment ideologues, the past was something from which to be emancipated. At best, the past imposed a sort of tutelage on a world still in its minority; at worst and more typically, the past chained the world in fetters, bound it in slavery, or lulled it to sleep in ignorance. The past was an obstacle to be overcome, not a precious legacy to be conserved. In the Enlightenment imagination, medieval Europe (according to the three-fold pattern of history habitual to the eighteenth century and seemingly impossible to shake off) was a time and place of superstition, error, barbarity, violence, darkness, and poverty. But the radical Enlightenment offered deliverance from the corruption and stagnation of the past and promised universal benevolence, peace, prosperity, liberty, equality, and reason. Above all, the glorious future would be rid of the pestilence of kings and priests.

Managing to strike all of these notes, Richard Price delivered his "Discourse on the Love of Our Country" in 1789 to mark the hundredth anniversary of the Glorious Revolution. Price praised the French Revolution and spoke with apocalyptic expectancy of world emancipation. He identified France as the Christ-Nation, quoting the prayer of Simeon over the Christ child and applying it to France.[34] Five years earlier, however, Price had already pronounced the same benediction over the American Revolution.[35]

True to Enlightenment presuppositions, Price saw America's victory over Britain as the harbinger of "universal liberty" and of the "rights of mankind." American independence opened a "new era in the history of mankind," bringing rapid progress, amelioration of the human condition, and the advancement of Reason, the seat of an empire of "liberty, science and virtue" that would spread over the whole world. America was the world's political messiah, characterized in ways similar to France a few years later. "Perhaps I do not go too far when I say," Price wrote, "that, next to the introduction of Christianity among mankind, the American revolution may prove the most important step in the progressive course of human improvement." At least he had the modesty to say "perhaps" and to assign American independence second place behind the Incarnation. America occupied a special place in providential, redemptive history. Americans were a sort of chosen people in whom, Price claimed appropriating God's covenantal promise to Abraham, "*all the families of the earth shall be blessed.*" Repeating the now familiar refrain from Francis Bacon and Ezra Stiles, he interpreted events in America as the fulfillment of biblical prophecy: "*many will run to and fro and knowledge [will] be increased.*"[36]

Price and the Enlightenment in general placed upon America an extraordinary burden of hope and offered Americans an enticing, secularized affirmation of their already expansive self-understanding. With echoes all the way back to Virgil, America was assigned the redemptive role of "the last universal empire upon earth"—the "empire of reason and virtue" and permanent peace.[37] This exaggerated expectation would reverberate all the way down to Woodrow Wilson's war message in 1917 in which he proclaimed that America intervened for the sake of "a universal dominion of right by such a concert of free peoples as shall bring peace and safety to all nations and make the world itself at last free."[38] Before that defining moment came, however, the light of America's self-understanding was refracted through yet more ideological prisms.

ROMANTIC NATIONALISM

In the mid-nineteenth century, the American redemptive myth, as inherited from the Puritans and reconfigured by the Revolutionary generation on both sides of the Atlantic, was further elaborated by varieties of Romantic nationalism and utopianism. In his brilliant satire, *The Blithedale Romance* (1852), Nathaniel Hawthorne wrote of the delusion of Brook Farm's "little army of saints and martyrs" that they "had taken up [the Pilgrims' high enterprise], and were carrying it onward and aloft, to a point which they never dreamed of attaining."[39]

Hawthorne's friend and fellow New England novelist Herman Melville developed this theme from another vantage point, "carrying it onward and aloft" to the point of identifying America as the world's "political messiah" engaged in "unbounded philanthropy." In an extended section from his novel *White-Jacket* (1850), Melville captured, in the eccentric voice of his seafaring narrator, the persistence, reworking, and expansion of the myth of the Puritan New Israel:

> Escaped from the house of bondage, Israel of old did not follow after the ways of the Egyptians. To her was given an express dispensation; to her were given new things under the sun. And we Americans are the peculiar, chosen people—the Israel of our time; we bear the ark of the liberties of the world. Seventy years ago we escaped from thrall; and, besides our first birth-right—embracing one continent of earth—God has given to us, for a future inheritance, the broad domains of the political pagans, that shall yet come and lie down under the shade of our ark, without bloody hands being lifted. God has predestinated, mankind expects, great things from our race; and great things we feel in our souls. The rest of the nations must soon be in our rear. We are the pioneers of the world; the advance-guard, sent on through the wilderness of untried things, to break a new path in the New World that is ours. . . . Long enough have we been skeptics with regard to ourselves, and doubted whether, indeed, the political Messiah had come. But he has come in *us,* if we would but give utterance to his promptings. And let us always remember that with ourselves,

almost for the first time in the history of earth, national selfishness is un-bounded philanthropy; for we can not do a good to America but we give alms to the world.[40]

As Schulte Nordholt aptly comments on this passage, "Inherent in a text of such exaggeration is a projection of the millennium, the golden future which grows beneath our hands. But such overstrained enthusiasm entails crossing well-defined boundaries both of orthodoxy and of human limitation."[41] It would require many years of harsh experience before many Americans confronted and reckoned with these boundaries, before many realized with Hawthorne that earthly utopias still need prisons and cemeteries, still face sin and mortality.[42] In the meantime, however, America's complicated messianic identity flourished. Liberal theologian Horace Bushnell likened the Puritan's divine errand to the Magi's quest in search of the Christ child, and America to a sort of manger for the new Christ: "Our sublime fathers had a high constructive instinct, raising them above their age and above themselves. God made them founders of a social state under forms appointed by Himself. This was the star of the East that guided them thither. They came as to the second cradle-place of a renovated Messiahship. . . ."[43]

Bushnell and his generation thought and wrote within the larger context of the spirit of their optimistic times. "Seldom," observes historian Robert Johannsen, "did [the idea of mission] attain such wide acceptance as in the middle decades of the nineteenth century, when the belief that the American people had been chosen to fulfill certain high and lofty purposes became a dominant theme in their democratic faith." "Born of revolution," he continues, "free from the restraints of tradition, and enjoying a unique geographic position, the young United States seemed to embody the hopes and ideals of men everywhere."[44] And these hopes and ideals, political, religious, moral, and economic, would not be achieved merely here and now for the American people but for all humanity and for all time.

The expansive temper of antebellum America was typified by such champions of Manifest Destiny as Democratic newspaper editor John L. O'Sullivan. His writing was filled with Romanticism's restlessness, boundlessness, vitality, and cult of originality. In an influential editorial, "The Great Nation of Futurity," O'Sullivan rejoiced that America was disconnected from the past and from every nation.[45] Americans were a people without an ancestry. America was an original nation, a new thing on the earth, and "connect[ed] . . . with the future only"—"*the great nation of futurity.*" O'Sullivan carried over the Enlightenment formula that the past was steeped in aristocracy, monarchy, and privilege while the future belonged to democracy, equality, and freedom. "Unsullied by the past," America was ready in the 1830s to advance into the virgin land of the open, boundless future. "We are the nation of human progress, and who will, what can, set limits to our onward march?"[46]

Typical of the rhetorical sacralization of the nation-state increasingly common in Europe at the time, especially in Italy, Germany, France, and among Poland's sentimental friends and exiles, O'Sullivan transformed America into a new Christ. Claiming for his nation the promise of Christ to His Church in the gospels, O'Sullivan exulted that America would champion its doctrine of equality and guarantee that "the gates of hell"—the powers of aristocracy and monarchy—"shall not prevail against it." "In its magnificent dominion of space and time," moreover, "the nation of many nations is destined to manifest to mankind the excellence of divine principles; to establish on earth the noblest temple ever dedicated to the worship of the Most High—the Sacred and True," a national "congregation" dedicated to the gospel of equality and brotherhood, proclaiming "peace and good will amongst men." The blessing and hope of the Incarnation announced in these tidings, however, had been loosed from their theological moorings and transported far from their orthodox meaning and intention:

> We must [march] onward to the fulfillment of our mission—to the entire development of the principle of our organization—freedom of conscience, freedom of person, freedom of trade and business pursuits, universality of freedom and equality. This is our high destiny, and in nature's eternal, inevitable decree of cause and effect we must accomplish it. All this will be our future history, to establish on earth the moral dignity and salvation of man—the immutable truth and beneficence of God.[47]

One of the most famous religious spokesmen for the American frontier at the time of O'Sullivan's secular gospel was the Reverend Lyman Beecher, head of a remarkable clan of preachers and reformers that included Edward Beecher, Henry Ward Beecher, Catherine Beecher, and Harriet Beecher Stowe. He witnessed American history from the Revolution to the Civil War. In his rousing 1835 speech, "A Plea for the West," Beecher captured his generation's millennial hope and expectation of earthly renovation.[48] His Romantic imagination seemed to slip all bounds as he spoke, and he sensed the same compression and acceleration of time that had stirred the revolutionaries of his childhood. As an epigraph to his speech he placed Isaiah 64:8: "Who hath heard such a thing? who had seen such things? Shall the earth be made to bring forth in one day? or shall a nation be born at once?"

Beecher's vision was unconstrained. He expected nothing less than for America "to lead the way in the moral and political emancipation of the world."[49] Sounding closer to the radical Enlightenment than to his Puritan ancestors, he predicted that through American inspiration "the government of force will cease, and that of intelligence and virtue will take its place; and nation after nation cheered by our example, will follow in our footsteps, till the whole earth is free." From out of a united America, East and West, will flow a flood of "benevolence into that river which is 'to make glad the city of our God.'"[50]

Other writers carried this imperative for world renewal even further, expecting that the United States might even have to intervene in Europe to right wrongs and liberate captives. A remarkable passage from an 1853 article in the *Presbyterian Quarterly Review* expressed this willingness to wage war on the side of the political messiah: "On the fields of Europe, among the rotten systems, reeking with lies and oppression, and in regions red with the blood of saints, the lines may be closed up, and we of the western world be forced to take sides, or let the issue for another long cycle go by default. The battle of Armageddon is yet to be fought." Tuveson cites these lines as a haunting anticipation of American intervention in the First World War and as part of the psychological preparation of the American people for the Armageddon of the Civil War and then the Great War.[51]

While generally more restrained than the Puritans' Yankee descendants by a sense of man's depravity and the limitations imposed by man's createdness, some segments of the South exhibited a similarly virulent form of romantic nationalism. On the eve of the Civil War, South Carolina Fire-eater Robert Barnwell Rhett cited the continued threat from the North to the Southern states' peace and safety and proposed to dissolve the existing union and form a new confederation. He connected the yearnings of the Southern people to the nationalist movements underway in Scotland, Ireland, and vanished Poland and to Italy's struggle for unification and self-government.[52] In an Independence Day speech in 1859, Rhett proclaimed the South's "restless energy," dissatisfaction with boundaries, irrepressible urge to expand, and "high mission" to help civilize the world. Rhett could not have more consciously identified his people's cause with the spirit of the age:

> There seems to be an irrepressible desire amongst all nations to extend their limits and their power. *Expansion is their law.* The lust for plunder or fame which stimulated an ALEXANDER and a GENGHIS KHAN, has long since given way to a system of colonial incorporation. By this means more barbarous peoples are civilized and improved, and the more civilized nations have become, the more intense seems to be their desire for expansion. At this moment the greatest conquerors are the most civilized nations of the world. France seeks expansion in Algeria and Egypt, Russia in Turkey and Upper Asia, the United States over this continent, and Great Britain all over the world. The restless energy which knowledge and civilization imparts, will not be satisfied with limits, but spreads abroad its eager enterprise and dominion. It is the destiny of human nature; and the Almighty may have imparted this desire for expansion to nations, in order that civilization and his true religion may be extended. The Caucasian race is not only to be the masters but the spiritual pastors of the world. As the Jews extirpated the heathen nations around them by God's command, so the weaker races may be destined to perish or to fall beneath the subjugation and tutelage of the superior races of the world. With no people on the earth is this policy of expansion more necessary than with the people of the southern States.[53]

Within two years of this speech, days after the first shots had been fired on Ft. Sumter, Henry Ward Beecher—son of Lyman Beecher and pastor of Plymouth Church, Brooklyn—explicitly linked the Union cause with European romantic nationalism. Preaching at Plymouth Church on April 14, 1861, and taking as his text Exodus 15:15 (a reference to the liberation of Canaan from hands of the ungodly), Beecher identified the American cause as "liberty here, and liberty everywhere, the world over." Like the Fire-eater Rhett, he looked for inspiration to an awakened Italy, Hungary, and Poland, and, unlike Rhett, to the emancipation of the serfs in Russia. "We, too," he declared, "have a right to march in this grand procession of liberty. By the memory of the fathers; by the sufferings of the Puritan ancestry; by the teaching of our national history; by our faith and hope of religion; by every line of the Declaration of Independence, and every article of our Constitution; by what we are and what our pro-genitors were,—we have a right to walk foremost in this procession of nations toward the bright future."[54] Like Christ in Gethsemane, he claimed, America had asked, "Let this cup pass from us!" But the war came, America's Calvary, and the nation was "called to suffer for our faith." "We shall be called to the heroism of doing and daring," he continued, "and bearing and suffering, for the things which we believe to be vital to the salvation of this people." In a direct appropriation of messianic promises from the book of Genesis, he reassured his congregation that "the scepter shall not depart."[55] The political messiah would prevail.

A decade later, speaking at the time of the Franco-Prussian War and sympathizing with a French nation "humbled" in a spectacle not seen since "Christ was lifted up on Calvary," Beecher again reminded his Plymouth congregation of God's plan for America in the providential work of world benevolence. Praising the fabulous growth of American power, wealth, opulence, and glory, Beecher believed that the nation by God's direction bore "a burden of humanity that its weal or woe will be like an eternal weal or woe, infinite, endless." Sounding more like Caesar than Christ, he prayed, "May God give us magnanimity and power and riches, that we may throw the shadow of our example upon the poor, the perishing, and the ready-to-be-destroyed, for their protection." Calling down a curse on anyone who would advocate war except for defense, however, Beecher cautioned that America had "no war that we want to wage except the war for righteousness in ourselves."[56]

The victorious Union had, of course, recently waged a "war for righteousness" against the South. But a new generation of American clergy, inspired by remnants of their Puritan heritage, the boundless promises of the Enlightenment, the aggressive Romantic nationalism of Bushnell and Beecher, and the emerging Darwinian naturalism of their own day, launched a new crusade. They longed to see for themselves "the glory of the coming of the Lord" and enlisted in God's ever-marching army in a new war for righteousness, first against Spain in 1898 and then in Europe from 1917 to 1918.

The Rise of the Messianic Nation

America's anointment as the world's political messiah did not end when demobilized troops returned from Europe in 1919. It did not end with America's opposition to the Treaty of Versailles, nor with America's refusal to join the League of Nations. The cumulative product of generations of reflection, experience, and anticipation, the American identity reached too deep and far to have been uprooted in a moment of supposed renunciation. Transcending party politics and most ideological boundaries, nearly all of the language of universality and emancipation, of the "city on a hill" and the world's rebirth, of light and dark, Messiah and Armageddon, reverberates down to the present moment. Like Woodrow Wilson before them, few modern presidents have been able to resist the allure of America's global redemptive consciousness.[57] In the 1940s, Franklin Roosevelt planned for a future refounded on four freedoms, freedoms that would prevail "everywhere in the world." In the fourth of these universal freedoms, freedom from fear, he anticipated a day when "no nation will be in a position to commit an act of physical aggression against any neighbor—anywhere in the world." In countless speeches from the 1960s through the 1980s, moreover, Ronald Reagan reached back to the earliest metaphors of America's "divine destiny" to reaffirm the nation's special calling as a "city on a hill."[57] Combining the Puritan errand with the Enlightenment dream of earthly regeneration, he also embraced Tom Paine's longing to "begin the world over again." And on September 11, 2002, George W. Bush, speaking with the colossus of the Statue of Liberty behind him, called America the "hope of all mankind" and appropriated the words of John 1:5 as if they described not just the Incarnation of Christ but the mission of the United States: "And the light shines in the darkness; and the darkness will not overcome it." To one degree or another and with varying motives and consequences, each of these men continued to speak of the United States as if it were the *Salvator Mundi,* following a pattern of thought that has endured for more than four centuries.

Given the troubling history of this tendency of the American imagination, however, especially as it played out in the Great War, it is worth returning to the sobering poem that serves as this book's epigraph. In "The English Graves," G. K. Chesterton ponders the meaning of the fates of millions of "simple men" who died far from the humble, narrow homes they had known. He was, of course, referring to his fellow countrymen, but his words apply almost as poignantly to the American soldiers of the First World War who lie buried in France, who fought under their nation's flag but were told they were saving the world.

I

A Vast Spiritual Migration

Tracing the Worldview of the Progressive Clergy

ON A MILD MONDAY MORNING in early November 1897, Presbyterian clergy, scholars, and laymen gathered within the gothic nave of "Old First" Presbyterian Church on Fifth Avenue near Washington Square to observe the 250th anniversary of the Westminster Standards, Calvinism's venerated confession of faith and a principal source of America's Protestant heritage. Professor Benjamin Warfield, Princeton Seminary's forceful defender of Biblical authority and of Reformed theology, described the confession that day as "a notable monument of spiritual religion." Warfield, who also served as editor of the conservative *Princeton Theological Review,* spoke for historic Protestantism and its inherited doctrines and creeds. Continuing the festivities that evening, a much larger group assembled at the Madison Square Garden Concert Hall to honor their "notable monument" further with a service of music and preaching.[1]

That same week in November 1897 witnessed a second commemoration as well. Eastward across the Brooklyn Bridge, in sight of lower Manhattan, an equally distinguished group convened a few days later at another prestigious urban church, the noted Plymouth Congregational Church. They came to celebrate Plymouth's fiftieth year of service in Brooklyn Heights and to remind themselves and the nation of that church's place at the forefront of progressive Christianity. The congregation sang the hymn "I Love Thy Kingdom, Lord" in a sanctuary decorated with autumnal chry-

santhemums and with banners reading "1857" and "1897." Plymouth
Church had been the pulpit of Henry Ward Beecher, one of nineteenth-
century America's preeminent liberal preachers, and its founding, therefore, represented quite a different achievement from the one celebrated
in Manhattan. Plymouth Church, while linked by its very name to the
Puritan heritage, had always, reported the *New York Times* that week, "held
such advanced ground upon all questions concerning the social welfare of
mankind."[2] Indeed, the Reverend Beecher had championed such causes as
modern theology, theistic evolution, social reform, and an activist, humanitarian mission for the modern church.[3] This was, after all, the aboli-
tionist congregation that had sent "Beecher's Bibles" to the Kansas Territory in 1855 to aid the Free-State cause. So, while the aging Westminster
Confession symbolized a rooted, orthodox Protestantism, Plymouth
Church's founding represented an activist, experimental, progressive
Christianity.

Plymouth's current pastor, Lyman Abbott, had assembled a group of
notable clergy to mark Plymouth's achievement, among them Washington Gladden and George A. Gordon, both prominent Congregational
ministers and authors, and William Jewett Tucker, president of Dartmouth
College. Each orator was famous for advocating both the "New Theology"
and a socially defined gospel.

Abbott himself had achieved some distinction as a leader of reconstructed Christianity and a crusader for good government. Plymouth's
pastor since 1888, he was also the respected editor of the *Christian Union*
(soon to be renamed the *Outlook*) and a nascent Rooseveltian progressive.
Abbott had begun his ministry in the Congregational Church on the eve
of the Civil War, and would for over forty years edit the weekly *Outlook,* a
magazine he transformed from a denominational paper into a national
journal of fashionable liberal opinion in both religion and politics. He was
well-known as a popularizer of modern theology, especially for his attempt to reconcile the Bible and evolution, to which cause he contributed
The Evolution of Christianity (1892) and *The Theology of an Evolutionist* (1897).
He was a popular essayist and conference speaker, and a tireless spokesman for international arbitration and world peace.

Fellow Congregationalist pastor Washington Gladden was a familiar figure at Plymouth Church. In the 1870s, he had been religion editor for Henry Ward Beecher's *Independent,* another widely read journal of current opinion. Gladden pastored several Congregational churches, beginning in Brooklyn in the 1860s and then in New York state and Massachusetts before settling in his nationally respected pulpit in Columbus, Ohio. By his own account, his theology was shaped by the teachings and close friendship of Horace Bushnell, New England's most renowned theologian since Jonathan Edwards. Bushnell had stressed an intuitive and experiential theology and thereby left a deep impression on the generation represented on the platform at Plymouth Church.[4] Like his followers, Bushnell had been no stranger to controversy. He had doubted the Trinity, posited a gradualist theory of personal redemption, and promoted the dual revelation of science and theology as the "one system" of an immanent God in harmony with his creation. Gladden later declared him to have been "the greatest theological genius of the American church in the nineteenth century." Building on Bushnell's foundation for the social gospel, Gladden made his own mark by challenging the contemporary church to take up the collective task of social reconstruction in a troubled urbanizing and industrializing America. From 1900 to 1902, he even served on the Columbus, Ohio, city council, putting his social gospel into practice and working to realize the kingdom of God on earth.[5]

The Reverend George A. Gordon was not destined to be as well remembered as Abbott and Gladden, but in the 1890s he was an esteemed spokesman for a modern, adaptive Christianity. He was born in Scotland to a strong Calvinist home and had immigrated to the United States in the mid-nineteenth century. He attended Bangor Seminary and Harvard, and then pastored Boston's prominent Old South Church. Like Gladden, he credited his theological liberalism to Bushnell's pioneering work. As a Congregational minister, Gordon popularized the New Theology, which he preferred to call "Progressive Orthodoxy" and which valued experience over doctrine and confessions. At Charles Eliot's Harvard he had studied under William James and was deeply influence by that philosopher's pragmatism. He remained friends with his former professor, corresponding with James during his Boston ministry and later presiding at his mentor's funeral.[6]

Joining these three theologians at Plymouth was William Jewett Tucker, Congregationalist minister, former Andover seminary professor, settlement worker, and, since 1893, the distinguished president of Dartmouth College. As one of the famous or—depending on one's theology—the notorious Andover Liberals, he had helped found the *Andover Review,* among the most important publications of Progressive Orthodoxy. While his essays for that journal had brought charges of heresy,[7] his address at Plymouth was reportedly "listened to with the closest attention."[8]

Abbott and his colleagues represented a distinct phase in America's complex religious history. They shared many formative experiences, emerged on the national scene together, flourished about the same time, and all died within a few years of each other and within the shadow of the Great War—Gladden in 1918, Abbott in 1922, Tucker in 1926, and Gordon in 1929. They were part of the same remarkable generation that had produced novelist William Dean Howells. With their passing, their progressive theology would seem as hopelessly old-fashioned as the orthodoxy they once criticized, their hopeful liberalism having been chastened by the spectacular contradiction of the First World War, by those "fearful convulsions of a dying civilization," as John Maynard Keynes would later describe the events of 1914 to 1918.[9] For the moment, however, for the years leading up to their nation's great adventure in the World War, they helped shape and define a religious and political movement, and determined to a large degree how that movement would interpret the cataclysm of the Great War. Together with their spiritual heirs—the rising generation of such noted liberal clergy as Shailer Mathews, Harry Emerson Fosdick, Henry Churchill King, and William H. P. Faunce—they served as highly visible and quotable spokesmen of their day's adaptive, meliorist, optimistic Protestantism.[10] Their names appeared frequently in the nation's leading journals. They contributed essays to the *Atlantic Monthly* and *Current Opinion,* while the *Literary Digest,* the *Century* magazine, and the *Nation* quoted their pronouncements on public issues. The *NewYork Times* and other metropolitan dailies followed their careers in New York, Boston, and Chicago. They counted local politicians, governors, and congressmen among their friends; hobnobbed with presidents McKinley, Roosevelt, Taft, and Wilson; tapped the resources of business tycoons Carnegie and Rockefeller; and traveled the world for the Young Men's Christian Association (YMCA) and numerous mission boards and even as foreign emissaries of the national government. These were the clergymen that progressive Americans consulted, quoted, and linked arms with in their efforts to define the new America and its expanding role in the world. Consequently, the progressive clergy, allied with the press, politicians, and big business, were positioned to influence far more than the nation's religious history. Nevertheless, despite the breadth of their political and social activism, their worldview and behavior during the war years was rooted in a particular theology.

Abbott's guests came to Plymouth Church to pay tribute to the Reverend Beecher's abiding influence in American theology, but they also intended to chart a course for their "new Puritanism."[11] This "new Puritanism" was to achieve everything the old system of faith and practice had fallen short of. Traditional Christianity, with its biblical literalism and notions of eternal retribution and individual redemption, seemed dangerously ill-equipped for the modern world. Progressive Christianity, in contrast, was to be intellectually respectable, credible, relevant, and liberating. In short, it would be a suitable spiritual companion to modern man as he entered the twentieth century. At a preliminary meeting in May 1897 commemorating Beecher's first Sunday in his Brooklyn pulpit, Lyman Abbott had praised progressive Christianity for having cast off the combined weights of Calvinism, the Westminster Confession of Faith, and the debilitating theology of Jonathan Edwards. Unlike the new theology, he declared, the old theology was "fatalistic in the very essence of its philosophy."[12] Having liberated their faith from a supposedly dead orthodoxy, these champions of the new Christianity sought to conform their creed to the modern spirit. Boston's George Gordon explicitly rejected the old theology, claiming that orthodoxy had not kept pace with the modern age. "For all thinking men who are in any measure open to the new light and spirit of our time," he told the Plymouth congregation, "Calvinism as an adequate interpretation of the ways of God with men, or even as a working philosophy of life, is forever gone."[13]

As a group, the progressive clergy found the Reformed theology of
John Calvin much too narrow and harsh, and of limited use in remaking
the world. They preferred instead the more benevolent, universalist, humanitarian conceptions of the Fatherhood of God and the Brotherhood of
Man—doctrines ripe with social and political potential. In his memoirs
published in 1915, Lyman Abbott reemphasized this progressive predilec-
tion. Recounting the changes in religion he had witnessed over sixty years,
he rejoiced that "for the conception of God as King, the conception of
God as Father [has replaced it]; for the conception of salvation as the rescue of the elect from a lost world, the conception of the transformation of
the world itself into a human Brotherhood, a conception which is the
inspiration of the great world-wide democratic movement."[14] For Abbott,
the spreading acceptance of the new doctrines signaled the triumph of
progressive Christianity over historic Calvinism and even over regressive
social systems. Significantly, Abbott blurred the distinction in his mind
between theological and political progressivism to the point that they were
a single movement, the joining of sacred and secular reconstruction that
so largely defined the worldview of his fellow modernist theologians.
Washington Gladden, for example, counted on the expansion of such ideas
as the Fatherhood of God and the Brotherhood of Man, as well as the
fusion of the sacred and secular and ideals of social solidarity, to bear
tangible results in the reordering of society, to "greatly accelerate the
progress of the kingdom," as he phrased it.[15] As Abbott reminded his Plymouth congregation in 1897, "the heresy and the moral reform were going along together."[16]

While progressive Christianity's skill at reconstructing institutions
would become clear as it tackled first the church, then American society,
and ultimately international affairs, its theology was grounded in a few
elemental assumptions about the way the world worked. First among these
assumptions was a belief in inherent, inevitable spiritual progress, in the
gradual tendency of the physical universe and of human history toward
the good, a process that determined the manner in which God achieved
His will. For the progressives, the world was in motion. But this was not
a random or inscrutable movement. Creation, humanity, and history were
not merely changing; they were changing in a clear direction, toward a

knowable goal, toward nothing less than the kingdom of God on earth. This idea of purposeful, teleological change dominated the intellectual world of the late nineteenth century. The law of evolution that was thought to control the natural world was presumed to direct the spiritual world as well. Plymouth's pastor Lyman Abbott believed that development in these two realms, the physical and the spiritual, was not merely analogous but also a synonymous, manifestation of a single force. "The law of progress," as he claimed, "is the same in both." Citing Herbert Spencer's belief in evolution as a unifying principle, he argued that "nothing is more certain than this, that we are ever in the presence of an Infinite and Eternal Energy from which all things proceed."[17]

The progressive clergy detected what they thought to be a comprehensive, universal process at work and developed from this principle a system that embraced all of life and thought. As William Jewett Tucker observed about the spiritual temper of his colleagues, "Gradually the desire and struggle for progress became the unifying purpose of the generation." Nearly ten years after turning the presidency of Dartmouth College over to his more famous successor Ernest Hopkins, Tucker observed in his autobiography, *My Generation,* that the atmosphere of the late nineteenth century had been characterized by an awareness of undeniable progress and a sense of anticipation. "One felt all the while," he recalled, "that he was living in the region of undiscovered truth. He was constantly made aware of the presence of some unsatisfied opportunity." For the churches in particular, this longing for new truth drew modern Christianity away from orthodoxy and toward a progressive theology. As Tucker pointed out, "the term which best expressed the character of the modernizing process as it went on in the churches was the term 'progressive.' It was, in fact, actually in use as a theological term long before it found so conspicuous a place in politics."[18]

The accuracy of Tucker's characterization of his times was reflected in comments from the pulpits and beyond near the turn of the century. The Reverend Newell Dwight Hillis—by 1900 successor to Abbott in the pulpit at Plymouth Church and, during the Great War, the most notoriously quotable of the progressive clergy—praised the emerging new day for the democratic spirit of cooperation and service, noting that "art, industry, invention, literature, learning, and government—all these are captives marching in Christ's triumphant procession up the hill of fame."[19] Hillis linked all social progress ultimately to Christianity's reign in the world. No one less than Christ himself, the captain of a modern army, was leading a conquered world in a grand victory parade. In the same spirit, but from a secular perspective, the *Encyclopedia Americana* in 1903 claimed that progress governed the whole natural and moral universe. And this observable forward motion had given to modern philosophy its faith in "meliorism," a principle of the natural world that the encyclopedia accepted as "a doctrine so firmly based on fact that none can controvert it." In a world of inevitable social betterment, pessimism had become "a contradiction in terms," and the pervasive "optimism" that resulted from this observable scientific process had given to "the mind a philosophical creed that renders life tolerable."[20] Progress, visible in every facet of life and ruling as the governing force behind existence, brought order to a world of change and moral purpose to a universe otherwise disturbingly random and meaningless. This faith in progress anchored the soul.

The progressive clergy often referred to their faith in progress by a more general principle they called "developmentalism," which they defined as an encompassing, meliorative force that controlled both the natural world and universal history. Consequently, all thought, including science, philosophy, and theology, had to be harmonized with this modern understanding of a world of constant motion and change. In 1909 Washington Gladden attributed the revolution in the nineteenth-century mind to this new developmentalism. To his way of thinking, even though he devoted so much effort to tangible social reform, the inner theological and philosophical changes of the age were far more profound than the environmental changes in the nation's urban and industrial landscape. He contended that "what goes on in the outer world, in truth, only registers the movements of mind." Gladden attributed the rise of the modern consciousness to the German thinkers Kant, Fichte, and Hegel, who had given the world "the historical sense, that showed the present to be the child of the past, that prepared the way for that doctrine of development which was to revolutionize human thought."[21] Once posited as the true nature of things, developmentalism gave the liberal church the context within which to understand creation, history, and even God Himself.

This pervasive faith in progress, while appearing simple-minded to a more jaded age, especially in the wake of the material and moral devastation of the Great War, was widely shared in Europe and America at the turn of the century, and was in some narrow ways well-founded, or at least explicable. As British historian Christopher Dawson pointed out not long after the First World War, such a dominant faith in progress was not as naïve as it is often portrayed. Continued advancement seemed reasonable in light of improved health and living conditions, increasing wealth and material goods, the general advance of European culture and its liberal political institutions, and the flowering of humanitarian reform. "Looked at from this point of view," Dawson noted, "Progress is no imaginary hypothesis but a solid reality of history." The mistake came in concluding that progress, rather than being the limited product of specific historical circumstances, was instead inevitable and permanent, and that it would necessarily make men "happier or wiser or better than they were in simpler states of society. . . ."[22] While arguably not naïve, the progressive clergy, along with much of their generation, nevertheless made this error of assuming that the developments they witnessed around them were inevitable, permanent, and beneficent. Acting upon this misunderstanding of progress, they extracted from it nothing less than a complete theory of the natural world, a philosophy of history, and a theology.

Drawing out developmentalism's implications for the natural world, the progressive clergy embraced and popularized a teleological view that, while evolutionary, deviated from orthodox Darwinism in some important ways. They tended to favor a particular variety of nineteenth-century evolutionary thought, namely, an older, more Lamarckian theory of biological development that bordered on pantheism. While William Jewett Tucker might later look back on the publication of the *Origin of Species* in 1859 as marking the point of his generation's "intellectual detachment . . . from the past," his fellow liberal clergy were uncomfortable with blind, designless, and wasteful natural selection.[23] Tucker placed Darwin at the center of his own intellectual upheaval, but other liberal clergy made no mention of the British naturalist, referring instead to evolution in a more general sense or possibly tracing their conversion to the developmentalist faith to Herbert Spencer's social theories. George A. Gordon, for instance, never mentioned Darwin or even biological evolution in his autobiography, an omission that seems inexplicable given his eagerness to adapt Christianity to the temper of his times. Likewise, Washington Gladden, in his *Recollections,* did not discuss Darwin or biological evolution. He referred instead to the "continuous process" of creation as posited by British geologist Sir Charles Lyell, who had expanded geologic time to accommodate millions of years of uniform, gradual change.[24]

Oddly enough, strict Darwinism, as historian James R. Moore carefully argued, actually attracted more adherents from the ranks of orthodox Calvinism, an alliance unexpected when reading back into the 1890s from the categories of the Fundamentalist-Modernist controversies of the 1920s. Princeton Seminary's own Benjamin Warfield, a contributor to *The Fundamentals* and a stalwart defender of Calvinism, apparently found a measure of Darwinism compatible with both the Genesis account and Calvin's teachings on creation.[25] Darwinism, with its brutality, inherent selfishness, and lack of design, seemed to pose more of a problem for the liberal theistic evolutionists, those like Lyman Abbott who preferred the more palatable Neo-Lamarckian theory which, with its emphasis on purposeful adaptation, its demand for an indwelling Force, and its faith in inevitable progress, made reconciliation between modern scientific theory and humanitarian theology much more manageable.[26] While evolutionary thought per se, then, did not define theological liberalism—that is to say, did not determine who would or would not be a progressive—a teleological, pre-Darwinian evolutionary cast of mind certainly characterized the progressive clergy's interpretation of the world. Overall, these clergy shared the perspective of their fellow theological liberal Joseph LeConte— the University of California naturalist who popularized Neo-Lamarckian theory in America—who was more concerned with evolution broadly defined, with a general understanding of "evolution as a law of continuity, a universal law of becoming," than with any particular version of biological change, be it Lamarck's, or Darwin's, or Spencer's.[27]

To this meliorist, benevolent, regenerative view of the natural world, the liberal clergy added a progressive interpretation of history as well. This developmental view of history displaced the Augustinian conception that had prevailed in Western thought from the collapse of the Roman Empire in the fifth century down to the late Renaissance. In a strict sense, Augustine himself had held to a developmentalist view of history, but not in the way the liberal clergy used the word. For Augustine, human history did indeed possess direction, stages, and purpose, but this sort of "development" was a process of decay, one without hope of renewal and one that led inevitably to destruction. Redemption would come, to be sure, but only outside of history and by the hand of a transcendent God.[28] While maintaining that history possessed meaning and ultimately accomplished the will of God, Augustine saw no reason to believe that God was incrementally transforming this fallen world into His kingdom. Rather than a literal, thousand-year reign of peace, the millennial kingdom existed as the spiritual kingdom of God's elect. It flourished as a union of the saints— both living and dead—in the one "City of God," while the groaning creation struggled on as the "City of Man" awaiting the consummation of the ages. In the meantime, God desired His people to seek an eternal, rather than a temporal, kingdom.

The progressive clergy, on the other hand, while retaining Augustine's conception of unilinear history, removed the key distinction between the City of God and the City of Man. They fused sacred and secular history into a quest for temporal salvation and redirected the historical process toward the goal of an everlasting Golden Age. Unlike Augustine, who claimed that destruction had awaited the human race ever since Adam's fall, the progressives believed that the flow of history bore humanity along to higher stages of development. In their skillful hands, history itself became a means of grace. Explicitly rejecting the Augustinian scheme of history, they united past, present, and future into a single redemptive process.

Shailer Mathews of the University of Chicago's Divinity School was among the most articulate of those theologians who rejected the Augustinian view of history in favor of historical progressivism. In a series of six lectures given at Harvard in 1916 and later published as *The Spiritual Inter-pretation of History,* Mathews mapped out a middle way that rejected the failed conceptions of Augustine's pure supernaturalism and the absolute naturalism of the new geographic and economic determinists. He spurned both schools of thought for being "dogmatic."[29] Mathews proposed as an alternative a unified theory of history that embraced the totality of human experience, or, as he phased it, "the total situation of man-in-nature." According to Mathews, Augustine's philosophy held no attraction for the modern mind because it could not account for factors that so visibly directed the course of events. He complained that Augustine's system did not recognize the influence of economics and other determinants on human behavior and was therefore incompatible with the modern understanding of the way the world worked. Just as precariously, Mathews warned, contemporary naturalism abandoned man to a mere animal existence and recognized little purpose or destiny for man as brute. He asked if life was indeed simply a matter of impersonal biological stimulus and response, merely "a mechanistic tropism." Or was it "a becoming rather than a mere being; a movement towards personal values; a world order to be constructed from within as well as from without; . . . a development away from animalism toward Godlikeness?" For Mathews, history possessed a distinct and discernable tendency, a teleology. It moved from the physical to the spiritual, from perdition to redemption.[30]

Mathews and his generation were not unique in adopting this view. To be sure, the progressive theologians' conception of history followed a long tradition of Western developmentalist thinking that had reemerged in the eighteenth century and then captivated the nineteenth-century mind under the influence of philosophers from Turgot to Hegel to Spencer.[31] According to these thinkers and their theological offspring, historical events fitted into a pattern of human progress. Thus, in the progressive clergy's interpretive framework, events in America's national life assumed a cosmic significance; each step in the nation's journey led inexorably to the City of God. Infused with such transcendent significance, what had been, for example, simply mundane politics or commonplace matters of foreign policy became, to the progressive clergy, theological events in a redemptive history. And this pervasive spiritualizing or sacralizing of matters of statecraft and public policy—a habit of thought and speech that appeared repeatedly among politicians, academics, and newspaper editors—held deep consequences for the direction of American policy as the Great War approached. For, as historian Richard Bishirjian has observed, "if salvation is thought to be intramundane, political life takes on new historical importance as it becomes enveloped in the history of salvation; and politics becomes the field of prophecy."[32] Certainly, by the time of the war, the progressive clergy were adept at practicing politics as prophecy. At the most fundamental level, they merged politics and religion.

The progressive clergy, then, did not expect salvation to come from outside of history in the Augustinian sense, but rather envisioned history as leading toward a definite goal, which was something quite distinct from a mere end. They replaced the Augustinian God *of* history with a developmentalist God *in* history. Lyman Abbott summarized this view of history succinctly when he wrote in *The Evolution of Christianity* that "the true historian . . . sees that there is a moral development; that events lead on to other events in the realm of spirit as in the realm of matter; that there is a God in history, as there is a God in nature—a God who is working out some great design among men, as there is a God who is working out great designs through all material and mechanical phenomena."[33] While the question of the Great War's meaning would prove troubling and awkward, it would not prove to be incompatible with this philosophy of history. Reaching for a handy image from John Bunyan's *Pilgrim's Progress*—a standard book in most American homes of the nineteenth century and a rich source of symbols and metaphors for preachers and politicians alike—the progressive clergy often pictured the totality of history in the role of Bunyan's Christian on his pilgrimage to the Celestial City, progressively freed from his burden and heading, episode by episode, stage by stage, to the Promised Land. And when the Great War exploded, it seemed natural to accept it as humanity's collective Jordan River, the last trial of faith before the splendor of Heaven.

By the turn of the century, a sacralizing, developmentalist philosophy of history was entrenched as a fundamental doctrine in reconstructed Protestant Christianity. The two most influential seminary textbooks of the day indicated the pervasiveness of this view: William Newton Clarke's

An Outline of Christian Theology, followed by William Adams Brown's *Christian Theology in Outline,* two texts that trained the younger clergy who
were later forced to find meaning in the Great War. Clarke, professor at
Colgate Theological Seminary, a mentor to Harry Emerson Fosdick, and a
leading academic of the New Theology, was confident that the evolutionary process initiated by God would inevitably carry humanity through
higher and higher stages of development. He spiritualized Jesus' Second
Coming into a progressive unfolding of this gradual and almost endless
process. "No visible return of Christ to the earth is to be expected," he
cautioned, "but rather the long and steady advance of his spiritual kingdom." Although the new era's approach might seem slow, he granted, it
nonetheless should be anticipated with confidence. "If our Lord will but
complete the spiritual coming that he has begun," Clarke continued, "there
will be no need of [a] visible advent to make perfect his glory on the earth."[34]

William Adams Brown echoed Clarke's expectation of a gradual fulfillment of Christ's kingdom, finding hope and meaning in
developmentalism.[35] Brown had joined the faculty of Union Seminary in
New York in 1892 and published his influential textbook in 1906. "To the
Christian," he argued, "the meaning of the universe lies in the fact that it is
the scene of the progressive realization of the kingdom of God." The implication of this process was clear to Brown: anything less than the kingdom of God had to be rejected as regressive and evil, as the adversary of
Christ's progressive reign. "So far as, at any time," he wrote, the world
"fails to realize the Christian idea, it is evil,—an enemy to be fought, and
if possible, to be subdued. So far as it is adapted to realize the Christian
end, it is good,—the revelation and the creature of God." Brown explicitly linked developmentalism with social reform, anticipating with social
gospel theologian Walter Rauschenbusch the "complete Christianization
of society." And like Clarke, he envisioned this transformation as an almost endless process and noted that the quest for perfection would be
continued even in the next life, where "we shall not be left with idle hands."[36]
One wonders what happened in progressive thought to the idea of Heaven
as a perfected state, but Brown was consistent in tracing out the implications of his universal idea. Redemption, as a process, would never really
be completed. Regenerative development would be perpetual.

The religious progressives migrated further intellectually by adapting much of traditional Christian theology to the new revelation of science and the new philosophy of history. Once the progressive clergy embraced developmentalism as, in William Newton Clarke's phrase, "God's method" for the natural and historical realms, then it followed that they would reinterpret the Bible and theology in light of this universal law as well. While much of this reinterpretation in the natural sciences, philosophy, and theology went on simultaneously and while the intellectual effect of these disciplines on each other was often unclear, developmentalism's scope and power were unmistakable. So pervasive had developmentalism become in the liberal movement in fact, that Pacific School of Theology professor James Buckham—whom Walter Rauschenbusch counted among the leading younger theologians concerned with the "relation between social life and religion"—could define the principle of development as the very essence of religion. Progress itself, he wrote, "means the recognition of the law of development . . . as of the very nature of the spiritual life." Rauschenbusch himself claimed that progress was "divine."[37]

The progressive clergy placed the Bible within this developmental scheme, understanding the books of the Old and New Testaments more as the product of changing historical experience than as inspired writings. Tucker recalled that historical criticism, or, as he defined it, "the application of the new scientific standards to the Bible," had caused an even greater debate than had Darwinism. It "awakened more concern, and stirred more bitterness, than the new hypothesis regarding the origin of man."[38] For most liberal theologians, inerrancy died when modern historical method put the Bible into a context of time and culture. The historicist perspective, as historian Sydney Ahlstrom concluded, "was a culminating and summary feature of the trend" away from the traditional view of revelation. Adopting a historical relativism, modernist theologians concluded that there was "no nonhistorical vantage point for man, only the history of changing conceptions of absoluticity."[39]

Thus, in the hands of the liberals, the Bible became a collection of historically conditioned religious experiences, an anthology of man's dealings with God rather than the revelation of God's dealings with man. And the progressive theologians were quite comfortable with this change. As

William Newton Clarke defended the new understanding of the Bible, it "was necessary, it was Christian, it was beneficent."[40] Moreover, they believed that this situation left them with both a responsibility and an opportunity. Each new generation was obligated to come to terms with a changing and improving understanding of God and His revelation, and then to express that understanding in a relevant way to its contemporaries. The principle of development as applied to the question of revelation, as James Buckham summarized it, "simply recognizes the *method* of revelation as continuous, accretionary, cumulative, and thus at once saves theology from the curse of becoming static and makes revelation a far more vital and normal reality."[41] In this way, God continued age after age to reveal Himself and His will through the entire process of history. History, then, was not only a means of grace, it was a revelation.

At an even more fundamental level, however, the progressive clergy used their doctrine of development to reinterpret God's character and activity, yielding a broader context into which they would fit their understanding of the Bible as an incomplete and imperfect revelation. Their theology replaced both the transcendent God of orthodoxy and the almost absent God of Deism with an immanent God at one with His creation; not quite a God of pagan pantheism, but rather a God who manifests Himself in His creation and accomplishes His will through natural, developmental processes, both historical and biological.[42] The implications of this doctrine of divine immanence were far reaching. As historian Kenneth Cauthen noted, "The combination of evolution and immanence goes a long way toward providing the basic context out of which liberalism came and in which it grew."[43] And, as would later be clear, these two ideas provided the basic context out of which liberalism interpreted the Great War.

Some of the progressive clergy identified immanence as fundamental to their own reconstructed theology. In his memoirs, Washington Gladden explained his view of God's immanence and expressed his hope that one day all of humanity would share this vision. God, he wrote, "is near us, in the very breath of our life, in the pulsations of our hearts, in the movements of our minds, living and working in us and manifesting Himself in every natural force, in every law of life. This is the truth which the world is beginning to understand, the truth of the immanent God; and when it gets to be a reality we shall not be afraid of losing our religion."[44] Meaning, apparently, that humanity eventually would be so closely attuned to God, would enter into a relationship so personal, so mystical, that systems of doctrine would become irrelevant. Similarly, William Jewett Tucker placed God's immanence at the head of the sequence of doctrinal changes that had led to the New Theology. "The first effect of the progressive departure in the field of strictly theological inquiry," he noted, "was to bring about a change in the prevailing conception of God. It changed the emphasis from the thought of His transcendence to that of His immanence." Tracing this change in theology to the revolution in the natural sciences, he concluded that it was to be expected that "the conception of God must be affected by the advance in our understanding of nature."[45]

The doctrine of divine immanence, like the developmentalist theory of history, was inseparable from the progressive clergy's rejection of Augustine's two cities. Their consolidation of the City of Man and the City of God into one holy metropolis united the work of man and the work of God; it fused politics and religion into a single redemptive work. As historian Arlie J. Hoover noted in his comparative study of the British and German clergy during the First World War, the doctrine of immanence verges close to pantheism, and thus "the cleft between sacred and secular is bridged; every secular pursuit becomes *ipso facto* a service to God, including love of country." Moreover, to the immanentalist mind, "culture is merely a continuous demonstration of God's will for mankind." By placing God within the historical process and by universalizing the kingdom of God, Hoover continued, "immanental theology practically erases the distinction between the two cities."[46] While this confusion might seem to have been an inconsequential by-product of the progressives' untethered imagination, its implications both for the church and for civil society were profound. To combine the two citizenships is to venture to build the City of God through human agency, to assume the place and activity of God Himself, to presume to know His will and conceive of oneself as the instrument of that will. Fusing the two cities can lead, in principle and in practice, to political absolutism by enlisting the transcendent order into the service of the secular state. In its most extreme expression, as philosopher Eric Voegelin noted, this fateful tendency appeared in modern totalitarianism. In these political movements "the Christian faith in transcendent perfection through the grace of God has been converted—and perverted—into the idea of immanent perfection through an act of man."[47] To maintain the distinction between the two cities means that there are realms beyond the reach of Caesar; to remove the distinction is to render all unto Caesar, even if one claims the whole while, as the progressive clergy certainly did, that one is rendering all unto God.

The progressive view of history, then, broadly considered, with its many variations in science and theology, replaced the traditional Christian conception of the cosmos as a world of constraints, of human society with a limited potential for improvement, and of history bound by a revealed and definite beginning and end. Developmentalism removed, as it were, the two bookends of the universe. The liberal clergy dispensed with Genesis and Revelation as the boundaries of human history; their evolutionary presuppositions introduced a vague, misty, and endless past and future in which their progressive drama could be played out. Coupled with a faith in an immanent God—who indwelt this process and thereby ensured its success—developmentalism ruled securely in the hearts of progressive Christians as they neared the Great War.

This optimism, however, did not mean that the progressive clergy thought the present world presented no challenges or responsibilities. In fact, quite the opposite was true. Underlying this general faith in progress, was an urgency, a sense of crisis that at times seemed almost to contradict their meliorist optimism. They defended the new thinking not merely as more enlightened and useful, but as the only path open in a world that had embraced an entirely new epistemology. They argued that they were simply responding to a theological and historical imperative. Change was inevitable; therefore Christianity had to refound itself on science's presumably more sure basis of truth. As eminent historian Ralph Henry Gabriel reflected in 1924 about the transformation in thought that had swept the church, "The super-structure of our culture has been rebuilt in adjustment to the new learning. The church has been no exception; like every other human institution it has been compelled to adapt itself to the intellectual development of the last two centuries."[48]

Convinced they were compelled to adapt their faith, the progressive clergy embraced the New Theology as essential to the very survival of Christianity in the modern world. The choice confronting them was not between two competing creeds, but rather between a new Christianity and no Christianity at all, between a modernist faith and modern agnosticism. Drawing on Jesus' analogy between a new faith and new wine, Lyman Abbott passionately defended the modernist solution to this dilemma. "We are living in a time of religious ferment," he warned in 1892. "What shall we do? Attempt to keep the new wine in the old bottles? That can only end in destroying the bottles and spilling the wine. Attempt to stop the fermentation? Impossible!" For Abbott the answer was self-evident: "Put the new wine into new bottles, that both may be preserved. Spiritual experience is always new. It must therefore find a new expression in each age."[49]

By calling the New Theology "new wine" Abbott may have conceded more than he intended, for the progressives were careful to note that what they were up to was not really the creation of a new theology but merely the restatement of the historic faith in different terms for the modern world. But while Abbott acknowledged some discontinuity between historic Christianity and his own religion, he believed that he offered to the contemporary world a faith that was impervious to the ravages of modern skepticism. Let the defenders of orthodoxy say if they would that the new Christianity destroyed the inherited faith, but Abbott stoutly denied that it produced unbelief. On the contrary, the new theology was, he wrote, "an endeavor to maintain faith by expressing it in terms which are more intelligible and credible." Thus, in a defense that perhaps summarized the whole movement in progressive theology, he argued that his goal was "not to destroy, but to reconstruct."[50]

This theme of "saving" Christianity by adjusting it to the modern mind pervaded the progressive clergy's rationale for reconstructing the faith of their fathers. Harry Emerson Fosdick—among the younger theologians who carried forward the modernist mission—recalled years later that the liberals in the church "deliberately, sometimes desperately," worked to "adapt Christian thought and to harmonize it with the intellectual culture of our time." To do otherwise and still have a thriving, meaningful Christianity, he believed, would have been impossible. Adaptation "was the only way in which we could save our faith, and its achievement was a matter of life and death." In the eyes of theological modernism, the struggle for men's souls raged among three forces: an orthodoxy that could not survive the scrutiny of science and philosophy; a purely secular modernism that would tolerate no faith at all; and a hybrid religious modernism that united Christianity with contemporary thought. Fosdick noted many years later that his concern had always been how "to be an intelligent modern and a serious Christian." He believed that modernism was the only alternative left open to a generation that otherwise "would not have been Christians at all unless we could thus have escaped the bondage of the then reigning orthodoxy."[51] Walter Rauschenbusch put it most succinctly when he warned in 1917 that by striving vainly "to keep Christian doctrine unchanged, we shall ensure its abandonment."[52] Having safely guided their modern faith away from the reefs of pure naturalism, the progressives agreed that Christianity also had to be diverted from an equally perilous obscurantism. If it was not acceptable to abandon "both the faith and the form" of historic Christianity, as Lyman Abbott feared the doctrinaire secularists would do, it was surely not possible to retain "both the faith and the form" as the narrow orthodox attempted.[53] From this point of view, conservatives were the unreasonable defenders of an antiquated traditionalism, stupidly unwilling to join the pilgrimage to a new and fairer land.

Standing at the other end of the theological spectrum, the defenders of orthodoxy agreed with the progressives' assessment of the problem: Christianity's survival in the modern world was most definitely at stake. But conservatives condemned the new hybrid faith as hopelessly heretical. Whether sounding the alarm from the parapets of Calvinist orthodoxy at Princeton Seminary or crying out from the more hodge-podge traditionalism of the emerging fundamentalist movement, the opponents of progressive Christianity believed that their liberal fellow ministers were leading Christianity down a broad path to sure destruction rather than to the Celestial City.

In an article for the *Princeton Theological Review* in 1915, J. Gresham Machen identified the conflict in the churches between liberals and conservatives as nothing less than a war of two worldviews. Writing as one of the last of the line of orthodox Princeton theologians that had included Charles Hodge and Benjamin Warfield, he warned that "two conceptions of Christianity are struggling for the ascendancy to-day." In the decades ahead, his resistance to the modernist tide provided a valuable contrast to progressive Christianity. At every point, he argued, modernism challenged such traditional Christian doctrines as the depravity of man, the radical discontinuity between God and man caused by sin, and the temporal state of the present world. Defending traditional Christianity from pragmatism, unbounded meliorism, and Divine immanence, Machen asked,

> Is Christianity a means to an end, or an end in itself, an improvement of the world, or the creation of a new world? Is sin a necessary stage in the development of humanity, or a yawning chasm in the very structure of the universe? Is the world's good sufficient to overcome the world's evil, or is this world lost in sin? Is communion with God a help toward the betterment of humanity, or itself the one great ultimate goal of human life? Is God identified with the world, or separated from it by the infinite abyss of sin? Modern culture is here in conflict with the Bible.[54]

Where the modernists saw continuity between God and man, Machen saw discontinuity. He chided the church for allowing the problem to go as far as it had and for not standing up more resolutely for its beliefs. He warned that the church was at a critical moment in its history and challenged it to decide between the two theologies. "The Church is in perplexity," he warned. "She is trying to compromise. She is saying, Peace, Peace, when there is no peace. And rapidly she is losing her power. The time has come when she must choose."[55]

Machen ended his barrage against the modernists by again summarizing the essence of the conflict and, significantly, by defending the Augustinian view of God, the universe, and history: "God is not a name for the totality of things, but an awful, mysterious, holy Person, not a 'present God', in the modern sense, not a God who is with us by necessity, and has nothing to offer us but what we have already, but a God who from the heaven of His awful holiness has of His own free grace had pity on our bondage, and sent His Son to deliver us from the present evil world and receive us into the glorious freedom of communion with Himself."[56] Machen agreed with the progressives that the world would ultimately be redeemed, but its deliverance would come by the hand of a transcendent God acting outside of human will and capacity. No conception could have been more alien to the progressives' belief in a salvific, revelatory, God-indwelt historical process.

While Machen and other traditionalists accepted the radical disconti-nuity between Christianity and the world, and maintained the distinction between the sacred and the secular, the progressives desired desperately to be one with the spirit of the age, to breathe the *Zeitgeist* around them. Such an ambition did not mean that they adopted wholesale any prevailing attitude or belief, but rather that they united their faith with what they thought to be the noblest aspirations of the times, especially with the re-formist idealism of the early twentieth century voiced by the Progressive Movement sweeping both major parties. They often referred to the "true" spirit of the age, to those ideals which reflected humanity's progress to-ward God's kingdom.

AFTER THE CELEBRATION at Plymouth Church in 1897, the commemora-tive sermons by Abbott, Gordon, Tucker, Gladden, and others were collected into a volume called *The New Puritanism*. The book's publisher realized the significance of the anniversary and how it symbolized the fundamental theological issues of the day. "The expansion both of knowl-edge and of wisdom in all departments of life during the Nineteenth Century has nowhere been more manifest than in religious matters," he wrote. "The general mental attitude in nearly all communions has changed, towards God and towards man." The publisher thought it especially appropriate "that the fiftieth anniversary of . . . so potent an influence as Plymouth Church . . . should offer an occasion for reviewing at large the vast spiritual migration of multitudes of Christian pilgrims to 'fresh fields and pastures new.'"[57]

By 1900 the vast spiritual migration of these pilgrims was complete. Like the millions of immigrants converging in New York harbor in search of a new world, these spiritual migrants passed through their own Ellis Island, an Ellis Island of the soul. They disembarked into the twentieth century carrying a meliorist view of the universe, a compelling faith in an immanent God, and a passion to unite Christianity with the spirit of the age. In addition to this intellectual baggage, the progressive clergy brought with them an irrepressible determination to redeem American society and even the world at large, to liberate humanity from its regressive past and bring it along on the pilgrimage to the Celestial City. Theological progressivism was far more than a body of speculative doctrine; as its proponents insisted so often, it was a "living faith," a faith to be pragmatically proved by its visible results in society. Believing the Promised Land to be within reach, the progressive clergy set out to redeem their churches, American society, and the world beyond through the power of an applied Christianity.

2

APPLIED CHRISTIANITY

IMPLEMENTING THE PROGRESSIVE WORLDVIEW

IN 1886, MORE THAN TEN YEARS before Plymouth Church's celebration of progressive Christianity, social gospel pioneer Washington Gladden offered to his publisher his new manuscript, "Applied Christianity." At first it seemed that this title would not pass the scrutiny of a certain Mr. Scudder, reader for the Boston publishing house of Houghton, Mifflin and Company, who balked at the word "applied." As Gladden recounted, Mr. Scudder "could not see the force of the adjective. I tried to show him that the whole significance of the book was in that adjective." Gladden fought for the title and prevailed, defending it as the essence of modern Christianity. The old message of individual redemption had to be expanded, he believed, so that the emerging urban and industrial order might be held morally accountable. For Gladden, as for the social gospel movement as a whole, what "the world needed most was a direct application of the Christian law to the business of life."[1]

This "direct application" of Christianity to the problems of the modern world challenged Protestantism's traditional understanding of the church's mission in the world and how its success was to be measured. The progressive clergy lived in an age that craved visible results, that demanded that its principles, values, and ideals prove their worth and viability. Religious modernism by 1900, as historian William Hutchison noted, was guided by Jamesean pragmatism, which "reunited thought and action by making experience the precedent of thought and workability the test of truth."[2] In a world oriented toward results, the ideal of "service" became fundamental to a reconstructed Christianity that down-played doctrines and creeds and in their place emphasized an activist, socially applied gospel.

This was the sort of "social service" gospel promoted just two years after Gladden's *Applied Christianity* went to press in Edward Bellamy's *Looking Backward,* a utopian novel about a collectivist American paradise of the year 2000. In this millennial vision, Bellamy featured a sermon that could have been delivered by any of the popular social gospel clergy of his day. Bellamy's fictional minister, Mr. Barton, rejoiced that the "new order" had discovered man's inner divinity and innate goodness, had recognized the fatherhood of God, and had at last achieved "humanity's ancient dream of liberty, equality, fraternity." Evolutionary progress had worked its miracle; in the New America everyone worked together in common service.[3] True to this shared vision, Washington Gladden and his fellow progressive clergy touted service—whether to the community, to the nation, or to humanity—as the essence of true religion. "There is no finer basis of fellowship between God and Christ and man," wrote Boston Congregational minister George Gordon, "than honest work, contributive to the welfare and happiness of the community and the world."[4] The exponents of the new faith, moreover, promoted service as vital to humanity's collective pilgrimage to the kingdom of God. "There is no surer way toward the New Jerusalem," Dean Shailer Mathews of the University of Chicago's Divinity School promised, "than the road of service to one's fellows made possible and heroic by an overpowering belief . . . in the eternal worth of humanity and in a developing providential order in human society."[5]

Embracing service, the progressive clergy rejected a radical discontinuity between Christians and the "world" and with it the picture of a chosen people beckoned to flee the City of Destruction. Instead, they saw the world as something for Christians to redeem, as a dominion waiting to be conquered. To that end they sought to apply the ethical teachings of Christianity to the full range of human activity, whether to local politics, national legislation, or international diplomacy. As William Jewett Tucker stressed in his 1897 Plymouth anniversary sermon, America at the close of the nineteenth century was embarrassed among the heathen nations because of the "vast amount of unapplied Christianity" evident within its own borders. The task of the church was to correct that deficiency, "to set Christendom in order—its cities, its industries, its society, its literature, its law."[6] Nothing was to lie beyond the sanctifying reach of applied Christianity; every tainted institution and sphere of life was properly the object of redemption and was to be prepared for its place in the emerging kingdom of God. In the new Decalogue engraved by the finger of progressive idealism, abstract "society" had to conform to the concrete ethical standards once reserved for individual Christians. To be sure, the admonition to "love thy neighbor" was as old as the Law of Moses, but in the new social order this commandment was to be applied to "sinful" institutions as well; sin was identified as residing not so much in the human heart as in society as a whole. From the seminaries to the pulpits, and into society and the world at large, progressive Christianity aimed at nothing less than national and international righteousness.

THE PROGRESSIVES' EFFORT to redirect modern Christianity's attention away from immortality in the world beyond and toward the immorality of the world under its feet began closest to home, within the institutional church itself. First through seminaries that emphasized social service and then through an interdenominational federation that aimed at national influence, the progressive clergy constructed an activist Christianity from the ground up.

By the beginning of the twentieth century, most of the prestigious seminaries had adopted liberal theology and among them provided an intellectual home for some of the movement's most influential leaders. While the voice of nineteenth-century modernism had been heard most forcefully from the pulpits of Bushnell, Beecher, and Gladden, the next generation would be known for its scholars at Yale, Harvard, Union Theological Seminary in New York, and the University of Chicago's new Divinity School. Seminaries were being transformed from institutions that sought primarily to inculcate a knowledge of Greek and Hebrew and systematic theology (and often to perpetuate denominational distinctions) into institutions that incorporated the emerging fields of sociology, psychology, and comparative religion. These modern institutions were not intended to be isolated from the distractions of the world. On the contrary, the reconstructed seminary, like the modern college with which it was often affiliated, strove to be recognized for its active, practical Christianity, for a faith engaged with a sordid but redeemable world. Brown University president William H. P. Faunce, a former New York pastor and veteran of both the social gospel and church unity movements, summarized the task of the progressive schools when he observed that "the modern college thinks of religion in terms of action." The Reverend Faunce believed that all college students, whether training for the ministry or another profession, needed to prepare for a life of Christian service. In fact, he warned, it was dangerous to the individual student's spiritual health to do otherwise, for "somewhere and somehow the student must express his faith through action or his faith will dwindle."[7] An applied Christianity was to be a vital, relevant, and sustaining Christianity.

Near the turn of the century, many of the nation's leading seminaries offered courses in the fundamentals of applied Christianity. Harvard and its offspring Andover led the way in the 1880s with course work in social ethics.[8] And in 1904 Union Seminary in New York added a faculty position actually called "Applied Christianity," endowed with $120,000 by Mrs. William E. Dodge, widow of the famed Congressman, philanthropist, and YMCA promoter. She desired, as she said, to "prepare the students of the Seminary to render practical service in the world, along the lines of its social needs."[9] In order to equip its students further for such "practical service," Union established close ties with both New York University and Columbia University, a step that enabled the seminary to offer a broader program of study.[10] The seminary also sponsored an annual Lincoln Day Conference for New York area social workers and was represented on the board of Union Settlement, which opened in 1895.[11]

Social settlements such as Union's were characteristic of the progressives' vision. Modeling their work mostly after England's Toynbee Hall, the founders of American settlements sought to apply the new social ethics by living among the very people they intended to help. Jane Addams's Hull House in Chicago is the best-remembered of the settlements,[12] but many others flourished in the nation's distressed urban centers. Seminaries cooperated with several of these homes, including Union Settlement, Andover House in Boston, and Chicago Commons.[13] Union Seminary professor William Adams Brown, who helped start Union Settlement, reflected in his autobiography on the natural affinity between the seminaries and the settlements. "The Settlement Movement," he wrote, "founded as it was on an optimistic view of human nature, fitted admirably the liberal philosophy in which we had been brought up. The central idea of the movement was contact. It was its aim to break down the middle wall of partition which . . . separated the haves from the have nots, and . . . to lay the foundation for more radical changes in the future."[14] Shailer Mathews tellingly commented that the settlements were "an expression of a new conception of Christianity which made service superior to theological orthodoxy."[15]

Joining the trend in seminary training toward practical service, Yale added a social ethics course in 1891, offering firsthand experience with the social conditions in large cities. As part of the class, students took annual trips to New York City, visiting University Settlement and other projects there. By 1910 Yale provided experience in such nontraditional ministries as professional social work. Professor Charles Macfarland taught "Pastoral Functions," a course designed to prepare Yale's ministers to head socially active churches, and he welcomed guest speakers such as John Mitchell of the United Mine Workers.[16] By the time of the World War, Yale had added the Horace Bushnell Chair of Christian Nurture.[17]

The thoroughness of Harvard's transformation into a training ground for an applied Christianity was revealed by President Charles W. Eliot in his noted 1909 address to the Harvard Summer School of Theology. In this lecture Eliot presented his conception of the "Religion of the Future," a rather unorthodox set of beliefs that rejected authority, tradition, personal regeneration, and Christ's atoning death in favor of a religion of divine immanence, rationality, social amelioration, service, and cooperation. The slogan of the church of tomorrow, he claimed, was "Be serviceable." He reminded the students that in their summer classes they had heard "how the ideas of democracy and social progress have modified and ought to modify not only the actual work done by the churches, but the whole conception of the functions of churches."[18] Eliot's speech drew considerable comment from the religious press, both condemnation and praise. Several denominational papers criticized his radicalism, and one Catholic bishop remarked that Dr. Eliot's new religion "will certainly not be Christianity." The *New York Times* dryly noted that it was not a religion anyone would ever die for. But praise came quickly from Union Theological Seminary, Eliot's Unitarian brethren, and the *Congregationalist* and *Outlook.* Lyman Abbott's *Outlook* commended his religion of service, disappointed only that he had not grounded his vision in the moral example of Jesus.[19] Whatever the press comment, Eliot's speech to Harvard's theology students further demonstrated the reorientation of liberal seminary training toward social service.

Overshadowing the record of Union, Yale, and Harvard as centers of Protestant liberalism, the new University of Chicago and its Divinity School attracted some of the most radical thinkers in religious modernism.[20] Among the seminary's more gifted and controversial scholars were Gerald Birney Smith, Shirley Jackson Case, and Shailer Mathews, members of a distinguished faculty that ensured Chicago's preeminence.[21] The seminary produced such widely read journals as *Biblical World,* the *American Journal of Theology,* and *The World Today.* Of *The World Today* Shailer Mathews wrote that "it was a new point of contact between religious idealism and political and social trends."[22] And, as Union's Brown would later note, such contact, like that provided by the settlement houses, was the key to many of the progressive clergy's reform efforts.

The new social emphasis in ministerial preparation made such rapid progress that by 1912 the eminent social gospel theologian Walter Rauschenbusch could observe that nearly all the notable seminaries offered courses in "Social Ethics" or "Christian Sociology."[23] Overall, their faculties gave direction, form, and substance to an applied Christianity, moving it from theory to practice. Protestant liberals believed that new social circumstances and new ideas demanded a new Christianity. Over the course of the nineteenth century they had crafted a new theology to accommodate the new learning, and then added to that reconstructed Christianity a redefined and expanded ministry for the sake of social change. Radical theologian Gerald Birney Smith of the University of Chicago's Divinity School summarized the role of the modern seminary well when he argued that theological training had to "deal with the bewildering needs occasioned by the shifting habits of people in modern industrial and spiritual life. An entirely new realm of theological training has been organized in order to prepare men to understand the social problems which are so intimately related to the religious life."[24]

Naturally, such enthusiasm for applied Christianity reached beyond the walls of the seminaries and, as intended, influenced the churches as well. Some seminary professors worked in both realms. Chicago's Shailer Mathews and Yale's Charles Macfarland, for example, were active in denominational federation, a movement aimed in part at broader social service through a united church. They believed that the church had to consolidate not just for the sake of the integrity of the body of Christ, but also as a practical matter. They intended to put the power and efficiency of a single organization behind the church's increasing social emphasis and its burgeoning missionary efforts. Most notable among the many church federation movements, and most germane to understanding the attitude of the clergy during the Great War, was the Federal Council of the Churches of Christ, launched in 1905.

In November of that year, several hundred delegates from churches across America assembled at New York's fashionable Carnegie Hall for the Inter-Church Conference on Federation. Leaders from twenty-eight denominations, representing an estimated eighteen million church members (at a time when the U.S. population numbered about one hundred million), attended the meeting. Commenting on the significance of the event, the *New York Times* noted that the conference spoke for "nearly all the Protestant faiths of the country whose aim is a world conquest for Christianity." President Theodore Roosevelt thought the occasion significant enough to send a personal letter to the convocation. Fresh from his diplomatic triumph in negotiating the Treaty of Portsmouth ending the Russo-Japanese War, Roosevelt reminded the church leaders of the opportunity for the West then opening in Japan. Anticipating the potential of church unity for missionary activity and, by implication, for international relations as well, he observed that he had "the very highest sympathy with the movement; . . . in addition to the great good it will do here, it is perfectly possible that the movement may have a very considerable effect in the Christianizing of Japan." Roosevelt assured the delegates that he had "a very real interest in what you are doing."[25]

The New York conference continued for a week and welcomed a broad range of participants to its platform. Social gospel activist Washington Gladden presided at one session, and the delegates also heard from retired Postmaster General John Wanamaker, Oberlin College's president Henry Churchill King, and Dartmouth's William Jewett Tucker, who discussed "Christian Citizenship." The Reverend Henry van Dyke, esteemed Presbyterian pastor, poet, and future ambassador to the Netherlands and Luxembourg under President Wilson, offered his conception of the "Ideal Society." Other distinguished speakers included Plymouth Church's Newell Dwight Hillis, Brown University's William H. P. Faunce, and Josiah Strong, president of the American Institute of Social Service and the author of numerous best-selling books advocating a muscular Christianity combined with a vigorous American foreign policy.[26]

In addition to King, Tucker, and Faunce, another college president spoke as well: Princeton's rising star, Woodrow Wilson, who addressed a special youth service on the timely topic "The Mediation of Youth in Christian Progress." Introducing him was long-time friend John R. Mott, the tireless YMCA administrator to whom Wilson as president would offer the post of ambassador to China in 1913 and later dispatch on two diplomatic missions, first to Mexico in 1914 and then to Russia in 1917. Consistent with his own interest in the YMCA, Wilson praised American youth for having put noble goals and ideas ahead of divisive "dogma." He proposed that in national service they should be guided by the question "*What would Christ have done in our day, in our place, with our opportunities?*" The possibilities of such a consecration to duty seemed limitless. "There is a mighty task before us," he charged, "and it welds us together. It is to make the United States a mighty Christian Nation, and to christianize the world."[27]

In laying out such expansive goals, Wilson repeated a theme heard often that week in New York. Throughout the conference, the delegates talked eagerly of "Christianizing" their communities, the nation, and the world. One by one they pricked the conscience of the church and the nation on issues ranging from betting on college sports to the need for more settlement houses. To help the churches work toward these goals, the conference's business committee presented a trial constitution for inter-denominational cooperation that included calls for "service for Christ and the world" and for "the application of the law of Christ in every relation of human life."[28] At a reception at the Waldorf-Astoria closing the conference, New York's Lt. Governor M. Linn Bruce encouraged the assembled church leaders to "bring about an ideal Church and an ideal State."[29]

To reach that "ideal State" the newly-formed Federal Council of Churches embarked on a mission to "Christianize" America with the social gospel. Walter Rauschenbusch claimed that the Federal Council's Philadelphia conference in 1908—its first official assembly as the Federal Council—marked a milestone in the social gospel movement, basing his claim on the fact that those sessions discussing social service attracted the most attention. The council that year also adopted the so-called Social Creed of the Churches, originally drafted as the Methodist Social Creed by social gospel leader Harry F. Ward.[30] At its next quadrennial meeting, in Chicago in 1912, the Federal Council expanded the Social Creed to include pronouncements on child labor, marriage and divorce, prohibition, worker safety, a shorter work week, and a "living wage."[31] But the council did more than issue opinions on the latest social concerns. Indeed, by taking advantage of personal friendships, and through direct lobbying efforts by its Washington Bureau, the federated churches positioned themselves to influence public policy. As one historian of the movement observed, "The Federal Council functioned as a state church by providing its members access to decision makers in government and business, and by speaking with a common voice more easily heard in public debate than the multiple voices of denominations."[32]

Of the success of the Federal Council in the years leading up to the First World War, General Secretary Charles Macfarland later wrote that slowly "departments were developed, associates were placed at my side, our ideals rapidly took substantial form and, in the providence of God, the Federal Council was a reality when world calamity came."[33] Thus, by the outbreak of the European War in 1914, an organized, activist church stood poised for national and international service.

. . . .

FEDERATION OF THE major Protestant denominations for the sake of social service revealed a change in the church's role in modern society. The church was no longer seen as a refuge from the world, as an enclave of the redeemed within Augustine's City of Man, but rather as a conquering army liberating the world and rebuilding the City of Man into the City of God. As William Jewett Tucker had proclaimed years earlier at Plymouth Church, "This is the vision of the latter day, not of a Church saved out of the world, but of a world redeemed by the Church."[34] The church no longer encouraged John Bunyan's Pilgrim to forsake all and turn his back on the City of Destruction, but instead urged him to drag the city of the damned along with him on the narrow road to redemption. Rather than being relieved of his burden of sin, the Pilgrim was expected to press forward with a new burden on his back in the form of the social gospel. Employing this metaphor from Bunyan's classic, Baptist leader, professor, and social activist Samuel Zane Batten claimed that "Christianity is not here to show men how to escape from the city of destruction and get away to the Celestial City; it is here rather to inspire men to labour and serve to transform the city of destruction into a City of God."[35] The modern church put on the armor of God to wrestle in flesh and blood with Apollyon and Giant Despair, the new adversaries who occupied city halls and corporate board rooms, impeding the progress of a pilgrim world.

Progressive theologians constructed a very broad definition of the church and its mission in the world, and included more and more of society under its sacred authority, to the point of not distinguishing between the church and the world. The kingdom of God encompassed all of humanity. Given such a wide field of legitimate action, the church was to make every area of life, every institution, an object of conquest. "The kingdom of God," wrote Walter Rauschenbusch, "is not bound by the Church, but includes all human relations."[36] Other theologians defined religion even more broadly, identifying genuine faith as simply anything that demanded devotion to something higher and larger than one's self. Even loyalty to one's country could count as religion. As Union Seminary professor A. C. McGiffert explained, "Whether it be art, or science, or philosophy, or patriotism, or humanitarianism, or the worship of God, that thus takes [a man] out of himself and lifts him into the region of the spiritual and ideal[,] the essence of religion is his."[37]

Not everyone was comfortable with this broadly defined kingdom and its crusading church. Indeed, by the time of the Great War a few churches had left the Federal Council, expressing concern over its progressive theology and social activism.[38] Moreover, some critics in the secular world also doubted the new role of the church in society. Writing in 1914, Princeton's stubborn classicist and doubter of progress Paul Elmer More saw the new earthly minded, humanitarian religion as symptomatic of the general decline of the age: "For one sermon you will hear on the obligation of the individual soul to its maker and judge, and on the need of regeneration and the beauty of holiness, you will hear a score on the relation of a man to his fellows and on the virtues of social sympathy." In short, More feared, humanitarianism had "usurped the place of religion."[39] The modern church often endured such stinging criticism for its relationship to society, but more often for its failure to fulfill its vaunted promises of social regeneration than for its eagerness to unite itself with the spirit of the age, as More complained. The progressive clergy's assumption that the church had both the ability and the duty to remake the social order was generally accepted by progressive America, which held the marshaled forces of "organized righteousness" accountable for any troublesome advance by the forces of "organized evil."

Despite criticism from various quarters, the progressive church pressed on with its critique of American society, focusing particularly on the remnants of nineteenth-century individualism, localism, and economic classical liberalism. Apart from Marxist and other marginal radical movements at the turn of the century, the most searching and sustained criticism of modern America came from the social gospel, a theological movement that by the outbreak of the Great War had spread well beyond the seminaries and pulpits in which it had been nurtured.[40] As historian Paul Carter noted, the social emphasis within Protestantism tended from the beginning to penetrate Christianity from the top down through the denominational press and bureaucracy, becoming by the time of the formation of the Federal Council a philosophy powerful enough to unite a broad range of otherwise dissimilar denominations. Nevertheless, despite its preoccupation with the so-called submerged tenth and related issues of labor, poverty, and social displacement, the social gospel remained a middle- and upper-class movement, most visible in the metropolitan pulpits of the East and upper Midwest.[41]

To be sure, the social gospel reached far deeper and wider than the elitist source of its advocacy might suggest; indeed, historian Susan Curtis found that calls for a socially responsive church were heard from cities across the Midwest and parts of the South.[42] Nonetheless, the leadership of the social gospel movement, those who were most visible and who reached the widest audience—the clergy who influenced the influential, so to speak—labored in the largest cities and moved within the highest realms of power, from the financial empires of Rockefeller and Carnegie, to the political dominions of Roosevelt and Wilson. In their efforts to reconstruct American life and thought, the progressive clergy were positioned to achieve that transformation. Their plans included every level of society down to the smallest rural community in America,[43] but to realize those ambitions they allied themselves with the nation's sources of power, money, and influence.

Sensing the rumblings of social discontent in the 1870s, as gauged by popular economist Henry George and others, the architects of the social gospel emphasized justice and physical redemption in this present world over spiritual salvation in the life to come. Consequently, they interpreted Christianity in terms of behavior rather than doctrine. They condemned moribund orthodoxy for its impractical talk of binding creeds and standards of faith, while they instead emphasized good deeds and standards of living. In his memoirs, Dean Shailer Mathews of the University of Chicago's Divinity School contrasted the two competing views of man and redemption. "The older evangelical orthodoxy," he wrote, "regarded the gospel as the message of forgiveness of sins by virtue of belief in Jesus as the atoning sacrifice. Faith in him was of course to be followed by moral life but the good news of salvation was not primarily moral." In contrast, the social gospel "was aggressively ethical. It naturally produced moral discontent rather than spiritual complacency."[44]

BUSINESS REPLY MAIL
PERMIT NO. 44 WILMINGTON, DE

INTERCOLLEGIATE STUDIES INSTITUTE, INC.
PO BOX 4431
WILMINGTON, DE 19807-9957

Dear Reader:

Thank you for purchasing this ISI Books title. Since 1953, the **Intercollegiate Studies Institute** (ISI) has fostered in successive generations an appreciation for, and a deeper understanding of, America's tradition of ordered liberty. **ISI Books** serves the Institute's broader national program by publishing books, guides, and other resources that consider afresh those perennial ideas which have shaped Western culture and the American experience.

If you would like to learn more about ISI and ISI Books, please fill out this postcard and drop it in the mail.

Name:

Address:

City/State/Zip:

Country:

E-Mail:

Phone:

I received this card in the book titled:

A UNIVERSITY IN PRINT
The imprint of the Intercollegiate Studies Institute

*Call **800-526-7022** or visit us at **www.isibooks.org**.*

In order to make the church "aggressively ethical," the social gospel required that Christianity redefine its theology of man and society. In *The Gospel and the Modern Man* of 1910, Shailer Mathews argued for the new solidaristic view of man in society. Mathews believed that social consciousness had become an inseparable part of the modern mind, a mind guided by a sense of historical process, the immanence of God in human events, and the empirical basis of truth. He further argued that the condition of the social order itself would determine the agenda of "really vital religious issues" facing the contemporary church.[45] This new solidarity meant that both sin and salvation, historically matters of supreme importance for the individual, were now social concepts. For Mathews, the new perspective—like the growing ideal of "service"—was attributable to historical development; society was moving inexorably from individualism toward collectivism, changing the very definition of sin. "As civilization develops," he wrote, "sin grows corporate. We sin socially by violating social rather than individualistic personal relations."[46] This view was much the same as the one promoted in Edward Bellamy's *Looking Backward*.

But if sin was social, then logically, for there to be any hope for humanity at all, salvation had to be social as well. As historian Richard Hofstadter noted, the social gospel embraced a Spencerian conception of social solidarity even though many of its leaders eschewed Spencer's brutal competitive model. To these reformers, "the social-organism concept meant that salvation of the single individual had lost its meaning, and that in the future men would speak with Washington Gladden of 'social salvation.'"[47] As Union Seminary's William Adams Brown explained the problem in his widely used textbook, *Christian Theology in Outline*, "the salvation of the individual can never be divorced as an end in itself from the establishment of the kingdom of God." "A man is saved," he argued, "only as he becomes a member of that society; that is, as he enters into right relations to his fellows, and so helps to realize God's plan for the world."[48] For the progressive theologians, redemption for any particular individual had meaning only in the context of redemption for humanity at large.

The more orthodox within American Protestantism continued to interpret the gospel primarily in terms of the individual. Society, if im-

proved at all, would be reformed as a by-product of the changed lives of
the converted. Modern Sodom and Gomorrah were more likely to be
spared for the sake of ten righteous than as a result of a higher hourly
wage or good sanitation. This is not to say that the orthodox clergy had no
interest in social improvement or in ameliorating the plight of the poor
and suffering. Their argument concerned the means employed and the
threat to the institutional integrity of the church and its primary and unique
mission. The conservatives feared that a preoccupation with temporal reform would lead, and indeed already had led, the church into doctrinal
heresy.

In contrast to such fears, Shailer Mathews hoped that the social emphasis would actually bring the doctrinally splintered churches together
"to fight their common enemy, not each other."[49] It seemed absurd to him
that with so much work to be done the church would quibble over such
matters as the authority of Scripture:

> With the sanctity of the home threatened by reckless divorces and even more
> reckless marriages, with a generation polluted by a mania for gambling, with
> saloons and brothels at its door, why should the church pause to manicure its
> theology? Facing a world in the darkness of heathenism, a submerged tenth
> rotting in our cities, an industrialism that is more murderous than war, why
> should the church stop to make a belief in the historicity of the great fish of
> Jonah a test of fitness for cooperation in aggressive evangelization?[50]

Combative evangelicals and modernists, he believed, had to remain united
within their denominations and to press on to greater unity for the sake of
the higher calling of a righteous nation in a righteous world.

United for service, the church had to convict America of its social sin
and of the need for repentance, impelled by a sense of God's justice. To
that end, the reforming clergy, much like the contemporary muckraking
journalists, appealed directly to the public conscience. "The social power
of the gospel will be commensurate with its power to rouse a hatred of
sin," Mathews wrote. But what kind of sin? Sin as defined personally and
judicially by Calvinism? On the contrary, a hatred "not of sin as a theological abstraction, but of sin as we have seen it actually working its way out in
oppression and sorrow and personal decay, whether it be in the world of

politics or of industry or of the home." New times had brought a new definition of sin and virtue: "Society needs to be convinced afresh of the elemental distinction between evil and good as redefined by the changing condition of our ever more complex life."[51]

Building on this redefinition of evil and good, Mathews further contended that God would hold the world to a strict accounting for its toleration of social sin. Although the progressive clergy offered a gospel imbued with brotherhood and a loving Father, they retained a strong sense of divine justice and of the inevitability of such judgment in a morally rational universe. In a striking comment, Mathews summarized the progressives' view of God: "It is sometimes said that modern thought is removing the punitive God from His universe. It seems to me, on the contrary, that it is bringing that God into the universe and even more into human life[,] . . . more a God to be feared than even the Jehovah of the prophets."[52] God was no sentimentalist, and His contemporary prophets still held their commission to preach justice and righteousness. Belief in progress in no way diminished the progressives' sense of evil and guilt. Journalist Mark Sullivan recalled of the prewar years that along with the spirit of progress "went a spirit of self-blame, a passion for putting on a hair-shirt as a spiritual luxury, a mood of accusing ourselves for having postponed so long the things we were now determined to accomplish in a hurry."[53]

A righteous America was the first order of business for the hair-shirted social gospel clergy, who were inclined to see sin in things and institutions rather than primarily in the human heart. Preaching in Des Moines, Iowa, in 1904, New York Congregational pastor Charles Jefferson called for a "new crusade" to save America, "our Holy Land," from the ravages of the modern Saracen. The forces of alcohol, vice, political corruption, and general lawlessness possessed the land, he warned. It was now time "to break the power of his mailed fist,—that is the object of the new crusade." But it was not only America that was to be rescued from the infidels. America itself would then redeem the world, serving as God's historically prepared nation, "through which the Eternal shall proclaim his will to all the sons of men." What the world needed, he continued with a nod to William James, was an American Christianity prepared to wage "a moral equivalent of war" in the service of humanity.[54]

The metaphor of war, especially of religious wars and crusades, was common to the Progressive Movement as a whole. At the 1912 Progressive National Convention in Chicago, at which the delegates sang such favorites as the "Battle Hymn of the Republic" and "Onward, Christian Soldiers," party candidate Teddy Roosevelt proclaimed to his fellow Bull Moosers that "Our cause is based on the eternal principles of righteousness. . . . We stand at Armageddon, and we battle for the Lord." Conservationist and Forest Service chief Gifford Pinchot, who served on the Progressive Party's platform committee at Chicago and was also active in the Federal Council of Churches, revealingly chose to describe the reform enthusiasm of the early twentieth century, especially the rising concern for "political morality," as a perpetual "war for righteousness."[55]

In its crusade to make America a Christian state, the united, activist church found staunch allies in a number of economists and social critics. Prominent among these was Richard T. Ely, perhaps the economist most often cited by the social gospel theologians. From 1881 to 1892, Ely taught political science at Johns Hopkins University and was one of Woodrow Wilson's seminar professors. By the 1890s, Ely was proposing that God worked primarily through the state to achieve His ends and that it was therefore the church's duty to see to it that the state was infused with Christianity and to remove any impediment in "the way of righteousness."[56] Ely's American Economic Association incorporated into its purpose statement a call for the "united efforts" of "the church, of the state, and of science" to address society's ills. Ely urged the church, the first member of this trinity, to seize the opportunities presented by economic crises to advance the realization of a just society. In later years he recalled that he had spent his life prodding the churches "to do their part to bring about a social order in harmony with the principles of Christianity." Significantly, he included the Methodist Social Creed—the very document adopted by the Federal Council of Churches in 1908—as an appendix to his autobiography.[57]

Similarly, George D. Herron, one of the most radical social gospel advocates, preached much the same message of social redemption through the power of the state. Herron began his career as a Congregational minister but joined the faculty of Grinnell College, Iowa, and lectured across

North America on "the Christian State." At Grinnell he taught "Applied Christianity" and assigned his classes Richard Ely's *Social Aspects of Christianity* and Washington Gladden's *Applied Christianity*. He warned America away from "selfishness"—his central theme—and taught that the state had to be "born again" in order to reach the "divine social kingdom." As historian C. Howard Hopkins noted, Herron believed that the redemptive forces in society could "be actualized only through the agency of the state." Eventually Herron's radicalism took him toward socialism and communism as the cures for society, and in 1900 he even campaigned for Socialist presidential candidate Eugene V. Debs.[58]

Following the same reasoning, Northern Baptist social gospeler Samuel Zane Batten contended that the most powerful forces affecting modern life were the state, Christianity, and democracy, all three of which were growing in strength and becoming universal. The challenge, therefore, was to combine these tides into a torrent that would sweep the world toward the kingdom of God. "Of one thing I am convinced," Batten exulted, "that one of the great needs of this present time is some large conception of the State . . . and its place in the purpose of God." The fundamental question remaining was "will the State become the medium through which the people shall co-operate in their search after the kingdom of God and its righteousness?"[59] Both church and state were necessary parts of God's kingdom, the two sacred halves, spiritual and physical, of God's reign. Batten even predicted that the two powers would "gradually merge into each other" and thereby forfeit their "identity in the perfected kingdom of humanity."[60] This union of church and state was a common hope among social gospel leaders. A writer for *Collier's* in 1912 perceptively concluded an article on the aging warrior Washington Gladden by noting that to Gladden "the United States of America is a theocracy."[61]

Ely's vision of the state as God's primary vehicle of His righteous will, Herron's similar dream of a redemptive state, and Batten's anticipation of heaven and earth merged into the "perpetual kingdom of humanity" all clearly indicated the progressive clergy's failure to distinguish the City of Man from the City of God and their desire to unite the forces of God and Caesar into a mighty army of earthly salvation. The American state was their messiah and the temporal world their millennial kingdom. What sociologist Robert Nisbet observed in a broader context applied equally to the progressive clergy: "Truly, in the New World as in the Old, the compounding of the idea of progress and the idea of the nation-state could result in an intensity of millennialism and messianism the like of which had never been seen on earth."[62] Who in America more passionately than the progressive clergy combined a religious faith in progress with a reliance on the state? It is in this context that such extraordinary paeans to the state as the Reverend William P. Merrill's poem from the *Christian Century* in 1917 must be understood. After hailing the dawning of the "day of the people," Merrill extolled the creative and redemptive power of the modern state:

> *The strength of the State we'll lavish on more*
> *Than making of wealth and making of war;*
> *We are learning at last, though the lesson comes late,*
> *That the making of man is the task of the State.*[63]

Universalizing the "man-making" powers of the state, the progressive clergy expected the worldwide triumph of their social ideals. As Samuel Batten said in 1911, "the superlative duty of men to-day is the Christianization of Christendom." Each Christian was obligated to work tirelessly until St. John's apocalypse was fulfilled, until "the Holy City of the seer's vision has become the reality of earth."[64]

This powerful sense of an impending new age gained wide acceptance among reformers in the first decades of the twentieth century, infusing them with a spirit of millennial fervency, the sort of expectancy and radical discontinuity between past and present that had made Bellamy's *Looking Backward* so popular. As a bemused Paul Elmer More observed on the eve of the Great War, "nothing is more notable in the Humanitarian literature of the day than the feeling that our own age is severed from the past, and opens an entirely new epoch in history."[65] In 1909, true-believer Shailer Mathews proclaimed that "a new age is imminent," and he promised that even though his generation "may not live to see our ambitions for a new social order fulfilled or some millennium dawn, . . . we shall at least have sold our lives dearly in fighting for the cause that, as surely as there is a God in heaven, must ultimately win."[66] Obedience to the scrutable providential flow of history was the essence of his generation's faith. The approaching epoch, the Future, the New Era—these dominated the vision of the progressive theologians. While traditionalists insisted on adhering to a known past, the progressives prepared for an imagined future, and, as was true of their LeContean version of the natural world, they emphasized "becoming" rather than "being." Mathews reflected this expectancy when he wrote, "A formal definition of modernness is not difficult. He is the modern man of any period who is controlled by the forces which are making Tomorrow."[67] The progressive's responsibility was to yield to those forces, to remove any impediment, and to make the world into what it was becoming. The future would be unified, egalitarian, civilized, peaceful, and democratic. The church, therefore, had to prepare the way. In every area of life the progressive clergy preached the wonders of "Tomorrow."

3

Applied Christianity Abroad

Foreign Missions, Internationalism and

the Expanding circle of Progressive Reform to 1914

The progressive clergy's zeal for national righteousness through an applied Christianity was matched only by their vision of international righteousness. And as with church unification and the social gospel, applied Christianity was central to this goal as well. Despite their historicism and increasing relativism, Protestant liberals on the whole believed in Christianity's distinctiveness, finality, and universality.[1] Moreover, they proclaimed Christianity to be the only foundation for the highest form of civilization. As William Douglas Mackenzie wrote in 1897, the year of the celebration at Plymouth Church, Christianity triumphed as the world's most advanced religion, before which all "lower forms of social organization" gave way. The church had been prepared for this moment in history, for "the deliverance of all tribes and races out of barbarism into the possession of Christian institutions."[2] By spreading Christianity, the missionary offered not merely spiritual hope, but also physical, material, and even aesthetic benefits as well. If the social gospel at home would reclaim society's outcasts through a better environment, then a socially oriented missionary movement undoubtedly would achieve the same feat on a global scale.

In the decades before the First World War, the American missionary movement flourished in its golden age. By 1900 about ninety missionary organizations were operating in the United States. Together they established thousands of overseas churches, colleges, schools, hospitals, and publishing houses. Their efforts enjoyed the support of many prominent Americans, including, most notably, John D. Rockefeller Jr.[3] The missionary fervor from 1890 to 1917 truly deserves the title "crusade," for these years were an era of unprecedented activity, funding, and enthusiasm.[4]

Although boasts of "uplifting" backward nations were common to both traditionalist and progressive Christians, the two groups were distinct in their objectives in spreading the gospel. For traditionalists, as hard as they might work to bring medical care and education to remote countries, their intention remained the saving of lost souls. For the liberals, however, Christianity was a means to another, and supposedly larger, end. It was a means to the socially defined kingdom of God. Making this very point, liberal minister and missions enthusiast Robert E. Speer denied that missionaries had ever gone forth with the simplistic picture foremost in their minds of rescuing perishing heathen, although in his own work he continued to emphasize the necessity of individual conversion in the building of a new society.[5]

Other liberal clergy more explicitly rejected a traditional view of the Great Commission. Such important interpreters of the modern church as G. Sherwood Eddy, Walter Rauschenbusch, Shailer Mathews, Henry Churchill King, and William H. P. Faunce all spoke for the new understanding of evangelism. The missions movement even engaged some workers who later denied that they had been concerned at all with the saving of lost peoples. G. Sherwood Eddy, famous at the time of the Great War as a national and international evangelist and as Asia secretary for the YMCA, admitted in his memoirs that he "held no ideas of a narrow orthodoxy of 'perishing millions' who were eternally lost. This I never believed and never preached at home or abroad." Eddy explained his conception of missions in 1914 when he wrote in the case of China and its neighbors that they needed a "physical gospel" of playgrounds, health services, and modern sanitation. As he looked back upon these years of optimism, he remembered his missionary zeal as "the flush of youth." The worldwide missionary campaign had been attractive to him as a crusade; it demanded selfless living for the sake of a cause and therefore appealed to his youthful romantic imagination. It "made an immediate challenge to our generation for the sacrificial and heroic, like the crusaders of the Middle Ages, like the battle-charge of Islam, or the communism-or-death alternative appealing to Lenin and his revolutionary followers."[6]

Adding his own perspective on missions from the forefront of the social gospel movement in 1912, Walter Rauschenbusch consigned the purely spiritual purpose of foreign evangelism to the oblivion of a bygone era. In the past, he noted, the missionaries had indeed worked to spread the gospel message as widely as possible. But now Christianity served more as a tool for broader social reconstruction. Echoing Theodore Roosevelt's concern in 1905 for a modernizing Japan, Rauschenbusch wrote, "To-day the leaders of the missionary movement are teaching a statesmanlike conception of the destiny of Christianity as the spiritual leaven of the East and the common basis of a world-wide Christian civilization." The representatives of Christ's church overseas were the advance guard "of the Christian nations in the effort to uplift the entire life of the backward peoples."[7]

Shailer Mathews unequivocally interpreted missions as a logical extension of the social duty of the churches. If the churches were to remain at the forefront of social change, then they had to be alert to the awakening of many peoples, not just of Americans. "With the nations being born anew through the influence of a new age," he urged, "the church must do something more than exhort the heathen to accept a sixteenth-century theology." He argued that the missionary impulse was much more than a religious effort; it was "a great social movement" as well. Through the benefits of education and medicine, and by exploiting contacts with political leaders in foreign countries, the missionary was able to change the face of the societies he adopted. As Mathews unblinkingly summarized it, "The missionary has been able . . . to revolutionize and reorganize civilization in the name of Christ." And, he continued, the internal missionaries within the United States performed no less a feat. These home missionaries, working to assimilate Eskimos, Indians, and immigrants, provided "training in the American spirit." Consistent with the progressives' meliorist faith, Mathews concluded that global evangelism ultimately would "guarantee that the entire world will be a better, a safer, and a happier place in which our descendants shall live." Presumably the burden for lost souls figured somewhere into this ambitious scheme, but Mathews's preeminent concern lay with a reordered, rationalized, advancing world.[8]

Explaining the political potential of this kind of modern missionary activity, Oberlin College president and progressive leader Henry Churchill King urged his fellow Americans to draw strength from their Puritan sense of "divine calling" as they faced the civilizing task ahead, because "every nation that means to count greatly in the world still needs the Puritan's feeling of commission from God." America had been summoned to extend "the sway of democratic principles" over the whole earth and "greatly assist, and not hinder, the existing democratic trend in the world."[9] Naturally, the spread of democracy required the spread of Christianity, but not of traditional Christianity. Concerned with the fate of the emerging Orient, King warned that for those nations to become truly modern, they would have to embrace modernity's religion as well. Only progressive Christianity could provide Japan and its neighbors with "a religion that will stand the rational and ethical test of the scientific spirit and of the social consciousness."[10]

In 1914, Brown University president William H. P. Faunce devoted an entire book to the social significance of foreign missions. Repeating a familiar theme, he called for the full application of the gospel to backward countries. In phrases identical to the arguments for applying the social gospel at home, he pleaded for a "complete message" of Christianity that worked toward "the entire transformation of both the individual and society." His book included photographic evidence of the practical results possible with a broadly defined evangelism, including pictures of schools, hospitals, and a wholesome orderliness intended to impress upon the reader the real work of the gospel.[11] Like Eddy, Mathews, and others, Faunce supported foreign missions primarily as a means to spread social gospel ideals, to reconstruct other societies in the way he hoped to reconstruct America.

WORKING TO RECONSTRUCT the church and American society, and to redefine the missionary enterprise, the progressive church's only remaining task was to consolidate the redeemed nations into a fraternal world order, building a righteous internationalism. In this way, the social gospel's version of the Golden Rule would reach beyond relations among individuals, beyond the workings of institutions and society, to govern relations among nations. Diplomacy would enter a new era the moment Christian nations began dwelling in the unity of Christian brotherhood, thereby fulfilling and universalizing in the world at large Christ's prayer for His church. While noting the dangers of economic and military imperialism, the progressive clergy's ideals were unmistakably expansive and imperialistic.

By the close of the nineteenth century, progressive Christianity was earnestly pursuing its distinctive version of internationalism. This humanitarian impulse was directed not toward a nonideological association of freely trading and competing nations but rather toward an internationalism guided by abstract notions of universal democracy and permanent peace, a world order benevolently led and dominated by America. The most notable advocate of this ambitious and revolutionary role for the United States was Josiah Strong. Although historians have generally interpreted him as an irrepressible expansionist, Strong's ultimate goal was the kingdom of God, which included bringing international relations under the rule of Christian ideals as part of its progressive reign. He saw internationalism as a logical application of social gospel ideals. He even considered the possibility that service to the world was more important than service to the nation, for, he wrote in 1900, "world life is something greater than national life, and world good, therefore, is something higher than national good and must take precedence of it if they conflict. Local, and even national, interests must be sacrificed, if need be, to universal interests."[12]

Like so many of his colleagues, Strong prophesied that the twentieth century would be a time of unprecedented opportunity for America. He argued that for a nation to be isolated was to invite stagnation and that, conversely, those nations that historically had the most contact with each other also enjoyed the most developed civilizations. For Strong, internationalism was part of the triumphant spirit of the age that included freedom, social progress, science, and aggressive missionary efforts. He was confident that mankind was, as he wrote, "about to enter on a new era, for which the nineteenth century has been the John the Baptist."[13] Loosed from the bonds of a crabbed isolationism, the Christ-nation would be free to share in the redemption of the world.

Other social gospel leaders joined Strong in his enthusiasm for a vigorous American internationalism initiated for the sake of Humanity. Washington Gladden, for instance, favored a close American alliance with Great Britain and claimed in 1891 that the two countries had to "stand together, in the coming days, for the defense and extension of Christian civilization."[14] Writing again on foreign affairs in 1909, Gladden proposed that America's international role was not only inevitable, but also that the nation was duty-bound to accept this new responsibility. In Gladden's vision of the future, the outdated tradition of isolation simply had to go. "From this destiny," he wrote, America "has steadily drawn back, but it is now inevitable, and she has no right to shrink from it. The well-being of the world is to be settled, more and more, by consultation and cooperation among the world-powers, and this nation must take her share of the responsibility." For Gladden, United States foreign policy was the social gospel writ large. "What a glorious new note it is that we hear resounding in [Secretary of State John] Hay's state papers," he exulted, "that the Golden Rule is and must be the foundation of international law."[15]

Although the social gospel advocates were committed to international peace, they were not necessarily true pacifists, an important distinction too easily ignored. Generally, they did not preach a nationally applied version of individual nonresistance, and certainly they were not what during the World War would be condemned as "peace-at-any-price men." They worked for ultimate, permanent peace and did not object to wars being waged in the meantime in the name of peace and humanity. Under the right circumstances, it was entirely possible for the progressive clergy to preach both peace and war at the same time. Gladden, for example, reconciled his ideals with the Spanish-American War because the conflict was a humanitarian cause. Indeed, he argued that humanitarianism was the only valid motive for a Christian nation to take up the sword. Rejecting both territorial expansion and isolationism, he envisioned a benevolent civilizing mission for the United States. In fact, for the sake of that mission, Gladden actually rejected the provisions of the Teller Amendment, in which Congress pledged that the United States would not take Cuban territory. Moreover, he even supported the United States' rule in the Philippines beyond 1902, believing that America had a Christian duty to nurture the Filipinos as well as to care for the Cubans.[16]

Several years after the war with Spain, however, Gladden cautioned that America's internationalism did not require the use of military might. He lamented that, while he admired President Roosevelt in many ways, "with his eagerness to increase our armament I have no sympathy; I believe that the day of disarmament is nigh, even at the doors, and that our nation is called of God to take the initiative in it." Rather than flex its naval strength, as Roosevelt had done with the Great White Fleet in 1907–1908, the United States should desire to impress the world with a metaphorical Great White Fleet of moral authority. "Our nation," he proclaimed, "is the one that can speak with [the] most commanding voice. It is her manifest destiny to lead the nations in the paths of peace, and her opportunity is here, for peace has already become not merely a possibility, but a stern economic necessity." Gladden did not question the fact that his nation had a "destiny," that its role was "manifest" and its duty world-wide; he feared simply that the galloping arms race would bankrupt every nation involved.[17]

Free from this ambivalence over America's use of force, Lyman Abbott enthusiastically backed American policy during the Spanish-American War, elaborating the brief conflict into "a crusade of brotherhood." He devoted extensive coverage to the war in his *Outlook,* boosting circulation in 1898 to one hundred thousand. As with many other expansionists, Abbott's argument relied chiefly on historical inevitability, a useful justification whenever the progressives lacked precedent for what they intended to do anyway. Simply put, America was fast becoming a world power, and therefore she was compelled to act like one. Such a course for the nation was a matter of moral duty.[18]

While Abbott, considering his close association with Theodore Roosevelt, might have been expected to think and talk like an imperialist, other liberal clergy preached from the same text, arguing that war was appropriate, or even required, under certain circumstances. In *The Social Gospel,* Shailer Mathews made this point when he argued that "non-resistance to evil might sometimes be the greatest of crimes." He argued that past wars had at times produced social progress, even though in modern times, war was—and really had to be in the progressives' logic—evidence of "the failure of civilization to embody the principles of Jesus." Like Gladden, Mathews predicted that Europe's massive arming would lead to trouble, but he was equally confident that wars would be eliminated as soon as nations were truly Christianized.[19] When at last the social gospel governed the world, international anarchy would end.

As was true of their domestic reform agenda, the liberal clergy's internationalism paralleled that of reformers outside the church. For example, Herbert Croly, founding editor of the *New Republic* and author of *The Promise of American Life,* called upon the United States to turn from its increasingly irrelevant tradition of isolationism and join "a world system" of cooperation with Europe and Asia. Such an entanglement, he acknowledged, might involve the country in European affairs, but notwithstanding America had "the general obligation of a democratic nation to make its foreign policy serve the cause of international peace." Like Gladden with his universalized Manifest Destiny, Croly placed America at the vanguard of peace. But ultimate and permanent peace might mean war in the short term. At some point, Croly warned, the United States, isolated in days past for the sake of its own peace, might be required to go to war for the sake of world peace. "Peace will prevail in international relations," he promised, "because of the righteous use of superior force." America could not shirk this responsibility since peace "would enable the European nations to release the springs of democracy."[20] Making a similar plea, but within a more explicitly religious context, Gifford Pinchot assigned America the supreme mission in world history. "Among the first duties of every man," he urged, "is to help in bringing the Kingdom of God on earth. The greatest human power for good, the most efficient earthly tool for the future uplifting of the nations, is without question the United States. . . ."[21] America's transcendent, righteous duty was obvious to progressives of all kinds, whether clerics or lay people.

To be sure, some religious liberals were consistent pacifists and rejected war in any guise as alien to the clear teachings of Jesus. David Starr Jordan, president of Stanford University and an outspoken and respected pacifist, warned his countrymen in the spring of 1914 of militarism's sure tendencies. "The greatest evil in our age is war," he wrote in the *Atlantic*

Monthly, and "the most menacing feature of this evil is readiness for war, which makes of peace a perennial farce, and the most widespread factor which makes for war is that form of patriotism which spends itself in distrust and hatred of other nations."[22] But though a principled opponent of war, Jordan was still an internationalist. Along with most of his contemporaries, he did not desire peace at the price of continued selfish isolation from the rest of the world. Contact and brotherly unity were still the answer.

Frederick Lynch, who in 1912 became secretary of the Federal Council of Churches' Commission on Peace and Arbitration and in 1914 headed Andrew Carnegie's Church Peace Union, also looked to the day when peace would triumph through international consolidation. He wrote admiringly of the national unity and growth of Germany and Japan, and was confident that the parallel trend toward consolidation worldwide would culminate in a "United Nations of the World." Before long, the new social spirit that worked to eliminate economic injustice and dishonest politics at home would end wars as well. He interpreted the two Hague conferences, attended by the great powers in 1899 and 1907 and initiated by Czar Nicholas II and Theodore Roosevelt for the express purpose of arbitrating international disputes, as signs of the "inevitable" drift toward cooperation in the twentieth century. Who could doubt human progress when the Second Hague Conference brought together "all the world in one room"? The potential seemed limitless for the third conference, scheduled for 1915.[23]

That war should become an anachronism in the modern world was among the progressive clergy's most cherished goals, and they proposed to rationalize international relations principally through a system of judicial arbitration. One of the most notable, yet historically neglected, gatherings of Americans in the name of world peace was the annual Lake Mohonk Conference on International Arbitration. Meeting each spring from 1895 to 1916, the conference was launched by Albert and Alfred Smiley, the idealistic Quaker brothers who owned the secluded Lake Mohonk lodge in upstate New York, a rambling Victorian retreat that hosted meetings on every reform issue from Indian affairs to world peace. Albert Smiley was so significant to the peace movement that Yale Divinity School's

Dean Charles Brown suggested that he belonged in an updated list of heroes from the New Testament book of Hebrews, noting that Smiley, too,
had "wrought righteousness."[24] Over the years the Mohonk meetings attracted such notable liberal clergy as Josiah Strong, Lyman Abbott, John
R. Mott, Charles Jefferson, Frederick Lynch, and Plymouth Church's
Newell Dwight Hillis. Also appearing at Mohonk were seminary professors William Adams Brown and Hugh Black, college president William H.
P. Faunce, *Independent* editor Hamilton Holt, and statesmen William
Jennings Bryan and William H. Taft.

Lyman Abbott delivered the opening address at Mohonk in 1896, and
claimed he sensed that those attending the second annual conference realized that something "unseen" was happening in the world. The hand of
God, he proposed, was moving the nations, especially the English-speak-
ing nations, toward peace, as evidenced by the reasonable resolution of
the Venezuelan crisis between Britain and America. This foundation of
cooperation had to be built upon, Abbott urged. An alliance of ministers,
politicians, and editors working to mold public opinion must "create the
sense, the consciousness that peace is far more glorious than war." The
American public needed to share the Mohonk vision of peace, a peace
beginning with the United States and Britain, and enlarging to encompass
the world.[25]

In his second address at Mohonk that year, Abbott told the Smiley
brothers' guests that the rule of law in international affairs would be the
natural fruit of "eighteen centuries of Christian civilization." It was not
important what individual men might think about the potential for peace;
the issue was rather, Abbott declared to immediate applause, "what God
Almighty is thinking about it." In almost gnostic terms, he characterized
the struggle for peace as one "between the animal and the spiritual" in
man, "between Christianity and barbarism." The obvious solution was the
rational rule of law through an international court of justice.[26]

The following year at Mohonk, William H. P. Faunce, then pastor of
New York's Fifth Avenue Baptist Church, chastised a city newspaper for
daring to call arbitration "sloppy amicability." What the editor failed to
realize, Faunce countered, was that arbitration was in fact the "ushering-
in of the kingdom of Jesus Christ on this earth." International peace was

part of the enlarging work of the modern ministry, the building of the
City of God. Modern pastors rightly refused to accept as their model "the
Pilgrim in 'Pilgrim's Progress,' who could go through the whole world,
from the City of Destruction to the Celestial City, without one earnest,
honest attempt to ameliorate the condition of the country through which
he passed." Clearly, Faunce protested, Christians were obligated to assist
in the coming "of the kingdom of the Prince of Peace among all nations."
In his 1898 address Faunce repeated an important principle from the liberal creed when he claimed that "the ethics of Jesus" encompassed more
than individual men and women and were in fact "the supreme standard of
national righteousness." Sounding very much like Josiah Strong, who happened to be in the audience, he argued that as an isolated Christian could
not possibly fulfill his duty to love his neighbor, so an isolated nation would
surely fail in its own international obligations.[27]

Ironically, the 1898 Mohonk Conference convened in the midst of the
Spanish-American War, but speaker Josiah Strong, like Faunce that year,
talked of the inevitability of world cooperation. After all, God Himself
was "committed to international arbitration," and the world was progressing
simultaneously toward democracy, "world-industry," and "a world-con-
science." The challenge was how best to sway public opinion, to reach the
"indifferent" majority. The key, Strong promised, was America's young
people, who were already organized into Christian Endeavor societies and
Epworth Leagues. "Enlist these young people and we have a machinery
simple, effective," he claimed. Through their devoted efforts any progressive measure could be enacted, for "the conscience of the millions would
be quickened, . . . the public opinion of the millions would be enlightened; and that means the consummation of the reform." "We can do it," he
concluded, "because we must."[28]

Faced with the potentially embarrassing fact of America's recent involvement in the Spanish-American War and subsequent accumulation of
colonial territory, Lyman Abbott in 1899 found it necessary to defended
just wars. "I cannot think that all war is wrong," he told his Mohonk audience. In fact, there were "some things worse than war." Some wars were
imperative and even beneficial, the inescapable extension of Christian duty.
Wars for freedom, self-defense, and in aid of the weak "may be the very

war of God Himself," he reminded the peace advocates. After all, if war had not come in 1861, America would have remained half slave and half free.[29] To admit that all wars were unjust by definition was to question the righteousness of the victorious Union cause. Like most of the others at Mohonk, Abbott did not favor a reactionary peace that relied on isolation or a cowardly peace achieved through nonresistance; he accepted the righteous character of wars fought for the sake of humanity and peace.

In the nearly twenty years between the Spanish-American War and American entry into the World War, the faithful clerical and lay peace advocates at Mohonk continued to discuss international arbitration. The annual conference continued to feature an array of distinguished speakers. In 1902, Union Seminary professor William Adams Brown connected internationalism to the social gospel. He looked with renewed hope at the growing spirit of self-sacrifice in America, a spirit upon which internationally minded statesmen could build their work. Across the country people were giving themselves to "the great cause of serving men," he observed. To Brown, the movement for municipal reform, relief for the poor, mass education, and foreign mission work led logically to the next task facing progressive Christianity: "This matter of international arbitration . . . is not an isolated thing. It is linked to every good cause everywhere; it is a part of the upward movement of our common humanity."[30]

By the time of the 1906 conference, there was actually some cause for optimism among those inclined to read contemporary events as prophetic signs of the promised deliverance of the world from the carnage and destruction of war. In 1906, for instance, President Roosevelt won the Nobel Peace Prize for his mediation in the Russo-Japanese War the year before, bringing the warring sides to the United States to discuss peace and producing the Treaty of Portsmouth. And then in April 1906, on the eve of the Mohonk assembly, the great European powers had met in Algeciras, Spain, to negotiate an arbitrated settlement to the volatile First Moroccan Crisis in which Germany had challenged France's colonial ambitions in North Africa.[31] Moreover, the United States itself, under the guidance of its internationally minded President Roosevelt, had even sent a delegation to this conference. True, the United States had sided with England and

France, but this had been an arbitrated settlement, an example of the type of practical results the Mohonk theorists had been arguing for.

An understandable sense of expectation and urgency, therefore, pervaded the Mohonk proceedings in 1906, but there were still grave matters to consider. After all, the world was still in the grip of a costly and ominous arms race. The audience that year was quite large; over three hundred invited guests filled the lodge. The roll of names included representatives from major colleges and universities, most notably Columbia and Yale, and members of the staffs of at least fifteen publications of national reputation, including the *Living Age* and Lyman Abbott's *Outlook*. Sensing the drama of the moment, Abbott warned in his address that the time had come for the nations to unite their armies into a single police force and harmonize their contrary wills in a court of arbitration. Otherwise, the greatest war in human history would soon explode. The choice was either to cooperate, or "build up armies and navies and get ready for the worst war the world has ever seen." The "common will," he promised, was "the sane way," "the righteous way." Only a "common international conscience, interpreted by a common international tribunal, expressing itself in a common international executive," only this can "make for righteousness, for peace, and for human welfare."[32]

Such talk of righteous internationalism was not limited to the Mohonk regulars. A few months after the 1907 Lake Mohonk meeting, international righteousness was again a prominent theme at the Fourth International Congress of Religious Liberals held in Boston. The similarity in emphasis was no coincidence given the list of honorary vice presidents. Those so honored included William H. Taft, Lyman Abbott, W. H. P. Faunce, Charles Jefferson, David Starr Jordan, Josiah Strong, and Mohonk's own Albert Smiley. Suitable to the occasion, Boston's Tremont Temple was decorated with the flags of many nations, and with placards bearing such messages as "After the way that is called heresy, so worship we the God of our fathers,"[33] reminiscent of Abbott's boast at Plymouth Church ten years before that "heresy" and the reform movements had always gone together.

At one session, before hearing from famed orator, utopian novelist, and Mohonk regular Edward Everett Hale, the international convention

sang a hymn written especially for the occasion. Their millennial tribute
to Boston and America rang through Boston's Symphony Hall:

> *O Pilgrim city by the sea,*
> *In thee we meet on kindred ground,—*
> *Pilgrims toward better things to be,*
> *By one high faith and purpose bound.*
>
> . . . .
>
> *And one the goal to which we press*
> *By toilsome paths as yet untrod,—*
> *Earth's longed-for reign of righteousness*
> *The shining City of our God.*[34]

Following the hymn, Hale opened his address to the packed hall by
praising the previous Congress of Religious Liberals, which had coincided
appropriately enough with the signing of the Treaty of Portsmouth. Confident of world cooperation, he promised that "as the 'United States' is
one nation, the united world is to be one empire of the living God." The
twentieth century was to be known not for its physical power, but for the
power of its ideas. At long last each man understood that he is the "child of
God" and labored in order "that God's kingdom shall come." Hale, a veteran of many reform crusades, a member of a Bellamy Club, and author of
the short story "The Man without a Country" penned during the Civil War
to inspire Northern devotion to the Union cause, assured the convention
that through the cooperative effort between God and man, God would
finally govern His earth. As a foretaste of that day, America had, in emerging united from the Civil War, claimed the power of union and answered
Jesus' prayer "'that they all may be one, as Thou, Father, art in me and I in
Thee.'" Consequently, America now stood boldly as "the great peace society of the world."[35]

In the audience at Boston was Hale's aged associate Julia Ward Howe,
whose famous "Battle Hymn" would be quoted endlessly during the Great
War. Her own reformist millennial vision had not dimmed over the years.
Indeed, in 1908 she thought she experienced a heavenly vision one night,
in which she saw a great mass of men and women united in the work of

reforming America and the world. "All were advancing with one end in view, one foe to trample, one everlasting goal to gain," she reported. "And then I saw the victory. All of evil was gone from the earth. Misery was blotted out. Mankind was emancipated and ready to march forward in a new Era of human understanding, all-encompassing sympathy and ever-present help, the Era of perfect love, of peace passing understanding."[36]

Back at Mohonk in 1909, impediments to Howe's "Era of perfect love" were on Frederick Lynch's mind. Lynch, who would soon head Carnegie's Church Peace Union, denounced the increase in armaments among the great powers and criticized the church for not being ahead of the world in its thinking. If the church ever expected the world to adopt the ethics of Jesus, it must "first educate itself into the ethics of the Master." He chided the congregations in England and Germany and at home in America for failing to object to "these great, pagan, overwhelming armaments." In active obedience to the Sermon on the Mount, the church's mandate was to reject war as it had already rejected the evils of slavery and prostitution. Thankfully, Lynch continued, the church was awake to its role in transforming the community, but now to avoid hypocrisy it had to apply the same ethical standard to nations: "What is right for one man is right for the State. What is wrong for one man is wrong for the State to do, and for the corporation." The danger facing the church was that while the rest of the world saw "great visions," it would continue to babble "baby-talk." One disgruntled member of the audience ridiculed Lynch's view of Christian ethics as "impossible" and "wild."[37]

Lynch's proposal that Christian ethics applied equally to individuals and nations alike found an ally in another Mohonk orator, William Jennings Bryan. Bryan was generally a theologically conservative Presbyterian and would make his reputation in the 1920s as a defender of Fundamentalism, a reputation that would overshadow his previous career and obscure his record in politics and foreign affairs. Bryan, a three-time Democratic presidential candidate and future secretary of state under Woodrow Wilson, was a long-standing anti-imperialist and foe of heavy armaments. He was on record against Roosevelt's heavy-handed intervention in Panama, recent incursions in the Caribbean, and the Taft administration's Dollar Diplomacy.[38] While theologically Bryan may have been something of an anomaly among Mohonk's liberals, he shared their faith in the progress of humanity and in the efficacy of arbitration. Indeed, as secretary of state he would arrange some thirty so-called cooling-off treaties with other nations. In his 1910 Mohonk speech, Bryan attributed his own hope for internationalism to three inspiring developments: the world's observable intellectual progress, its movement toward popular government, and humanity's moral progress. "Let no one think that the world is getting worse," he chided. "There is a moral progress in the world; there is a recognition of the doctrine of brotherhood such as has not been known." Bryan argued that the peace movement was biblical; the same moral principle that governed men governed nations. After all, Christ himself "taught us the power of love, not the power of the sword."[39] Bryan had been making similar claims repeatedly on the Chautauqua and YMCA lecture circuit and even internationally in his famous "Prince of Peace" speech in which he argued for the application of the "Gospel of the Prince of Peace" as the "only hope" in the world "of the substitution of reason for the arbitrament of force in the settlement of international disputes."[40]

By 1911, the Mohonk Conference could boast that from its modest beginnings in 1895 it had grown to the point where it now enjoyed the support of chambers of commerce across the country, as well as the backing of over three hundred colleges and universities. Each year, the conference committee sent thousands of copies of its annual report to libraries free of charge. In 1911 those assembled again heard from the ever-popular William Jennings Bryan, who called on the United States to "rise to the responsibilities of its position" and put the commandments of God into action unilaterally, and then watch the effect on a startled world.[41]

That same year, at the urging of the Federal Council of Churches, April 2 was recognized as "Arbitration Sunday" and the Clerical Committee at Mohonk challenged the churches to "be foremost in the blessed work of the establishment of peace."[42] On behalf of the Federal Council, founding secretary Elias B. Sanford promised "hearty cooperation in those plans that look for a close co-ordination of religious and peace organizations of every name in this propaganda for peace and the principles of a world-wide brotherhood."[43] And cooperate they did. According to Frederick Lynch, the American Arbitration and Peace League forwarded to the U.S. Senate over thirty thousand peace sermons delivered on November 26, 1911, and the New York Peace Society sent information on arbitration treaties to more than 150,000 churches. Lynch was certain that the Senate betrayed the will of the people when it failed to ratify pending arbitration treaties, a disconcerting neglect of duty that prompted him to join the call for the direct election of senators.[44]

At the final Mohonk meeting before the outbreak of the Great War in 1914, Lynch unveiled what promised to be the greatest organization yet attempted for enlisting the church in the cause of peace: Andrew Carnegie's Church Peace Union. Carnegie was president of the New York Peace Society, and his Church Peace Union followed his earlier effort at world peace through the Carnegie Endowment for International Peace, endowed in 1910 with $10,000,000, with President Taft as its honorary head and former Republican secretary of state Elihu Root as president. Launched in February 1914, the Church Peace Union included Protestant, Catholic, and Jewish clergy. Among those summoned to Carnegie's New York City home for the first meeting were a number of Mohonk's faithful, including William H. P. Faunce, *Independent* editor Hamilton Holt, the Reverend Charles Jefferson, Frederick Lynch, and the YMCA's John R. Mott. Others present included Dean Shailer Mathews, Federal Council of Churches' General Secretary Charles Macfarland, missions enthusiast Robert E. Speer, and William P. Merrill, the pastor who in his poetry would soon praise the man-making power of the state. Carnegie endowed his union with $2,000,000 and even provided another use for the funds once war had been banished from civilization, an optimistic clause he had also included in his Endowment for International Peace.[45]

Lynch explained to the Mohonk audience that the first task of the Church Peace Union was "to get all the pastors to preach peace sermons." Often cooperating with the Church Peace Union, the Federal Council was active in this concerted effort to sway public opinion. In 1913 and again in 1914 the council organized "Peace Sundays" similar to the Arbitration Sunday of 1911. In 1913 alone it sent thirty thousand peace pamphlets to ministers across the country, lobbied state and national church organizations to pass peace resolutions, and supplied the religious press with articles and editorials. In preparation for the 1914 Peace Sunday it sent fifty thousand letters to pastors and issued a "Peace Hymn" to five hundred daily newspapers.[46] Most important, Lynch also revealed at Mohonk plans for an international church conference to be held in the summer of 1914,[47] designed to give tangible form to the progressive church's quest for international righteousness. The Church Peace Union and the Federal Council planned for the conference to open in Konstanz, Germany, on August 1, 1914.[48]

ON THE EVE of the Great War, the progressive clergy were certain that in bringing God's kingdom of righteousness to the world they had a valuable ally in President Woodrow Wilson. Other politicians made claims to speak for national and international righteousness. Theodore Roosevelt, after all, had been fighting the Progressive Party's "never-ending warfare for the good of humanity," as he promised while standing at Armageddon and battling for the Lord in the 1912 presidential race.[49] But the election had gone to Wilson, and the progressive churches found in the new president a man sympathetic with their cause, a man who as president of Princeton in 1905 had spoken at the Federal Council of Churches' organizational meeting. Shortly after his inauguration in March 1913, the Federal Council delivered a greeting that praised the president for his social gospel ideals:

> Your warm and sympathetic sense of our democracy; your conviction expressed
> in so many ways . . . that our social order must be fashioned after the Kingdom
> of God as taught by Jesus Christ; together with your public faithfulness and
> your personal faith, lead the churches of the nation to look with confidence to
> the performance of the serious and solemn duties of the coming years.[50]

The leaders of the Federal Council were correct to see reflected in Wilson their own vision of America as the servant-nation of the world. During his first term, Wilson spoke freely of his desire to see America assume the messianic mantle of the suffering servant. In Brooklyn in May 1914, for example, Wilson invoked such ideals as "duty," "service," and "sacrifice," and justified his Mexican policy as an act of national self-sacrifice: "We have gone down to Mexico to serve mankind if we can find out the way. We do not want to fight the Mexicans. We want to serve the Mexicans if we can. . . . A war of aggression is not a war in which it is a proud thing to die, but a war of service is a thing in which it is a proud thing to die."[51] As America had served humanity in Cuba and the Philippines, it was to do so once again in Mexico under Wilson's leadership.

But Wilson's enthusiasm for service was not limited to Mexico. At Arlington National Cemetery in June, he claimed that it was America's "duty" and "privilege" to "stand shoulder to shoulder to lift the burdens of mankind in the future and show the paths of freedom to all the world."[52] Indeed, so he claimed on Flag Day, the American banner stood for "the right of one nation to serve the other nations of the world . . ." and it "has vindicated its right to be honored by all the nations of the world and feared by none who do righteousness."[53] The unstated, but obvious, corollary was that other nations had a great deal to fear if they did not act righteously. Referring to the flag again on July 4, Wilson repeated his promise that another nation need not "fear America unless it feels that it is engaged in some enterprise which is inconsistent with the rights of humanity." He predicted that one day all nations would realize that Old Glory was "the flag, not only of America, but of humanity."[54]

With humanity's flag unfurled in the summer of 1914, Wilson had designated himself as the world's guarantor of righteousness, the very role for the United States that the progressive clergy had been championing for at least twenty years. Meanwhile, the nation's clerical prophets of peace left for Konstanz to plan for international righteousness. This was to be their most ambitious advance yet in applied Christianity, the full expression of a progressive mind accustomed to intervening for the sake of domestic righteousness and already disposed to engage the United States in world affairs.

4

Fit to Serve All Mankind

The Progressive Clergy and the European War, 1914–1917

In the early morning darkness of August 1, 1914, Frederick Lynch and Charles Macfarland traveled by express train from Paris to Basel. As American delegates for Andrew Carnegie's Church Peace Union and the Federal Council of Churches, they made their way across western Europe toward the lakeside town of Konstanz in southern Germany—just north of the Swiss border—for the opening of the international peace conference sponsored by their two church organizations. But on that summer night it appeared that their venture had suddenly taken an ironic turn. Their train halted abruptly. Told by a guard that the Germans had torn up the tracks and closed the border with France, they quickly realized that Europe had plunged into the very catastrophe that the church delegates were assembling to prevent.[1]

The general European war had erupted after five weeks of diplomatic maneuvering following the June 28 assassination of Archduke Franz Ferdinand, the heir to the Austrian Hapsburg throne. The archduke had been shot while on a state visit to Sarajevo, capital of the recently annexed province of Bosnia. His life had been claimed by a young Serbian nationalist, who as a member of "The Black Hand" had pledged himself to fight for a united Serb state in the Balkans, free from Austrian control. Events after that troubling day in the Bosnian capital seemed to flow inexorably toward war. Early in July, Germany pledged to Austria—an ally along with

Italy in the Triple Alliance—its backing for military action against an ambitious Serbia. Assured of Germany's support, the Vienna government on July 23 issued a detailed ultimatum to Belgrade, so objectionable to the Serbs as to nearly guarantee its rejection. A surprisingly cooperative Serbia agreed to most of Austria's demands, but by this time both sides had mobilized their armies. Unsatisfied by Serbia's response, Austria declared war on July 28, one month after the death of Austria's royal heir. At this point, so the Germans argued, the war could have been contained and localized as the latest in the series of Balkan controversies that had afflicted the region in recent years. But two days later the Russian empire mobilized its forces and came to the aid of its Serb brothers, the Czar's Slavic client in the region. Alarmed by the Russian action, fearing a two-front war, and needing to implement its war plans quickly or not at all, Germany responded by mobilizing for war and closing its borders with Russia and France, both members of the opposing Triple Entente. On July 31, an enthusiastic France began mobilizing its own forces and all hope of averting a general war vanished.[2]

The armed camps of the Entente and Central powers, precariously counterbalanced for decades, now in the first week of August marshaled their forces for a show of strength and resolve that would soon escalate. The years of industrialization and nationalism, of economic and imperial rivalry, of an unprecedented arms race on land and sea, had culminated in a general European war. Some critics of the old diplomacy and balance-of-power politics had predicted such dire consequences for unrestrained ambition, but other, more hopeful observers had argued that such a war was far too irrational, too contrary to enlightened national self-interest, ever to occur. And yet this destructive war, the very conflict that the civilizing, progressing world supposedly had transcended, had come crashing in. The modern world's faith that it had laid aside the "arbitrament of the sword" as an archaic, wasteful, and barbaric means of settling disputes, now faced the greatest military contest the world had ever known.

When peace delegate Frederick Lynch realized what was exploding around him, he seethed with contempt for Europe's irresponsible governments, calling them "avaricious and unscrupulous." Interpreting the war largely as the grotesque culmination of capitalist exploitation, he believed

that the world's best hope at this critical moment was for Europe's oppressed workers to face "the fact that they were simply dupes, fools, pawns,"
the pathetic victims of "military cliques" and "capitalists."[3] He assumed
that the laboring classes were essentially pacifist and that they would recognize their common interest and oppose the evil scheming of their op-
pressors, but Socialist parties across Europe answered the call to arms, as
Lynch would soon witness.

Remarkably, Lynch saw reason for hope in the midst of this tragedy.
He counted on the horror of modern war to work a transformation within
the soul of the apathetic churches, which would then convert their nations to the paths of peace. He was confident that "this catastrophic collapse of the nations will at last convince the Church that Jesus Christ has
no part with a civilization that can bring forth nothing better than Hell for
all Europe."[4] The lesson that generations of peace advocates had been trying to teach would now be indelibly impressed upon the nations at war. As
Lynch and Macfarland finally wound their way on toward Konstanz by
another train, Lynch, struck by the beauty of the passing countryside in
contrast to the horrors unfolding elsewhere, observed that "only in the
heart of man was there tumult, passion, enmity, and revenge. Nature was
in tune with God. Man was getting in tune with the Devil."[5]

Andrew Carnegie's Church Peace Union had arranged the international conference at Konstanz as the centerpiece of its growing effort to
enlist the churches in the peace movement. The conference aimed at elevating international relations to, in Lynch's words, a "high ethical plane."
In 1910 Carnegie had established his Endowment for International Peace,
in 1913 he had opened his lavish Peace Palace at the Hague, and in February 1914 his Church Peace Union had been generously funded with two
million dollars to help "Christianize" world affairs. The hope of enlisting
the churches had long been shared by the Peace Union's close ally, the
Federal Council of Churches, of which Lynch's traveling companion,
Charles Macfarland, was secretary. In fact, the Church Peace Union had
evolved directly out of the Federal Council's Commission on Peace and
Arbitration. Among other delegates selected by Carnegie's Peace Union
and the Federal Council to attend the meeting in Konstanz were several
familiar faces: Ernest H. Abbott of the *Outlook,* Union Seminary's William

Adams Brown, the Federal Council's Sidney Gulick and Samuel Z. Batten, and a number of New York pastors.[6] About twenty-five of the Federal Council's representatives were able to reach Konstanz.[7]

The conference opened on Sunday, August 2, the very day Germany, determined to take Paris swiftly, demanded passage through a vulnerable Belgium and sent its troops into Luxembourg. Delegates from twelve countries, including a lone representative from Germany, assembled for prayer in the very room where five hundred years earlier the Council of Konstanz had met to decide the fate of reformer Jan Hus. Lynch recalled the prayer meeting as a moment of emotional trauma so intense that he felt the kingdom of God itself about to come rushing in. As he rose to pray, he envisioned himself as nearly a Christ-figure. "My heart was bleeding for the sins of the world," he sighed. "I saw the mad orgy of lust, vice, drunkenness, hatred, cruelty that was to be loosed, and I felt for once something of what Christ felt in Gethsemane." And yet despite the present ordeal, he expected a renewed world to emerge from the war, a world cleansed by a "second Reformation" in which nations would submit themselves to the same ethical precepts once erroneously applied only to individuals.[8] The next day Germany declared war on France.

With the war crowding in on them and realizing they needed to leave Germany, the delegates discovered that the last train from Germany would depart on Monday. Unwilling to disband the conference, however, they decided to remove to London, where they would resume their meetings August 5. On August 4, Germany launched its momentous invasion of Belgium, and Britain followed through on its treaty obligations to Belgium and declared war on Germany. The far-flung empires of Britain, Germany, France, Russia, and Austria-Hungary were now at war. The Balkan crisis had become a world war. From London, a frustrated Ambassador Walter Hines Page wrote President Wilson that he was visited by two peace delegates who had fled from Germany with few of their belongings. In the confusion swirling around Page at the American Embassy, their pleas for help seemed trivial. They seemed to Page to think they were immune from the suffering of war. Page told them to "thank God you saved your skins." He concluded from all the petty petitions besieging his office that "everybody has forgotten what war means—forgotten that folks get hurt."[9]

By transferring their church conference to England, the American delegates landed where their sympathies evidently had been all along. Lynch, for one, attributed the war to German intransigence, and the conference's sponsor, Andrew Carnegie, defended his native Britain. Although still numbering himself among the "advocates of heavenly peace," Carnegie blamed the German empire for refusing to heed England's peace overtures. Germany may have been ignorant of the consequences of such stubbornness, Carnegie conceded in a telegram to the Neutrality League of London, but nevertheless "Britain was in honor bound to protect Belgium." Likewise, Lynch praised England for its attempts "to restrain both Russia and Germany."[10] Both Lynch and Carnegie, though advocates of brotherhood and peace, were quick to name the "aggressor nation" in the midst of confused international circumstances, circumstances that at the moment hardly allowed for a judicious reading of events. Lynch and the other delegates in the opening days of the war had already forged an emotional alliance with Britain and were quick to include the empire among the peacemakers.

Taking a broader view, Lynch assigned ultimate responsibility for the present chaos to the unrestrained militarism raging on all sides. Yet at a deeper level, underneath the material explanations for the war, he found an inner, spiritual foundation for the conflict. And if the war were rooted in spiritual causes, then logically the church of Christ had to share some culpability. He criticized the institutional church for having neglected the message of temporal peace for so many years. If it had preached the message of peace with its present moral urgency fifty years earlier, then the Great War never would have come. "Who is to blame for this war?" he asked directly. "*The Church is to blame.*" Drawing this same conclusion, the Federal Council's Sidney Gulick attributed the church's failure to its conventional belief in both an individualistic gospel and a transcendent kingdom of God, two doctrines preached at the expense of equality and brotherhood.[11] Lynch's and Gulick's points were predictable, the same principles of "international righteousness" that had been developed at peace conferences over the last few decades. And in one sense this was a self-

serving explanation of the underlying responsibility for the war; it met
the progressive clergy's purposes by fitting the war into their case for a
church-led social reconstruction.

This desire to see the churches active in international affairs produced
one lasting result of the otherwise disappointing peace conference at London: the inception of what became known as the World Alliance for International Friendship through the Churches. Lynch and Macfarland were
among the American members of the organizing committee, which also
included such familiar church leaders as Shailer Mathews and John R.
Mott, and the *Independent*'s Hamilton Holt, a respected editor later instrumental in founding the League to Enforce Peace. Throughout the early
years of the war, Carnegie's Church Peace Union maintained close ties
with the alliance and with the Federal Council of Churches' Commission
on International Justice and Goodwill. Indeed, Carnegie's millions funded
both. Additionally, the Church Peace Union helped fund Oswald Garrison Villard's American League to Limit Armaments (1914) and the American Union against Militarism (1915), and coordinated its activities with
the Committee on Moral Aims of the War and with the League to Enforce
Peace.[12]

Reporting on the delegates' work in London to the Federal Council
of Churches back in the United States, Macfarland seemed almost to welcome the war for the ultimate good it would produce for humanity. The
consensus of the church conference, he reported by cable, was "that the
old political order is breaking down, and that . . . it will crumble to pieces.
The churches have the prophecy of a new order that will save the nations."[13] The upheaval of war would yield fertile ground for the new world
order. In a formal report to the Federal Council of Churches signed by
Lynch and Macfarland, the American delegation summarized its view of
the war: The European conflict was simply the inevitable collapse of "un-
christian civilization." The church's task therefore was to sanctify the divisive "spirit of patriotism" by directing its powers away from international
rivalry and toward social gospel ideals. "Like our laws and our culture,
our education and commerce and industrialism," read the report, "so too
our very patriotism must be pervaded by the mind of Christ and ready for
the discipline of the Cross—the sign and symbol, not merely of brotherly

love, but of international love, over against the short-sightedness and self-ishness of individuals and peoples."[14] The activist churches were accustomed to infusing the "mind of Christ" into the social order, and now they sought to apply to selfish nations the transforming gospel of internationalism.

This line of reasoning paralleled that of the British novelist, socialist, and promoter of world government H. G. Wells. A noted advocate of international reorganization for perpetual peace, his ideas served as something of a model for liberal thought in America. In an article published in the *New York Times* on August 5, the day the peace delegates resumed their work in London, Wells called the war "righteous" and claimed his homeland wielded a "sword drawn for peace." German ambition, he argued, thwarted civilization's progress, and the spoiler had to be confronted. With German militarism defeated, Europe could then pursue the ways of peace and end the bloody age of armaments. He hated war, he told his American readers, but this was war of a different order. The war's outbreak had not destroyed his hope for peace but rather had provided the very means to achieve it. This was a war for peace.

As postwar revisionist historian Walter Millis noted in reference to Wells's essay, "the 'war to end war,' like the war to end 'autocracy,' had entered the American ideology long before President Wilson had ever thought of endowing it with the great power of his rhetoric."[15] But of course Wilson was already on record as eager to serve mankind, and the step from this principle of self-sacrifice to a war of "service," or of peace, or of democracy, or of any number of noble ideals, proved very small. Wells's logic revealed how easily the progressive mind floated between pacifism and war. In this regard, the German ambassador to the United States, Count von Bernstorff, later reflected that he had fatefully misread the American mind: "The juxtaposition in the American people's character of Pacifism and an impulsive lust of war should have been known to us, if more sedulous attention had been paid in Germany to American conditions and characteristics."[16] Perhaps this tendency of the American temper is what Harvard professor Irving Babbitt had in mind when he reflected that his countrymen were "the most pacifist and the least peaceful of people."[17]

At first, however, it seemed unclear to progressives whether the war presented an obstacle to the approaching new order or a catalyst to the world's redemption. Some greeted the news with heads shaking, having for years predicted the inevitable collapse of the old order, yet shocked by so swift a descent. Writing in the *Independent*'s first issue of the Great War, Lake Mohonk participant and former president William Howard Taft called the war "a cataclysm." In his view, all the work of past centuries toward a saner world order had unravelled. It meant nothing less than "a retrograde step in Christian civilization."[18] In the same issue of this magazine founded by Plymouth Church, an editorial writer interpreted the war more hopefully as the great dividing line of history, the separation of the modern world from the ancient. The conflict was to be the final battle between the Enlightenment and the Middle Ages, between the new dispensation and the old, between the coming age of international reason and the receding days of petty national ambition. The *Independent* blamed small-minded European autocrats for the world's troubles, calling the war the work of "Head Devils" who were "mad with the lust of power, drunk with their own egotism," but who now had "signed their own doom." "Their days are numbered," the *Independent* predicted. "The monarchs must go— and they will."[19] Apparently, if nothing else, the war would carry the world over from the age of monarchy to the age of democracy.

Similar early optimism about the consequences of the war issued from the editorial staff of the *Christian Century*. After admitting the depth of their "sympathies with England" as that nation struggled "to preserve the peace," the *Christian Century*'s editors anticipated that there would be "a new birth of Democracy in Europe" because of the war. By the sheer magnitude of the catastrophe, "the reign of universal peace" would be brought closer. Indeed, "the worse this war the sooner and the more lasting the peace that is to come." Yet while predicting ultimate success, the editors— for the time being anyway—saw the war as a setback to most of their reformist ideals. The war meant "an awful relapse." The delicate fabric of world unity had been badly damaged by the events of July and August, and "many things must be begun all over again." Nevertheless, "with God's help we'll do them better next time!"[20]

In contrast to the optimistic progressives, professor J. Gresham Machen at Princeton Theological Seminary expressed a more measured view of events in Europe. Like so many of his theological opponents, he had studied abroad in Germany. Yet for some reason Machen's fondness and sympathy for Germany seemed more durable than that of his liberal colleagues, an attitude all the more striking given his contempt for modernist German theology. In a letter to his mother dated six weeks after the opening of the war, he called Britain's alliance with Russia and Japan "an unholy thing" that had been fashioned for the sole purpose of subduing Germany, Britain's "progressive commercial rival." The idea that this was to be a war for democracy he found manifestly absurd. Britain, in his estimation, was "the least democratic of all the civilized nations of the world." Responsibility for the war rested with Britain's drive for imperial supremacy, he argued, an ambition that deprived Germany of "a place in ocean trade" and actually prevented international peace. This was not a war of ideals, but rather a war of economic competition.[21]

A few weeks into the war, the Federal Council of Churches asked President Woodrow Wilson to proclaim a national day of prayer.[22] Sunday, October 4, was so designated. For the moment, the progressive clergy seemed to be able to hold the war at some emotional and intellectual distance. Despite their sympathy with Britain and the Allied cause, they sensed the conflict's deep tragedy for all involved and desired a quick and genuine peace. And yet the logical tendency of their militant idealism was indicated from the start. Lyman Abbott's *Outlook* in New York published the text of Wilson's proclamation and advised its readers what to pray for. The most pressing need, the editors suggested, was for an international peace based on righteousness. Shaping up as the final battle between militarism and peace, the war separated "the reign of the sword" from "the reign of the conscience." Petitions should be offered to God asking Him to send the day of peace founded on justice, because "enduring peace—the peace of God—can dwell only in righteousness and judgment."[23] The *Outlook* desired no mere end to the war, but rather the lasting peace that would follow divine justice. The progressives, at least the militant branch represented by the *Outlook,* sought a certain kind of peace, the right kind of peace—a perpetual, righteous peace. Similarly, taking hope from the Day of Prayer, the *Christian Century* in Chicago thought the fact that a neutral power such as the United States showed such prayerful concern over a distant war was clear evidence "of the reality of the 'international mind.'"[24] Ostensibly, the success of the Day of Prayer was a sign that the American people had transcended their provincialism and were coming to understand the burden of service.

In New York on the Day of Prayer, Wilson's secretary of state, William Jennings Bryan, addressed the congregation of the Free Synagogue assembled at Carnegie Hall. Opening the service, Rabbi Stephen S. Wise read a prayer written by social gospel leader Walter Rauschenbusch. The prayer stressed not only America's neutrality but also the ideal of national service. Wise asked God to "grant our people a sober and neutral mind, fair and friendly to all nations, remembering our own sins, and when the hour comes may our nation be fit to serve all mankind as the spokesman of peace and the healer of wounds." Following Rabbi Wise, Secretary Bryan told the congregation that it was inevitable in the modern world that America should be a neighbor to all. "No nation can live or die unto itself alone," he claimed. The same obligations that bound neighbor to neighbor also united nation to nation, and it was to be America's privilege to "put itself in a position to render a larger service to the world than it otherwise could—and with nations, as with individuals, service is the measure of greatness." Despite his subsequent reputation as an isolationist, Bryan in the autumn of 1914 unmistakably sought American engagement in the noble task of world redemption, to be the world's servant as Wilson had promised just weeks before the war erupted. Bryan, although a pacifist, envisioned a large role for the United States as an international servant. Later that same Sunday, Bryan repeated these themes at the Reverend Charles Jefferson's Broadway Tabernacle, speaking to the largest crowd ever to have filled the metropolitan church. Andrew Carnegie, the sponsor of the Church Peace Union and so many other peace organizations, sat in the audience to hear the secretary's plea for peace.[25]

Meanwhile, President Wilson, his daughter, and his son-in-law, Secretary of the Treasury William Gibbs McAdoo, attended Peace Sunday services at Washington's Central Presbyterian Church. Seated in the crowded sanctuary, they listened to the prayers and sermon of the Reverend James H. Taylor. He prayed for a mediating role for the United States, certain that America would help bring peace to Europe, and he defended Christian idealism. Far from indicating any failure of Christianity, he assured the president and the congregation, the European war stood as clear evidence of what awaited those nations that abandoned Christian principles.[26]

At Washington's Episcopal Church of the Epiphany, a few blocks from the White House, the Reverend Randolph McKim claimed that the president had made history by asking the American people to pray not for their own safety, but for the peace of Europe. Such a request, according to McKim, was "an act of supreme altruism, it is a recognition of our relations to the whole world." By proclaiming a day of prayer, Wilson had reinforced the internationalist mind, reminding people that the well-being of all humanity inescapably involved the United States. Even so, for the moment, McKim said he was thankful that a policy of neutrality and the vastness of the Atlantic Ocean kept the war far away. Later that day, McKim addressed a crowd of some six thousand on Mount St. Albans in northwest Washington, site of the unfinished Episcopal Cathedral of Sts. Peter and Paul, known familiarly as the National Cathedral. McKim preached at the "Peace Cross," a twenty-foot stone monument erected in 1898 to mark the end of the Spanish-American War. Now the faithful gathered around the cross once again to recall the world to the ways of peace. British Ambassador Cecil Spring-Rice attended the afternoon ceremony.[27]

While this sort of rhetoric and activity was most evident in metropolitan pulpits in the North and East, the Day of Prayer was observed beyond the circle of national progressive elites. One Baptist pastor in Newberry, South Carolina, urged his congregation on Peace Sunday to contemplate the war's transcendent significance. He promised that as they prayed together for the world's plight they would "learn the sooner to 'love our neighbor as ourselves.'" He praised Wilson, a man whom God had sent "to the kingdom for such a time as this," for his efforts to infuse foreign policy with an unyielding sense of "righteousness." By his conduct to date, Wilson had "nailed the flag of righteousness to the mast of our nation" and so far had kept the nation at peace. This familiar interpretation of the war and of Wilson's leadership suggests that the progressive clergy's arguments for a righteous internationalism had penetrated deep into American society. And yet, perhaps reflecting the more conservative temper of his local congregation, this South Carolina pastor concluded that true peace would come only with the spread of the gospel, and to that end, he urged, as much energy should be put into missions as into war.[28]

Not only the religious press and the pulpits pondered the relationship of Christianity to the war. Secular newspapers also grappled with the religious significance of the events they reported, suggesting the American public's yearning to grasp the war's deeper, theological meaning. In the first weeks of August 1914, many editors pointed out the disparity between progressive expectations and degenerative reality. The *New York Herald* dared to wonder, "Is Christian civilization a failure?" The *Sun* despaired, "Is there no other last argument of nations?" The *Lewiston* [Maine] *Journal* attributed the war to the forces "of a false national ambition and of imperialism and special privilege fighting against Christian internationalism." On a more confident note, the *Chicago Tribune* saw the war as the final conflict between barbarity and civilization, between autocracy and democracy, between the divine right of kings and the divine right of the people:

> This is the twilight of the kings. Western Europe of the people may be caught in this debacle, but never again. Eastern Europe of the kings will be remade, and the name of God shall not give grace to a hundred square miles of broken bodies. It is the twilight of the kings. The republic marches east in Europe.[29]

The consensus among the "right thinking" press seemed clear. The *Tribune* took the same view as the *Independent* two months earlier: This was a war between the age of monarchy and the age of democracy. From the beginning of the war, many Americans interpreted the tumult as no ordinary rivalry among nations, but rather as an abstract war emptied of its historical content and infused with a transcendent significance, as a total war between absolutes: democracy against autocracy, Christian civilization against pagan barbarism, Good against Evil.

Considering the temper of the times, it is not surprising that Americans interpreted the Great War as an event of profound religious significance. The early twentieth century was pervaded by a deep religious sensibility—at least by a certain kind of religious temper evident in the era's metaphors and images, a spiritual atmosphere in which Teddy Roosevelt's stand at Armageddon in the 1912 election accompanied by the strains of "Onward Christian Soldiers" made sense. To ignore this feature of American life circa 1914 is to miss the key to understanding the way many Americans interpreted world events. One indication of this spirit is the attitude of the secular press. Metropolitan newspapers often featured local and national church events. They reviewed the latest books by eminent theologians, and regularly dispatched reporters to find out what prominent pastors had to say about current social and political issues. The *New York Times,* for example, regularly sampled the sermons of the city's pulpits, ranging from Charles Jefferson on Broadway, to William Merrill at the Brick Church, to Newell Dwight Hillis in Brooklyn. Religious questions were of immediate popular interest in the early twentieth century.

American popular literature of the Progressive Era also reflected this pervasive religious temperament. In 1915, literary critic and radical individualist Randolph Bourne identified "redemption" as the dominant theme of current popular literature. Embarrassed by the invariable tendency of American authors to reform their characters by book's end, he admired controversial novelist Theodore Dreiser for his ability to resist this propensity. One book he especially criticized was the best-seller of 1913—novelist Winston Churchill's *The Inside of the Cup,* a melodrama of one minister's struggle to apply the social gospel in his fashionable urban church. The novel so captivated the American public that it still held third place in sales for 1914. While Bourne complained that the book had not escaped the "*idée fixe* of American fiction," the *Bookman* attributed Churchill's success to the fact that occasionally a writer will "express in the form of fiction certain problems which for the time being lie very close to the conscience of the people." The *Bookman* accurately predicted that the novel would one day be nothing more than "dead embers," but its popularity at the time suggests just how pressing religious questions were to the American mind on the eve of the Great War.[30]

The publishing industry in general revealed the same public interest in religion. Publishers were rationally sensitive to the demands of their market, and religious themes had always sold well; at times, only the number of new titles in fiction outpaced those in religion. To be sure, by 1914 the combined disciplines of sociology and economics surpassed theology in the number of new volumes, but with the coming of the European war theology regained first place—a reversal *Publisher's Weekly* had predicted and a reversal that highlights the war's neglected theological dimensions. Moreover, in 1914 more new books appeared in religion than in any other category, including fiction. Nearly three new titles were published every day to meet demand! Although the publishing industry as a whole suffered a downturn during the war, religion continued to sell well, remaining among the top categories.[31] Americans had a redemptive literature as well as a redemptive history, and they looked for a redemptive war.

Other evidence more directly reveals that Americans in 1914 needed little prompting to seek out the religious significance of the war. In December 1914, *Everybody's* magazine posed to its readers the question "What is a Christian?" The editors published several of the more than five thousand replies—coming mostly from laymen—and asked "redemptive" social gospel novelist Winston Churchill to comment on what they revealed about the state of American Christianity. Significantly, many of the letters focused on religion and the war, even though *Everybody's* had not mentioned the war in its inquiry. According to the editors, the letters placed no blame for the war on Christianity itself, but rather on the general failure to apply Christian principles to everyday life. Christianity had not faltered. Those institutions charged with "spreading and intensifying the spirit of Christianity through the centuries" had failed. The war merely demonstrated to a startled humanity how far the world had yet to travel to reach the kingdom of God.[32]

The editors also reported that their readers were willing to fight for their country, and that they believed that a war of self-defense was fully justified and that a Christian must "be a fighter for the things that make all society better, must be the deadly destroyer of its enemies." In the minds of the majority of the letter-writers, *Everybody's* concluded, "Christianity means service to God and man." Americans in the first months of the war remained confident in "the higher destiny of mankind."[33]

WHILE THE LETTERS to *Everybody's* disclosed the reading public's predisposition to interpret the war as a religious struggle, they also pointed to one of the war's most troubling questions for the mind of progressive Protestants: the haunting fear that somehow Christianity had failed. Progressive theology had promised so much over the past few decades, but in the face of its greatest challenge, the sort of challenge it had claimed to be equipped for, the activist church appeared to be powerless. The daily war headlines mocked every word the progressive clergy had uttered. As the world order crumbled in 1914, it appeared that the church would be held at least partly responsible for the catastrophe. And this accounting seemed only fair. After all, had not the progressive church promised a New Era? Union Seminary professor Hugh Black acknowledged that "on every hand we hear of the failure of religion in the face of the tragedy of Europe. It is true that organized religion has failed, but the failure is equally true of other organized powers."[34]

By thus trying to share the blame with other institutions, Black may have helped divert attention from the church, but he avoided the fundamental question of the reconstructed church's failure to fulfill one of its key promises, the earthly reign of the Prince of Peace. In the *Century* magazine in February 1915, essayist Edwin Davies Schoonmaker found proof of the church's failure in the public commentary that followed the destruction of Reims Cathedral by German artillery. Schoonmaker complained that the French cathedral's loss had been mourned as the loss of a great art treasure, rather than as the loss of a place of Christian worship. While a later generation might see the reaction to the bombardment of Reims Cathedral as an indication that this sort of indiscriminate destruction had not yet become an accepted feature of twentieth-century warfare, this essayist complained that "the beauty of the nave has outlasted the religion of the altar." "Apollo has triumphed over the Christ," he sighed, perhaps unable to anticipate that Mars would triumph over both. But this further insight would have served only to prove his point. Falsely believing that its own power had advanced along with the rest of civilization, the church suddenly found itself without moral authority. And as to its promise to bring peace among men, Schoonmaker scolded, "After eighteen hundred years it is as easy for men to thrust bayonets into one another as it was in the heathen world. Is it not apparent that the church has collapsed?"[35]

Unwilling to concede Christianity's collapse, New York preacher John Haynes Holmes took another approach to the problem of the church's supposed failure. An ardent pacifist and radical theologian, he wondered how anyone could blame Christianity for the war when the conflict was so obviously the result of anti-Christian ideas. "I see in this stupendous tragedy," he told his congregation at the Church of the Messiah, "the failure of battleships and standing armies to safeguard international peace; I see the failure of militarism to train great peoples in the virtues of gentleness and honour; . . . I see the failure of the idea that force can rule the world and so ruling bring happiness and health to men." But the failure of Christianity he would not admit. Christianity had yet to rule the nations of Europe, and their pagan societies, tottering under the weight of militarism, had "finally and forever crashed to ruin." Holmes seemed to be conceding more to the church's critics than he intended, for this was the very point the scoffers made: The contemporary church, contrary to its promises, had not fundamentally altered the world's condition. Nevertheless, Holmes refused to be daunted by events and interpreted the present turmoil as an opportunity for those who still anticipated the coming kingdom of God.[36]

Lyman Abbott's *Outlook* similarly placed blame on the nations at war rather than on progressive Christianity. Europeans claimed to be part of "Christendom," yet behaved like barbarians.[37] But as much as it condemned Europe for violating pacifist Christian ideals by going to war, the *Outlook* defended the compatibility of Christianity and war under certain circumstances, in the way its editor Lyman Abbott at Lake Mohonk had noted the blessings of certain progressive wars. According to the *Outlook,* to admit that war could not be used as a tool of national policy would have been to question the legitimacy of the Union cause during the American Civil War, to return to a consistent theme in Abbott's thought. The *Outlook* praised such wars of "service," reasoning that the "Civil War rendered a greater service to the South than to the North." In fact, "the South's prosperity dates from Appomattox Court-House." The European war would spread similar spiritual and material blessing, for "if the Allies succeed . . . they will render an incalculable service to Germany." Furthermore, since the Great War was a righteous cause, Christians were justified in using the hymns "Onward, Christian Soldiers," "The Son of God Goes Forth to War," and "The Battle Hymn of the Republic" to define the essence and meaning of the war. After all, "the spirit of Christianity is not inconsistent with the spirit which fights to the death to save the oppressed from the oppressor. A noble expression of the Christian spirit is the line, 'As he died to make men holy, let us die to make men free.'"[38]

Some critics seized on the war as evidence of the failure of a particular kind of Christianity, namely, the old orthodoxy, that dark force accountable for so much suffering in the church and the world. Echoing Sidney Gulick in his lecture at Konstanz in August 1914, imperialist Josiah Strong faulted individualistic thinking for neglecting humanity's collective needs. In a review of Strong's most recent book, *The New World-Religion,* one writer recognized the tendency to blame the church for the world's swift regression, but noted that Strong continued to trust in the true "spirit of Christianity" to rescue the world from its folly. As Strong wrote, "The spirit of Christianity, as shown forth in the social teachings of Jesus, is not only far from being a failure, but is the only power which can bring the human family through its hour of trial and ultimately realise the goal intended for it, which is nothing less than the coming of God's kingdom to earth." The transformation of the world would come, Strong promised, as soon as people decided to cooperate with God in His redemptive work.[39]

Recognizing the seriousness of the self-doubt that the international conflict engendered in the modern church, Baptist minister Harry Emerson Fosdick offered a hopeful interpretation of the church's distress. Well aware that there were those who "in exasperated disillusionment" were ready to discard Christianity "upon the scrap-heap," he found reason to rejoice in the midst of mourning. The church's anguish meant that as once the church had struggled with the morality of slavery, now Christians finally understood the incongruity between their reforming faith and the sinful world and its archaic institutions. Aware of this intolerable dissonance, they would surely see to it that it was warfare that died, and not Christianity. Moreover, and most important, popular agonizing over the morality of war signaled that people at last accepted as a fundamental doctrine of their faith the social applicability of Christianity.[40] The belief that Christianity was at heart a social religion and was therefore responsible for mending a broken world had finally penetrated the American mind. The public's re-action to the war, their apparent understanding of it as a challenge to their theology, proved the point. Whether this change in theology to a more socially defined Christianity was as widespread as Fosdick and others sug-gested, the appearance in the press of the "failure of Christianity" theme suggests the importance of the question, at least to a segment of the read-ing public.

BEHIND THE PERVASIVE question of whether or not applied Christianity had failed in the face of war lay an even more fundamental doubt: Had God Himself failed? In light of the developmentalist presuppositions of the liberal Protestant mind, this was an inescapable problem and a vital matter to resolve. Since an immanent God was supposed to be working out His evolutionary plan for humanity, propelling the world ever closer to the fulfillment of His kingdom, the calamity of the war raised serious doubts about His intentions. Even more alarming, the ancient question of theodicy—justifying the presence of evil in God's creation—erupted in a very tangible way in the war. It would seem that if God was in control, he was perverse; if not perverse, then He was certainly not in control.

As earlier generations of liberal theologians had been unable to rec-oncile the biblical account of miracles with their view of immutable natu-ral law—believing that God had yielded His autonomy to an orderly sys-tem—so the progressive generation contended that in the moral realm God also operated according to an equally immutable moral law. God Himself did not transcend these laws of nature which governed the devel-opment of both the physical and moral universe. In the progressive scheme of things, good ultimately and invariably triumphed and evil inevitably failed, even within the limits of this present fallen world. The relationship between sowing and reaping in the moral universe was as fixed, invari-able, and predictable as cause and effect in the physical universe. God's moral law, however, did not function impersonally and mechanically, but with clear purpose. Just as biological evolution in the developmentalist view tended toward Creation's ultimate physical perfection, so moral progress achieved its moral perfection. In all His activities, God worked for man's betterment.

But times of crisis seemed to challenge this comfortable notion. Of course, questions about God's moral character were not new at the time of the Great War. Indeed, the ancient Greeks had puzzled over the problem of evil, and the Deists had struggled with the rationality of the 1755 Lisbon earthquake. Subsequently, in the nineteenth century, the liberal clergy had removed the doctrine of eternal punishment from their theology in order to retain their belief in a benevolent God.[41] In 1897 Boston Congregational minister George A. Gordon, who attended the Plymouth Church anniversary that same year, had wrestled with the question of God's goodness and the rationality of His universe. Gordon was concerned specifically with the redemption of souls after death, but his attempts to make God conform to a humanitarian sense of morality led him to the same conclusions that later would be reached during the Great War. Gordon reasoned that if God did not provide a means of salvation after death, then He was not a "moral being." As he warned, "The moral view of the universe, by which is understood the utter righteousness and fatherly kindness of the Supreme Being, must fight for its life." God, as a developmentalist, immanent God, had to be working toward the total redemption of His universe. Logically, His ambition, His "eternal passion," had to be "to make righteousness sovereign over all his moral creatures."[42]

Protestant liberals rationalized the embarrassing presence of warfare in this meliorist universe in several ways. Oberlin College president Henry Churchill King, never doubting that the universe conformed to his own human sense of rationality, was left with the classic dilemma: "either God is good and not omnipotent or he is omnipotent and not good." He argued that the war could be understood only as an unavoidable part of an evolving, trouble-filled world swayed by man's free will, a world that instilled character and taught lessons otherwise impossible to learn. "An imperfect developing world," he wrote, "is needed for the development of moral character in man."[43]

Lyman Abbott's *Outlook* confronted time and again this same question of God's purposes. Immediately after the outbreak of war, it reassured its readers that they need not doubt humanity's continuing progress. God, employing the present war as a means to a glorious end, was teaching the world to turn from its evil ways: "When, in the long education of the race, climbing slowly and painfully from the dust, there come ascendencies of a barbarism which men thought extinct, . . . despair and fear have no place; to brave men and women crises are moments of revelation and growth." When, in the face of trials, men continue to trust God's plan, "the spiritual education goes forward to make hatred and war more and more the survivals of a vanishing past."[44] War was not an inevitable part of human existence to be managed and limited, but rather the remnant of a receding era of barbarism. War belonged to the past. Oddly, the *Outlook* actually turned war's presence in the world into evidence of war's certain extinction. The world was heading toward peace, so war could not, by definition, be an enduring institution. Proof was not necessary to this tautological reasoning from ideals. One reader wrote to praise the *Outlook* for its reassuring editorials, knowing they would "do much to bring about a peace of mind and to strengthen faiths in this world crisis."[45]

At the end of August 1914, the *Outlook* repeated its claim that for some ultimate good God was allowing humanity to suffer the consequences of its behavior. While each European power had its own war aims, God had His war aim as well: the defeat of German militarism and autocracy. This was God's war. The *Outlook* maintained "that a Power greater than that of all the warring peoples is directing the purpose of the war. That purpose is the end of military autocracy in Europe."[46] Later, the editors admitted that many had been too quick to talk of Christian nations and a Christian world. But this was a time for hope, not for discouragement; "despair has no place in a world for which Christ died and in which millions of men, however mistaken, are ready to lay down their lives for country or for honor." Moreover, the war was to be the vehicle of the world's education: "the world must patiently go to school until it has learned those great lessons of justice, self-sacrifice, and helpfulness which will make wars and rumors of wars" things of the past.[47] Just how nations learned "helpfulness" by slaughtering their neighbors, the *Outlook* did not explain. But if this were God's war, fought for God's purposes, could it be long before the progressive clergy felt compelled to enlist on God's side and battle for the Lord?

Calling for justice again in October, Abbott and his colleagues argued that peace would never come by mere wishing; it had to be built. They rejoiced that on the recent national Day of Prayer "petitions for immediate peace" had not been heard, but rather prayers for structural changes that would remove the causes of war. As early as November 1914, the *Outlook* framed the conflict as a Wellsian war against war. While not using that precise phrase, they clearly envisioned the Great War as the last war the world would ever know. The nations at war, struck by the insanity of their acts, would put away militarism forever as a tool of diplomacy. "To have faith in God is to believe that he knows what his children need," the editors asserted; "that he dares to allow them to take their own way and learn by bitter experience the lesson which they would not learn from teaching; and it is so to learn that lesson from this terrible experience that it will never have to be again repeated."[48] The horrors of warfare became acceptable, rational, and strangely reassuring when interpreted as instruction and discipline from the hand of a cosmic schoolmaster.

While Protestant liberals accommodated the war into God's progressive, educative plan for His creation, they also attributed the war to a similar facet of God's character: the operation of His immutable moral law. God superintended history, and just as biological creation obeyed His evolutionary natural law, so human behavior was subject to a rational, observable natural law of morality. The universe functioned according to an inviolable pattern of cause and effect, of sowing and reaping. The nations of Europe ignored God's moral law and suffered the consequences. It was only a matter of time before the good would prevail and evil crumble. Forgetting what patient Job had learned—that at times in this fallen world wickedness triumphs and the righteous suffer according to the inscrutable will of an omnipotent God—these progressives believed that perfect justice operated here and now. The universe was not just ultimately, transcendently moral, but presently, immanently moral.

Typical of much liberal thought in this regard was New York pastor Charles E. Jefferson. He believed that Germany had to suffer the consequences of its behavior. The war had compelled this pacifist "to reconcile the love of God with the wrath of God," and he appealed to the grinding wheels of divine justice in order to make sense of the war. A just God could not allow wickedness to succeed in this world, he warned, and the "nations which sin beyond forgiveness are simply blotted out." Only one conclusion was possible: "We live in a moral universe. We are in the grip of moral laws."[49] Righteousness prevailed over Jefferson's former pacifism, which yielded to a militant sense of international justice. The distance between pacifism and war was short indeed.

Even after witnessing a full year of modern total war, the progressive clergy remained certain that God was purging and perfecting the world. The *Outlook* in 1915 claimed that "God's presence in the affairs of men was never more impressively evident, than in this terrible crisis." Indeed, the editors continued, the war had rescued the world from its "false goals" and its disturbing tendency toward luxury and immorality. Selfish materialism was "dying on the battlefields of Europe." The world was purer because of this war; in fact, it had been reborn. "God is in his world and the soul of the world is alive again."[50] A year of the most tragic war yet known to mankind had done nothing to shake these progressives' faith in a renewable world. If anything, it had intensified it. This was a regenerative war. As late as March 1917, Lyman Abbott still wrote of the war's capacity to educate humanity in the higher things and concluded that "the lesson always has been and always will be worth all that it costs."[51]

5

With Battle Banners Furled

The Varieties of Progressive Pacifism, 1914–1917

In the more than two and one half years between August 1914 and American entry into the European War, Protestant liberals continued their prewar pursuit of world peace, defended social gospel imperatives, and accommodated the war into God's developmental plan for the ages. Unresolved, however, remained the question of America's role in the European War. Whether pacifists or militarists, Protestant liberals never doubted that the United States had a vital role to play. They never argued over the propriety of American entanglement in world affairs. Rather, they struggled with varieties of internationalism. The use of American influence, whether moral or military, to direct world affairs no longer troubled their consciences; the days of meaningful isolation had ended nearly twenty years earlier with the Spanish-American War and America's departure into world empire under McKinley, confirmed by Roosevelt, Taft, and Wilson. Regardless of the details of the progressives' various views on preparedness and armed intervention, they shared the assumption that America was to be, as Wilson promised, a servant nation. The enduring question that divided them was how America would best perform its duty to serve humanity and achieve international righteousness.

Protestant liberals divided themselves into three attitudes toward the American mission for world peace: militarist, Tolstoyan, and juridical. The Federal Council of Churches' Sidney Gulick applied these useful labels in

1915 to the three major types of "pacifism" then prevalent among religious progressives. It is noteworthy that each side in the debate presented itself as pacifist; all claimed to be working toward ultimate world peace, and in this sense all were idealists. They argued over means, not ends. The militarists among them stressed national rights, the "Tolstoyan" pacifists called for absolute nonresistance, and the juridical peace advocates invoked international law and a universal Golden Rule.[1] These three groups represented the range of approaches to world peace within progressive circles until April 1917 when American entry decided the issue on the side of the militarists and world planners instead of the noninterventionists.

Among the militant "pacifists," few spoke more forcefully for their views than Lyman Abbott and his colleagues at the *Outlook,* including the belligerent contributing editor Theodore Roosevelt, who early on called for vigorous national preparedness and then for intervention. Just a few months into the war, the *Outlook* recommended American military readiness, putting the magazine in the vanguard of the national campaign for increased armaments on land and sea. The editors argued that the world could not rely on mere talk of peace for its safety but instead had to trust in the determination of democratic peoples, backed by physical strength and unswerving resolve, to spread liberty and justice. International righteousness would never come through weakness:

> It is because The Outlook believes that righteous liberty in this world demands more than the mere lip service of our great democracy, that righteous liberty in the end can be obtained only through the spread of the democratic ideal for which this Nation stands, and that the spread of this ideal depends not only upon the desire and the will but also upon the power of our people, that we have long advocated the adequate military preparation of our American democracy.[2]

Clearly, the United States had to be ready to spread the "democratic ideal" to the world, bringing "righteous liberty" to all. This destiny would not be fulfilled if Americans listened to those who advocated nonresistance, whom the *Outlook* ridiculed as kin "to those who might hope to abolish individual murder by abolishing the civil police, or fires by the abolition of insurance."[3] Lyman Abbott returned to these analogies time and again during the war, and he intended the United States to be the agent of worldwide law and order. America was not to prepare militarily merely to defend its borders from invasion and to protect its vital interests, but also to spread its political ideals. Whether or not the *Outlook* realized that this expansive mission turned the United States into a potentially revolutionary force in world affairs, a force to topple empires and undermine established governments, the magazine's enthusiasm for these ideals was unmistakable.

The practical good sense of Abbott's international police force and global fire insurance seemed indisputable, especially after the dramatic events in the war at sea in the spring of 1915. On May 7 a German submarine torpedoed the British liner *Lusitania* off the southern coast of Ireland. The nation that had "crucified" Belgium now added another sin to its record of abuses. Nearly twelve hundred of those traveling from New York to Liverpool lost their lives, including 128 Americans. It little mattered to public opinion that the German Embassy had warned embarking passengers of just such an eventuality and to stay off the Cunard liner. The scale of the tragedy simply would not admit the nuances of mitigating circumstances or the complications of any moral ambiguity. The sinking seemed so obviously barbaric that it served only to advance Germany's rapid demonization.[4] Although these were not the first or the last American casualties to German submarine warfare, the enormity of the tragedy struck Americans deeply. As historian Arthur S. Link noted, "the sinking of the *Lusitania* had a more jolting effect upon American opinion than any other single event of the World War."[5] In terms of public relations alone, the sinking was a disaster for the German cause.

Responding quickly to the sinking, Lyman Abbott shot off an angry telegram to the *New York Times*, denouncing Wilson for his apparent weakness in the face of such obvious German aggression. He compared Wilson to a spineless President James Buchanan on the eve of the Civil War, events that the elderly Abbott had lived through. It took a man of Abraham Lincoln's stature, Abbott recalled, to avoid pointless discussion and to act decisively. "In such a crisis," he charged, "courage is a duty and timidity a crime; dread of war creates peril of war, and no decision is so bad as indecision." By failing to respond forcefully, he argued, Wilson actually had brought the United States closer to war, and a war to be fought on Germany's terms, not America's. German submarines engaged in sophisticated piracy, not in civilized warfare, and for such behavior that pariah nation should be excommunicated from the company of civilized peoples. "America should disown all fellowship with a power which perpetuates massacre of unarmed citizens on the high seas and calls it war," he concluded.[6] Similarly, the *Christian Century,* though officially pacifist, did not withhold moral judgment from Germany. It saw the sinking of the *Lusitania* as the "latest desperate deed of barbarism," an act that proved that Germany was truly insane.[7]

On May 10, with the *Lusitania* incident still in the headlines, Wilson spoke at Convention Hall in Philadelphia to a crowd of fifteen thousand, including four thousand newly naturalized citizens. He discussed the imperative of international unity and of America's role in the world family. He talked of America's unavoidable contact with other nations, of its moral authority, and its need to set an example of self-restraint. In short, he thought it possible for a nation in its integrity to be "too proud to fight."[8] The crowd responded warmly, but in so describing the nation's position, Wilson seemed to reveal the very weakness Abbott thought he detected in the president. Roosevelt had nothing but contempt for Wilson's sentiments. And the *New York Times* thought the president missed the mood of the people.[9]

But on May 13 Wilson issued a strongly worded response to Germany that stressed the rights of Americans and the obligations of international law and called upon Germany to end unrestricted submarine warfare and to pay reparations. Ex-president Taft called the note "admirable in tone . . . dignified in the level the writer takes with respect to international obligations." It was also praised, naturally, by the British government and press.[10] As hard as it may have been, even Abbott had to admit he was pleased with Wilson's handling of the affair. But the *Outlook* staff pushed for "National action" to back up the president's words. Roosevelt called for an immediate break with Germany. Abbott defended the somewhat contrived right of Americans to travel on belligerent ships and did not question Wilson's efforts to fit submarine warfare into existing international law. Under the circumstances, he found neutrality immoral and demanded that the "crime" of the *Lusitania* be punished. "Patient waiting has done nothing," he insisted. "Protesting words have done nothing. In the presence of wholesale assassination The Outlook is not neutral. We believe the time has come for National action."[11]

In the same issue, the *Outlook* reinforced its point by quoting from the Reverend Leighton Parks of St. Bartholomew's Church in New York. Parks used the analogy of the church and wayward members that Abbott had employed in his earlier telegram to the *Times*: "Let our brother, Germany, be unto us as a heathen, one who has cut himself off from the congregation of Israel, and a publican. . . . Let us say to Germany, 'You have placed yourself beyond the pale, and we cannot for the time being have anything to do with you.'"[12] These biblical images were repeated so often during the war that they ceased to be mere analogies and instead substituted for the complex and often ambiguous reality of international relations. By 1915, some progressive church leaders had already cast Germany in the role of the wayward sinner who needed to be disciplined and brought back into the loving church of nations.

Within a week of the *Lusitania*'s sinking, the Navy League, an ambitious and highly visible preparedness organization founded in 1903 on the British model, held its annual dinner at the Hotel Ansonia in New York. Prominent speakers included Admiral Frank F. Fletcher, Assistant Secretary of the Navy Franklin D. Roosevelt, and Lyman Abbott. In his address as reported by the *New York Times*, Abbott admitted that the present war had caused him to reevaluate the nearness of world peace, of the approaching Golden Era when nations would settle their disputes through sensible arbitration. As long as nations as obstinate as Germany remained in the world, Abbott reasoned, the civilized peoples had to continue to fight for order. He warned that an ambitious Germany, left unchecked in Europe, combined with a naïve disarmament policy at home, would lead the world to "anarchy." The only alternative was armed defense, and Abbott was ready: "We ask the nations of the world to join us in opposing that nation which tramples under foot international law and the rights of man. We must plant the seed of international brotherhood with swords at our side."[13] Abbott saw no contradiction between militarism and brotherhood. Indeed, an enforced international righteousness would achieve world fraternity. A righteous war would bring permanent peace.

The same week as the Navy League's banquet, the rector of the Episcopal Church of the Epiphany in Washington, D.C., Randolph H. McKim, preached on "The National Crisis," having in mind particularly the case of the *Lusitania*. McKim ranked among the most vocal of the militant clergy. A Confederate veteran, McKim naturally appealed to historical sentiments and analogies different from those used by Abbott, pleading, for example, for the integrity of the Founders' Republic rather than for the universalization of Lincoln's imperishable Union. Nevertheless, McKim was at least as militant in his call for righteousness, and he joined Abbott and Roosevelt as a member of another preparedness organization, the National Rights League.[14] He cautioned his congregation that "war may sometimes be necessary." He carefully distanced himself from the absolute pacifists who found both warfare and military service inherently evil. He argued instead that "Christian soldiers" embodied the highest Christian virtue, namely "self-sacrifice." Repeating a theme already familiar by 1915, he admonished his listeners that a "just peace" had to be "based on righteousness."[15]

The cry for righteousness was heard back at Lake Mohonk as well in 1915. Its annual meeting opened in the midst of the *Lusitania* crisis, and consequently American military preparedness became the conference's immediate focus. Over the years Mohonk speakers had stressed the importance of the United States setting an example for the world by disarming unilaterally. But in 1915 Princeton University president John Grier Hibben, Wilson's successor and another member of the National Rights League, created a stir at the conference and in the press when he called for national preparedness. The nation had to stand for "righteousness," he told the assembled peace advocates. "We dare not indulge ourselves in the enjoyment of the blessings of peace, while we turn deaf ears to the cry of distress, or to the summons of a righteous cause." With applause that must have sounded strange in the Quaker lodge, the audience of pacifists answered Hibben's militant summons to service.[16]

The following morning, the *New York Times* commented on the "almost jarring dissonance" of Hibben's speech at peace-loving Mohonk. But on reflection the editors recalled that Mohonk never had been the home of radical pacifism anyway. They knew that Hibben would "have no critics among those who realize that war is a relative, not an absolute, evil, just as peace is a relative, not an absolute, good." The *Times,* confident in the good sense of the American people, attributed Hibben's warm reception to the fact that "the tendency toward indiscriminate condemnation of war, always narrowly confined, has now almost disappeared."[17] The pacifist clergy could easily reconcile themselves to both preparedness and wars of service.

Summarizing many progressives' reaction to the sinking of the *Lusitania,* the *Outlook* printed a commemorative poem:

> *No riot cry for vengeance blinds*
> *Our passion for a righteous world;*
> *With bitter hearts but steady minds*
> *We stand with battle banners furled.*
>
> . . . .
>
> *Not craven heart nor palsied tongue*
> *Keeps back our fingers from the sword,——*
> *The courage men have left unsung*
> *Still waits in service to the Lord.*[18]

The poem was typical of much of the wartime language that flowed from the militant pacifists. It combined the sacred and the secular, stressed America's selflessness, and promised action at God's appointed time. The message was clear: America's present inaction should fill Germany with fear. Germany should beware of rousing the sleeping giant across the Atlantic. Though the flags for the moment were closely furled, the United States stood ready to battle for the Lord against His enemies.

Abbott continued to campaign for preparedness in the months after the *Lusitania* incident and was active in such high-profile preparedness organizations as the National Security League, formed in December 1914 to gear up the nation for a conflict with Germany.[19] At a four-hour public meeting at Carnegie Hall in June sponsored by the league, preparedness advocates heard from former Democratic presidential candidate Alton B. Parker, from former and future secretary of war Henry L. Stimson, as well as from the ubiquitous Lyman Abbott. Abbott ridiculed Secretary of State Bryan for urging the president to bar Americans from traveling through the war zone. Bryan, fearing that Wilson's *Lusitania* protest guaranteed war rather than peace, had resigned the week before. The audience burst into applause when Abbott complained that "it is hard sometimes to keep one's patience."[20]

The militant pacifists gained another opportunity to rhapsodize on the meaning of the war when President Wilson designated a second day of prayer for Thanksgiving Day, 1915. On G Street in Washington, just two blocks from the White House, the Reverend Randolph McKim used the occasion of the Day of Prayer to ask his congregation at the Church of the Epiphany to ponder whether or not they had fulfilled their "duty to mankind." While praising the American people's aid to Belgium and Serbia, their sacrificial giving to the Red Cross, and the devoted service of some in medical corps, he severely criticized the United States' conduct over the past fifteen months. He was angered that the administration had never made any formal protest to Germany over the "crucified nation" of Belgium. He was disappointed that Wilson had not followed with force his stern protest to the sinking of the *Lusitania*. In vain, McKim complained, "we believed that those brave words would be followed by deeds as brave." In short, "nothing has been done to vindicate the insulted majesty of our Republic!"[21]

Little more than a year before, McKim had prayed at the Peace Cross on Mount St. Albans in Washington, but now in his Thanksgiving Day sermon he urged the United States to sever diplomatic relations with Germany. Doing so, he argued, would unite the will of the country, silence "disloyal citizens," and throw "the immense weight of our influence" against Germany onto "the side of humanity and law and liberty." Cutting diplomatic ties was worth the risk, he reasoned, for the Central Powers were already infiltrating the United States and planning sabotage. In the face of such danger, he asked, "should we fail of our duty in a great world crisis when the blood of our citizens cries to Heaven for vengeance because we are *afraid of the consequences?*" The time for neutrality had ended, and the American people demanded "strong and resolute action." McKim had no fear that his political comments were inappropriate for a sermon. On the contrary, he believed that Christian duty compelled him to condemn "selfish ideals." Moreover, he contended that ministers, by virtue of their supposed neutrality in political affairs, had a special obligation to speak out; they were "unaffected by the currents of politics or of commercial interests."[22]

By the end of 1915 it was clear that international "righteousness" was to be the guiding principle of American foreign policy, at least among a vocal segment of the militant pacifists. But such enthusiasm was not limited to the church. No less a political force than Theodore Roosevelt had joined the agitation for a righteous world. He was a formidable ally of the forces of militant pacifism, for he, too, considered himself to be a true peace advocate, but of a peace built on righteousness. In this regard, Roosevelt was an idealist. He was a peacemaker of some record, having won the Nobel Peace Prize in 1906 for his mediation in the Russo-Japanese War and the Moroccan Crisis. And in his Annual Message to Congress in December 1905, he explained his vision of an ethical world:

> We can . . . do nothing of permanent value for peace unless we keep ever clearly in mind the ethical element which lies at the root of the problem. Our aim is righteousness. Peace is normally the hand-maiden of righteousness; but when peace and righteousness conflict then a great and upright people can never for a moment hesitate to follow the path which leads toward righteousness, even though that path also leads to war.[23]

Permanent peace required righteousness; righteousness would likely require war. Peace through righteousness through war. This was the militant pacifist mind at work.

To achieve and maintain this pure peace, Roosevelt proposed as early as September 1914 a "world agreement among all the civilized military powers" to found a "world league for the peace of righteousness." The *New Republic* later haunted him with this suggestion when he attacked Wilson's own league proposal. Roosevelt's plan went beyond the arbitration treaties already familiar to most Americans, and instead pledged the United States to defend peace with force of arms. He did not desire to arbitrate international crimes; they had to be met with force.[24] Within two years Roosevelt abandoned his plans for a league and instead became one of the most impassioned critics of the idea. The *New Republic* wryly observed that Roosevelt's apparent hypocrisy "makes some of us sceptical of his title to be considered the undisputed Chief of the Kingdom of Righteousness."[25]

Roosevelt placed justice ahead of personal safety and distinguished between selfish wars of aggression and idealistic wars of "conscience." As the *Outlook* interpreted his position, he held "that a large share of the present peace agitation comes from those who place physical comfort above conscience; who are swayed by the horror of war, rather than by the horror of injustice." Surely Germany's war against Belgium bore no moral comparison with Belgium's war against Germany. The *Outlook* relied on the common sense of "those who look for the firmer establishment of democracy" to concur with Roosevelt that the high justice to be won by the present war belonged on the same moral plane as the achievements of the American Civil War.[26]

Despite what the *New Republic* might later think of his right to do so, Roosevelt spoke tirelessly during the war of the need for international righteousness. Indeed, it was the theme of a collection of his articles published in 1916 under the title *Fear God and Take Your Own Part*. Roosevelt dedicated this vigorous call for preparedness to Julia Ward Howe, and included the entire text of "The Battle Hymn of the Republic" at the front of the book. He admired her, he wrote, because in an earlier time of national testing "she preached righteousness and she practised righteousness." Moreover, "she embodied that trait more essential than any other in the make-up of the men and women of this Republic—the valor of righteousness."[27]

Roosevelt was well aware, however, of the nonresistants' admonition to imitate Jesus' meekness in the face of His enemies. But the former president preferred to point to the more militant Jesus who had cleansed the temple of money-changers. The proper Christian behavior in the face of injustice was to demand the end of that injustice even at the expense of peace. As Jesus had been willing to sacrifice peace for the sake of justice, so America had to risk her safety for the sake of a cleansed temple of mankind. As Roosevelt explained it, "sometimes it is not peace, but war which is the proper means to achieve the [righteous] end." America had to dedicate itself to that goal, for the nation was "a mighty Republic conse-crated to the service of God above, through the service of man on this earth." Functioning as a political incarnation of the Church Militant, America was "a people sworn to the great cause of liberty and justice, for themselves, and for all the sons and daughters of mankind."[28] Evidently, America's obligation reached beyond even that of an international Good Samaritan and approached that of a messiah, appointed to give its life as a ransom for many.

WHILE LYMAN ABBOTT and other militant clergy unambiguously advo-cated national preparedness and retribution in the name of peace and protested German violations of American neutral rights, another group of progressive clergy advocated peace through national nonresistance. This circle included such respected pastors and authors as Frank Crane, Wash-ington Gladden, Charles E. Jefferson, John Haynes Holmes, and former Secretary of State William Jennings Bryan. This second variety of "paci-fists" did not disagree with the militarists' vision of an internationalist America. On the contrary, its advocates just as passionately desired American involvement in achieving world fraternity. But for them, the hope of humanity lay not in taking whip in hand and cleansing the temple, but rather in applying Jesus' injunction to turn the other cheek. By applying the sheer moral weight of principled nonresistance, the United States would shame the rest of the world into turning to the paths of righteous-ness.

One such advocate of radical pacifism was newspaper columnist and former minister Frank Crane, whose articles appeared in more than thirty newspapers nationwide, reaching millions of readers. As early as August 13, 1914, he envisioned the war culminating in world government, in poet Alfred Lord Tennyson's long-anticipated "Parliament of man," a phrase the progressive clergy quoted endlessly. Within a few days Crane was call-ing on the United States to show the way to that world unity. In Septem-ber 1914 he pleaded, "Rise up, America! Take the lead! For what other nation can?" Crane saw America as the appointed nation emerging at the appointed time, and he believed that "the eyes of humanity" were fixed upon Woodrow Wilson. "Mr. Wilson, your hour has struck," he wrote in

December, as if his column were an open letter to the president. "The United States of America is the logical nation to inaugurate this movement [for world federation] for which destiny has now prepared mankind." The time was ripe for action, and "every preacher in the land will laud you from his pulpit."[29]

In February 1915, Crane responded sharply in the *Outlook* to that magazine's January article "Christianity and War," which justified the Christian's use of force. Crane appealed to rationality, progress, and democracy in his rebuttal, claiming that "an intelligent, twentieth-century, democratic Christian should refuse to go to war." The commandment "Thou shalt not kill," which restrained the Christian from harming his own neighbor, also prevented him from inflicting any violence on his country's neighbors. He called war "the greatest conceivable crime." Participating in it constituted "the deepest possible offense toward Almighty God."[30] While Abbott and Roosevelt appealed to the example of a militant Jesus and welcomed wars for justice, Crane embraced a Jesus whose "social enthusiasm was humanity." Once Christians rejected narrow patriotism and instead embraced Jesus' "enthusiasm," wars would vanish from the earth. Crane argued that Christians had to "bend every energy" to the cause of peace and build a community of nations governed by an international court that possessed an international police "to enforce its decrees." Unfortunately for the consistency of his argument, Crane found himself in a logical corner by advocating the use of force to resist force. Delighted that Crane conceded as much, the *Outlook* gleefully responded that the success of his plan required "'one international armed force TO ENFORCE ITS DECREES.' which would be war."[31]

Also enrolled in the ranks of "Tolstoyan" nonresistance was Washington Gladden, the conscience of "applied Christianity." Like Crane, he protested preparedness and American military intervention and shared his belief that the war would bring international cooperation and open the way for continued human progress. In a letter to the *New York Times* in 1915 he prophesied that America's moment of opportunity would come when the warring nations of Europe were exhausted. In the meantime, the United States stood in no danger whatsoever from Germany. Appealing to a common theme, he argued that the war already had impressed its horrors so deeply into the soul of humanity that such a conflict would never be repeated. Christians around the world would see to it that their respective nations repented of the evil of war and turned from their perversity. Gladden assumed, as he informed the *Times,* "that it will be plain to a good many millions of average human beings . . . that war, at its very best, is a hideous insanity, a fiendish foolishness; and that a demand for putting an end to it, such as the Heavens have never heard, will arise from Christendom."[32] Like so many of his fellow clergymen, Gladden found a certain rationality in the war by promising himself that it would somehow straighten out a twisted world.

In 1916, Gladden won an essay contest sponsored by Andrew Carnegie's Church Peace Union with his entry "The Forks of the Road." He argued that military preparedness meant "the flat repudiation of all that is central and vital in Christian morality." He did not deny the need at times for defensive wars, as in the case of invaded and occupied Belgium, but he warned that the cry of national defense was more often than not a pretext for wars of aggression. The real tragedy of the World War to Gladden was that the "Christian" nations acted so contrary to "the laws of the Kingdom of Heaven." He had devoted his life to applying Christianity to collective national behavior. In another essay in 1916, Gladden contended that by arming itself the United States was defying God's law of brotherhood in the same way that Europe had done with such tragic results. He was amazed that after witnessing the consequences of unrestrained national ambition in Europe for more than two years, the American people would now consent to their own nation's preparations for war. It was clear to Gladden that the European nations were reaping what they had sown: "They would not obey the law [of love], but they cannot escape its penalty. Hell is the penalty of the disobedience of God's law and war is hell." And now, by arming itself, America was about to experience the same inevitable workings of God's moral law. Gladden could only respond, "It's a mad world, my masters!"[33]

Aside from Gladden, perhaps the most thoughtful and widely read spokesman for nonresistant pacifism was the now little-remembered Congregational minister Charles E. Jefferson, pastor of the Broadway Tabernacle in Manhattan, where William Jennings Bryan had delivered his words of peace to a packed house on the Day of Prayer in 1914. This was the same minister who in 1904 had urged the church to mount a new crusade to rid the American "Holy Land" of the modern Saracen. Jefferson was also a founding member of the League to Limit Armament, joining in that antiwar organization with Oswald Garrison Villard, Jane Addams, George Foster Peabody, and Lillian D. Wald.[34] He regularly attended the Mohonk Conferences and was present at Andrew Carnegie's home in 1914 for the inaugural meeting of the Church Peace Union,[35] in time becoming the chairman of that body's executive committee. Like Gladden, Jefferson condemned war and all preparations for it. Writing in the *Independent* in August 1914, he disputed the militarists' claims that armaments would ensure peace, arguing that increased spending on defense merely fueled the raging conflagration of war. Armaments were not "instruments of reason or righteousness."[36]

In February 1915, Jefferson gave a series of six lectures on "Christianity and International Peace" at Grinnell College, Iowa, where George Herron had once taught "Applied Christianity." He identified the kingdom of God as Jesus' "central idea" and directly related it to the quest for world peace. Repeating a familiar social gospel refrain, he reminded his audience that "the city of God is no longer a distant goal in the clouds to be reached after this life is over, it is rather a city which is to be brought down out of heaven, and given a place on the earth by the prayers and labors of men." For the City of God to descend, the selfish, warring world had to be transformed into a brotherhood. Not surprisingly, Jefferson placed the United States at the forefront of that effort. Americans, he warned, had to "think soberly about our nation and its mission to the world," for the United States had not "begun to do yet what it is in the mind of God we shall do." Indeed, "if we use the powers which heaven has given us we can mold and guide the world."[37] As was typical of even the most consistent pacifists within the church, Jefferson actually encouraged the use of a certain kind of national power and believed that America possessed a divine calling to inaugurate the kingdom of God on earth.

Persuaded that not only the fate of the temporal world, but also the very survival of Christianity itself depended on permanent peace, Jefferson insisted on the church's involvement in international affairs. Although

Christianity had for centuries accepted the principle that earthly powers were divided between the church and the state, between God and Caesar, Jefferson believed that Caesar, characterized by militarism, had to submit to the authority of the church. Short of this, Christianity would be swallowed up by Caesar. "The church cannot survive if militarism is to rule," he told his Grinnell audience. "Christianity must languish if Caesar is to sit on the throne. A house divided against itself cannot stand." Whether conscious or instinctive, this was the same dualistic, all-or-nothing argument that Lincoln had used to explain the impending Civil War. Despite the fact that the church had existed side-by-side with Caesar for nineteen-hundred years, Jefferson called on the twentieth-century church to demand the usurper's removal. "The American pulpit is recreant to its highest trust," he scolded, "if it does not insist in season and out of season upon the introduction of Christian principles in national policies, and if it does not demand that the attitude of our nation to all other nations shall be that of a Christian man to his brothers."[38]

In 1916, Jefferson delivered the Merrick Lectures at Ohio Wesleyan University and once again spoke on international peace. Specifically, he took as his theme the lessons of the war. Sounding much like his colleagues, he speculated that the war was "a text book for the instruction of humanity in spiritual things."[39] The European war was God's revelation, and through it the world learned to hate war:

> Millions of men are in the trenches. It is well that they should be there, for it is only there that they can learn what war is. It is well that the war is going to be a long one, because important lessons are not easily learned. . . . There is nothing which Europe so needed to know as what war is. And there is nothing which our Republic needs more to know.[40]

Oddly, Jefferson found reason to believe that the war demonstrated humanity's essential virtue. He optimistically claimed that "the war teaches us to believe in man." Faced with the greatest war in history, Jefferson was inspired by the plentiful examples of heroism, self-sacrifice, and the power of human will and patriotism. These were Christian virtues, he reminded his Ohio audience, and their flowering in wartime meant that there was genuine hope for humanity. Nothing less than a new earth would emerge from the war. In the midst of battle, the kingdom of God itself approached: "Through the smoke of battle I see a fairer world. Across the fields of blood there streams the light of a brighter day." "An era is ending," he promised. "A new era is being born." And the people of the United States would be the instrument of the world's redemption, for "by patient effort we shall baptize all the nations into the spirit of goodwill, and bring the whole world into complete subjection to the gracious will of the Prince of Peace."[41]

Another outspoken nonresistant pacifist was John Haynes Holmes, Unitarian minister and pastor of New York's Church of the Messiah. He assumed one of the progressive church's most radical positions on social questions and war. In 1909 he helped organize the National Association for the Advancement of Colored People (NAACP) and in 1915 he was one of the founding members of the American Union Against Militarism, along with Addams, Villard, Max Eastman of the *Masses,* and Rabbi Stephen Wise.[42] Holmes advocated "passive resistance," but with the emphasis on resistance. He would combat evil. Pacifism was no cowardly surrender to the world's sin, but rather a battle waged "not as the devil fights, but as God fights," that is, with moral force, not physical.[43] Despite his call for this variety of sanctified nonresistance, Holmes, as fully as any other liberal minister, envisioned America leading the world into the Promised Land. American ideals would one day "conquer Europe," he wrote, quoting celebrity pacifist David Starr Jordan. "And when was there such an opportunity to fulfil this duty as at this hour of world agony?" Punished by an exhausting war, bankrupt and devastated, Europe would inevitably look with longing eyes at America's imperishable ideals. America could not betray the world and herself by misguidedly pursuing "security not in love but in power." To do so would mean the end of the American empire.[44]

Another warning against America seeking safety in militarism came from Wilson's first secretary of state, William Jennings Bryan. Though not a religious liberal, Bryan was involved with the Federal Council of Churches and regularly attended the Lake Mohonk Conferences. He shared his more progressive friends' faith in a certain expression of American internationalism, even as he firmly resisted their more ambitious schemes. In a long but stirring speech at the final Mohonk Conference in 1916, Bryan criticized the League to Enforce Peace, and was able to address his remarks directly to its founder, William Howard Taft, who was seated in the audience. Bryan favored closer international cooperation and as secretary of state had crafted numerous "cooling-off" treaties, but he feared that Taft's league would violate America's tradition against entangling alliances and also guarantee wars in the name of peace. Moreover, Bryan predicted, the League to Enforce Peace would involve Europe in the Western Hemisphere in violation of the Monroe Doctrine. In no way did he want the United States to be a world policeman, and he opposed American entry into the Great War. Reflecting his Midwestern, agrarian, populist roots, he predicted that such involvement would place an enormous war debt on future generations, sacrifice countless American lives—he feared half a million dead—and mean that America would lose a neutral's unique ability to mediate.[45] In general, Bryan favored a more Tolstoyan policy of nonresistance for his nation, believing that the strength of America's moral influence alone would sway the world toward peace more effectively than any amount of military coercion. But Bryan was already out of Wilson's cabinet, and this minority opinion would not shape the administration's policy.

THE THIRD GROUP of clerical "pacifists" as identified by Sidney Gulick and distinct from the militants and the Tolstoyans were the "juridical" pacifists. These were the advocates of world organization and rationalization, of collective security in the name of international peace. Industrial tycoons like Andrew Carnegie and John D. Rockefeller had brought their organizational skills to bear on a competitive market, and in its own sphere the Federal Council of Churches strove for similar order among the competing Protestant denominations. The similarity of these two impulses was made explicit in 1917 by John D. Rockefeller Jr., in a speech to the Baptist Social Union:

> Would that I had the power to bring to your minds the vision as it unfolds before me! I see all denominational emphasis set aside. I see co-operation, not competition. In the large cities I see great religious centers. . . . In small places, instead of a half dozen dying churches, competing with each other, I see one or two strong churches, uniting the Christian life of the town. I see the church

molding the thought of the world as it has never done before, leading in all
great movements as it should. I see it literally establishing the Kingdom of God
on earth.[46]

Extending this vision, Rockefeller, Carnegie, the Federal Council of
Churches, and allied foundations and organizations planned for habits of
cooperation to replace the supposed anarchy of international competition.
The juridical pacifists hoped to achieve a sane, managed, orderly world.
And this group was perhaps closest to President Wilson—in friendship and
in its approach to world peace.

Naturally, Carnegie's Church Peace Union publicly opposed preparedness and wanted the European War to end without American armed intervention. In December 1914, Carnegie's organization endorsed Wilson's
stand against large increases in defense spending. Believing armaments to
be futile, the Church Peace Union—of which Faunce, Jefferson, Lynch,
Macfarland, Shailer Mathews, and Wilson's friend John R. Mott were all
members—approved $10,000 for a campaign "to rouse the people of this
country to a realization of their duties in regard to the terms of peace in
Europe and the threatened growth of militarism here."[47]

For the spring of 1915, the Federal Council of Churches, which shared
many of its leaders with the Church Peace Union, planned a week of prayer
for a "righteous world peace." The council issued guidelines for local congregations on how to conduct the event, proposing, for example, that on
Tuesday they pray "that the warring nations may be guided to the securing
of a righteous world peace, and that the hearts of the stricken peoples may
be prepared for a new era of human brotherhood." In the midst of the
week of prayer for a new international order, the churches were not to
neglect the social order, but should remember to petition God "that a just
and humane and truly Christian social order may replace the present order through peaceful processes directed by the cooperative forces of all
lovers of righteousness and men of good will."[48]

Wilson addressed a Columbus, Ohio, meeting of the Executive Committee of the Federal Council in December 1915, ten years after his speech
to one of the Federal Council's first sessions. The Executive Committee
included Charles Macfarland and Shailer Mathews, and Washington Glad-

den, who ministered in Columbus, was in the audience. Echoing the council's social gospel presuppositions about the proper task of Christianity, Wilson told them that "the most vitalizing thing in the world is Christianity." He downplayed theology and emphasized his habitual themes of social service and self-sacrifice. Christianity, he cautioned, was not useful in the world if it existed as merely "a valid body of conceptions regarding God and man," but rather only as it worked to translate those ideas into life. Wilson's object in coming to Columbus, he told the committee, was "to remind the church that it is put into this world, not only to serve the individual soul, but to serve society also." He argued that in some ways saving society took precedence, "because you have got to save society in this world, not in the next. . . . We have got to save society, so far as it is saved, by the instrumentality of Christianity in this world."[49]

Wilson also compared Christianity to the highest form of patriotism, noting that they were both "the devotion of the spirit to something greater and nobler than itself." The key to changing the world lay in unselfishness, he urged, "and the church is the only embodiment of the things that are entirely unselfish—the principles of self-sacrifice and devotion." And as the church was the example of spiritual service, the United States was the example of national service. From its very founding, Wilson continued, America's

> object in the world, its only reason for existence as a government, was to show men the paths of liberty and of mutual serviceability, to lift the common man out of the paths, out of the slough of discouragement and even despair; set his feet upon firm ground; tell him, Here is the high road upon which you are as much entitled to walk as we are, and we will see that there is a free field and no favor, and that, as your moral qualities are and your physical powers, so will your success be. We will not let any man make you afraid, and we will not let any man do you an injustice.[50]

Using images from Bunyan's *Pilgrim's Progress,* Wilson posited that America had been founded, had "its only object for existence" in fact, to bring humanity up to the "high road," to a path of safety and justice on which to progress unmolested. Wilson could not have better tailored his address to this audience. The leaders of the Federal Council had devoted themselves to the uplift of humanity, and they were ready to follow Wilson as he led America into greater "mutual serviceability."

The day following his speech to the Federal Council, Wilson appeared before Columbus's Gridiron Club, again noting the parallel between patriotism and Christian idealism and the contribution of both to fulfilling America's mission. Patriotism, he proposed, "bids every man subordinate his own interests to the interests of the common weal and to act upon that, though it be to the point of utter sacrifice of himself and everything that is involved." In the same way, Christianity causes a man to turn from his own interests to serve others. Both patriotism and Christian idealism bring the individual to the point where he aligns "every thought and action with something greater than himself." By so purging their own souls of any selfish ambition, Americans would be able not only to save themselves but also to redeem all mankind. "I believe, and you believe," he reminded his audience, "that the interests of America are coincident with the interests of the world, and that, if we can make America lead the way of example along the paths of peace and regeneration for herself, we shall enable her to lead the whole world along those paths of promise and achievement." Having united its own fragmented individual ambitions into one hope, the nation would "make conquest of the spirit of the world."[51]

By the time of these two speeches in Ohio in 1915, Wilson seemed to be on a clear path toward war. He had issued two strong warnings to Germany over the *Lusitania* incident, provoking a weary and conscience-stricken Secretary Bryan to resign in June over the pro-ally stance of the administration and Wilson's apparent movements toward war. Then in November, at a banquet sponsored by the Manhattan Club at New York's Biltmore Hotel, Wilson announced his plans for a four hundred thousand–man army and for a navy on a par with Britain's, a goal beyond even the dreams of Lyman Abbott and the Navy League. Wilson called for arming the nation to keep Prussian militarism at bay. Republican editor William Allen White later recalled that he had watched Wilson take a new step in his presidency that November evening. "Neutrality had gone out of his heart," White remembered. "He was a partisan of the Allies against Germany. He took the country with him eventually." Bryan now publicly rebuked the president, calling his policy "a menace to our peace and safety" and, even more damning, "a challenge to the spirit of Christianity." By arming, America was imitating the European powers.[52]

Considering his two Ohio speeches in December that promoted the patriotism of self-sacrifice, Wilson appeared headed for some sort of American action. Even though he called for preparedness for the sake of peace, the Church Peace Union protested his actions. The union argued in December that it was manifestly not the duty of Christian America to increase the amount of armaments in the world, but rather, its statement countered, it was "the duty of God-fearing men to increase in the world the stock of good-will, and to devise means by which the recurrence of the present world tragedy may be rendered impossible." To this end, the resolution continued, religious leaders had to devote every effort and nourish "in men's hearts the divine ideals of human brotherhood."[53]

This statement may have been the official position of the Church Peace Union, and some of its members, such as Charles Jefferson and Frederick Lynch, no doubt agreed with it. But a contrary version of pacifism offered by other members of Carnegie's union and of the Federal Council required a very muscular and aggressive American policy. They did not blush to advocate an ambitious role for the United States in world affairs, although for the time being they stopped short of calling for war. But as the Wilson administration drew closer to entering the European War, several of these leaders advanced to an openly more interventionist stance.

The Federal Council's Sidney L. Gulick, for example, published *The Fight for Peace* in 1915, a book prepared jointly for the Federal Council of Churches' Commission on Peace and Arbitration and for the Church Peace Union. He repeated themes common in liberal Christianity's view of the war and of American foreign policy. The present war, he argued, had not proven Christianity a failure; on the contrary, Christianity's power to mold international relations "has never been adequately tested." This reasoning, that Christianity had not yet fully been applied, served as an easy escape for those who otherwise would have had to face the evident failure of a social gospel foreign policy. And defending what he termed "Golden Rule Diplomacy," Gulick called for its wider application rather than for any reevaluation of its premises. To reach this new epoch in international relations, Christians had to emulate Christ and be "ready to suffer with Him in the redemption of the world, transforming it from what it is into what it ought to be."[54]

Gulick was the author who divided American pacifists according to the means they advocated to achieve peace, whether through military force, judicial arbitration, or Tolstoyan nonresistance. He conceded that while the "juridical pacifist"—as he styled himself—and the militarist might seem to be irreconcilable, they both rejected nonresistance, and both embraced "righteousness and justice." Significantly, he dismissed the remaining distinctions between the two groups as "chiefly matters of emphasis, expression and spirit." The duty of every Christian was "to establish the Kingdom of God on a world-wide scale through methods of *international righteousness and helpfulness.*" According to Gulick's line of reasoning, by building the kingdom on earth, Christians even shared in the atoning work of Christ; through an analogous "suffering love," Christians helped "redeem the world." Gulick's foreign policy proceeded from a fundamental point of liberal theology: the secularization and universalization of the doctrine of the Atonement. Once translated from theory into practice, he proclaimed, "the doctrine of the Atonement, rightly grasped and lived, throws new light on all man's problems. It becomes a mighty living force for the redemption of the world. For Christ's redemptive work is not complete till all His disciples have shared with Him in His suffering for the sin of the world, that they may share with Him its redemption."[55] Gulick had hit upon an important principle; the Apostle Paul had also instructed the early church about sharing in Christ's suffering. But it is hard to imagine that Paul had the Roman Empire's foreign policy in mind when he penned this advice. Yet as the title of Gulick's book made clear, for modern, progressive Christians, completing Christ's redemptive work in the twentieth century required *The Fight for Peace.*

Church Peace Union secretary Frederick Lynch, while critical of the preparedness movement, shared Gulick's vision of America as the redeemer nation. At Mohonk in 1915, in a speech that sounded very much like a page from Woodrow Wilson, he called upon America to follow "a high Christian course" to the end "that it may not only stop this war—that is the minor thing after all—but that it may somehow or other lead the nations up to a plane where not only international law will not be violated and not only the rights of neutrals will be protected, but all the world will see that the time has come to put this business aside forever," arriving at last at "that sweet Kingdom of God."[56] In a book published the following year, *The Challenge:The Church and the NewWorld Order,* Lynch repeated this messianic hope and pleaded with the churches to "preach a new patriotism, a patriotism that is not so much concerned with saving the nation as it is in having the nation be a Christ-nation to the other nations of the world.""The time has come," he proclaimed, "for the Church to take Jesus by the arm and have *faith* in His teachings, and go forth bravely to apply them to the world." Though still desiring that the United States stay out of the war, Lynch nevertheless could not have concocted a grander role for America than as the "Christ-nation" in world affairs: "those who are truly Christian are anxious to have the United States become the saviour of impoverished, distracted, disrupted, groaning Europe, after the war is over."[57]

An immediate test of America's claims to saviorhood came not in Europe but in Mexico.To most Americans, mention of war in 1916 would have brought to mind the Mexican situation. Since 1914 Wilson had talked of the need to "serve" the Mexican people and in April 1914 he had sent troops to Veracruz. He failed to unseat General Victoriano Huerta from power, but in early 1916 "service" on Mexico's behalf was still on his mind. He told a NewYork audience that, as the United States had demonstrated in Cuba in 1898, "a nation can sacrifice its own interests and its own blood for the sake of the liberty and happiness of another people."[58] Exasperated by Pancho Villa's raid into New Mexico in 1916, he ordered troops back into Mexico, this time to capture Villa.[59]

Mexico proposed a negotiated settlement to the controversy and suggested a meeting of three representatives from each side. Hoping to avoid a full-scale war with Mexico, Wilson agreed to delegate three American "commissioners" to negotiate peace: Judge George Gray, Secretary of the Interior Franklin K. Lane, and theYMCA's John R. Mott. A Catholic priest in Connecticut was so incensed thatWilson would choose a man as strongly identified with Protestant missions as Mott to deal with Catholic Mexico, that he threatened to "advise every Irish Catholic in the State of Connecticut to vote against" Wilson in the upcoming presidential election.[60] Wilson's

closest advisor, Colonel House, had actually proposed sending a Catholic
negotiator, provided he "was more of a Wilson man than a church man."
With Mott on board, the Joint Commission met through the fall of 1916,
but the situation in Mexico was soon eclipsed by the impending U.S. entry into the European War.[61] Writing after Wilson's reelection that autumn, Mott linked the two crises and thanked Wilson for being a man of
"responsiveness to backward, oppressed and struggling peoples and . . .
for dealing in a large and truly Christian way with the present unprecedented world situation."[62]

Among those seeing the situation in Mexico in 1916 as an opportunity for the United States to exercise a benevolent policing power was
Shailer Mathews, dean of the University of Chicago's Divinity School,
president of the Federal Council of Churches, and a member of Carnegie's
Church Peace Union. A police action in Mexico, he decided, "will be both
defensive and vicarious." In other words, American soldiers would be fighting as servants of the Mexican people, a familiar Wilsonian theme and an
attitude that could justify almost any military intervention. Admitting
America's paternalistic attitude toward its southern neighbor, Mexico
Commissioner Franklin K. Lane observed, "There is a great deal of the
special policeman, of the sanitary engineer, of the social worker, and of
the welfare dictator about the American people. . . . It is one of the most
fundamental instincts that have made white men give to the world its
history for the last thousand years."[63] Lane recognized the power of the
humanitarian, social gospel, Wilsonian impulse to shape history.

But could this "social worker" war with Mexico be a pacifist war as
well? Could it be part of the historical movement toward world peace the
way the Spanish-American War had been some twenty years before? Could
it be a progressive war? Shailer Mathews thought so and easily reconciled
intervention in Mexico with his pacifist principles. In fact, he argued that
such a use of force by the United States was not only justifiable, but obliga-
tory. He warned that "the immediate duty of every Christian who is loyal
to the ideals of peace is to separate peace as a world-policy from police
duty thrust upon us by conditions we . . . could not control." In an explicit
advocacy of war as a useful and proper tool of the social gospel, Mathews
charged that "a policeman protecting social ideals from maniacs and thugs

is an exponent of more efficient social service than a Good Samaritan binding up the wounds of victims of civic neglect."[64]

Earlier, in Washington in May 1916, Mathews had addressed the first annual meeting of the League to Enforce Peace, a largely Republican organization that William Howard Taft, Hamilton Holt of the *Independent,* Harvard president A. Lawrence Lowell, and others had founded the summer before in Philadelphia to promote peace though collective security. Cynical essayist Randolph Bourne, the critic who had complained of America's incurably "redemptive" literature, dismissed the proposal as "a palpable apocalyptic myth."[65] Nevertheless, the league served as one of the most influential interest groups on behalf of a league of nations, and President Wilson endorsed the league idea at its 1916 meeting.[66]

The League to Enforce Peace was notable for bringing together the various strands of pacifism and internationalism. Distinctions among various kinds of progressive pacifism became less meaningful as America neared intervention. Taft, in a letter to ten thousand pastors, called for an international system of law and military defense to end war, portraying warfare as an impediment to "religious, social and industrial progress."[67] This was the same analysis of the war he had offered the *Independent*'s readers in August 1914. Significantly, the Church Peace Union's board voted to allow its trustees to participate in the formation of the league. The two groups eventually coordinated their efforts, and Taft later reciprocated by becoming a trustee of the Church Peace Union.[68] Taft, of course, also attended the Mohonk Conferences. The league's "National Provisional Committee" included some of the most familiar names in Protestant liberalism: Lyman Abbott, novelist Winston Churchill, columnist Frank Crane, editor Hamilton Holt, W. H. P. Faunce, Washington Gladden, David Starr Jordan, Frederick Lynch, Charles Macfarland, and many others. The league focused on the development of international law and enforcement, and in one historian's estimation it "became the most influential pro-league organization in the United States and perhaps the world."[69] Abbott, Gladden, Daniel Smiley from Mohonk, and Shailer Mathews all became vice presidents of the league, while Frederick Lynch and Hamilton Holt sat on its executive committee.[70]

At the league's 1916 meeting in Washington, Mathews praised Taft's organization as "an ideal that dares call upon nations as well as individuals to sacrifice." For the sake of justice, the new league would emphasize the duties rather than the rights of nations. "We hope," Mathews continued, "that by its program it will be shown that spirituality, common sense, and cooperative patriotism may be united into a splendid, devoted effort to give to the other nations the justice which we claim for ourselves." Anticipating his critics, Mathews countered that he did not care if the church devoted itself to a plan that might seem naïve: "I would rather prepare for Utopia than for Hell"—repeating a line from Teddy Roosevelt and suggesting that these were the only two options any longer open to the world in 1916.[71]

Brown University president William H. P. Faunce—another league member—was also among the "juridical" pacifists, and, like Mathews, called for justice before peace. Faunce had been a regular speaker at Lake Mohonk and was a member of the Church Peace Union, and at one time had opposed preparedness. The evolution of his thought is instructive. In October 1914, at Brown's 150th anniversary celebration, he had mourned the attack on "the Christian ideal . . . by the arrogant militarism of Europe." By June 1915—the month of the founding of the League to Enforce Peace—he favored an international league, urging Brown's graduates to fix their gaze on "the hope and vision of a league of all the nations to maintain an enduring peace." War was part of the withering past, he told them, and it was up to the rising generation to fight for peace: "War is old, pathetically old, tragically futile, hopelessly antiquated. Peace, heroic and sacrificial, is the new vision which only young men can believe in."[72] By advocating a league he moved decisively toward righteous interventionism.

By April 1916, Faunce had abandoned his pacifism altogether. He had always accepted the taking up of arms for national defense, but now he put the more abstract principle of international justice ahead of his desire for peace. Standing before a meeting of the American Council of the World Alliance for International Friendship through the Churches—the organization born out of the disappointing Konstanz peace conference in 1914—he declared that he valued "justice" above simply an end to the European

War. By sounding so much like Teddy Roosevelt and Lyman Abbott, he created something of a stir in the audience. This peace advocate of some record admitted that he no longer desired merely to stop the war: "We do not want the war stopped until peace can be established on the basis of justice. For myself I believe it must be fought out." Like a disease, he suggested, the war had to rage until it ran its course and left the body. Not the end of this particular war, "but the prevention of war, is the task that summons today the Christian forces of the world." True pacifism, he argued, was impossible in a world rebelling against Christ and His dominion: "I cannot for a moment accept the doctrine of Tolstoy so long as I follow a Christ whose whole life was a resolute resistance to evil."[73] The League to Enforce Peace was on record by late 1916 as opposed to a premature end to the war.[74]

This notion of a premature peace was central to the evolving progressive attitude toward the war. Ending the war without achieving righteousness would betray the cause of Christ Himself. Progressive Christians no longer interpreted the war as simply the collapse of Europe into the pit of economic and military imperial rivalry, but rather as the alignment of the world into the ultimate imperial rivalry, the one between paganism and Christianity, between the empire of Satan and the empire of God. Germany and the other autocratic empires lagged behind on the continuum from barbarism to Christian civilization. To stop so historically productive a war short of its promise would be unthinkable. Clearly, then, for some of the clergy the European War by 1916 had already assumed the character of a holy war. The "pacifists"—as they continued to call themselves—embraced war as a means to righteousness. Seminary professor John Wright Buckham assured the readers of *Biblical World* that "pacifism does not mean passivity" and "does not renounce physical force." And, he continued, this kind of pacifism certainly did not mean a peace based on selfish isolationism. Allowing Europe to fight out its own wars "may have been justifiable for our nation in its infancy; it is not now. The pacifists do not advocate any such peace policy as that. Their motive is not safety but service. They would have ours not a hermit nation but a humanitarian nation."[75]

Despite the Protestant liberals' careful classification of themselves into militant, nonresistant, and juridical pacifists, these categories were never as clear in practice as they were in theory, and in hindsight such precise labels tend to obscure just how much the various groups agreed. Members of all three groups, for example, continued to work together at Lake Mohonk; the League to Enforce Peace enjoyed support from the jingoist Abbott as well as from the anti-preparedness Gladden; and while Sidney Gulick distanced himself from "Tolstoyan" pacifism, the Tolstoyan pacifist John Haynes Holmes wrote admiringly of Gulick. Frederick Lynch cooperated with the Church Peace Union, the Federal Council of Churches, the League to Enforce Peace, and the American Union Against Militarism. Their varieties of pacifism, especially as they bore upon modern America's image of its role in the world, were virtually distinctions without a difference. Whether they were "realists" or "idealists" mattered little in a foreign policy debate that ranged within such narrow limits.

Progressive clergy across the spectrum tended to agree on the "meaning" of the war and cherished similar hopes for its results. They shared the *New Republic*'s assessment in 1916—more than a year before American entry—that "the great lesson of the war for the American people . . . is that American isolation has come to an end."[76] For most of the progressives, neutrality in this war had never meant isolation or simply national self-preservation. Wilson told the Associated Press in 1915 that his policy of neutrality did not derive from "indifference." Neutrality, he said, "is not self-interest." On the contrary, "the basis of neutrality is sympathy for mankind." Neutrality was a means to service. Indeed, America was "the mediating nation of the world." The American people had transcended history by creating a nation free from selfish ambition, and such a nation was "free to serve other nations." Wilson confessed to the opinion-makers in the press that he was "interested in neutrality because there is something so much greater to do than fight: there is a distinction waiting for this nation that no nation has ever yet got. That is the distinction of absolute self-control and self-mastery." The American people "are trustees for what I venture to say is the greatest heritage that any nation ever had—the love of justice and righteousness and human liberty."[77] Wilson and the progressive clergy inhabited the same universe of words and ideas. They gave the same eccentric meaning to "neutrality" and "peace" and the same definition to the sacred words "service" and "righteousness."

WHETHER AMERICA'S CALL to service meant armed intervention in Europe or even arming for national defense was another matter. Not all the progressive clergy agreed. Some of the more militant pacifists joined preparedness organizations and even marched in preparedness parades. In New York on May 13, 1916, for example, the city's militant clergy joined 140,000 marchers in the Citizens Preparedness Parade. Flag-waving crowds lined Fifth Avenue, where the fashionable churches and grand hotels wore patriotic decorations for the occasion. The National Security League was one of the parade's sponsors. From morning till after dark, row upon row of participants marched northward up Manhattan. Esteemed guests included Mrs. Theodore Roosevelt, Alton B. Parker, Henry L. Stimson, Thomas A. Edison, and former Secretary of State Elihu Root, founder of the Army War College and recipient of the 1912 Nobel Peace Prize. Two hundred bands accompanied the veterans of the Spanish-American War, area National Guard units, women's groups, bankers, insurers, businessmen and actors, craft unions, manufacturers, importers and exporters, and students from local high schools and from Columbia University. The city's clergy followed behind the architects and just ahead of the wholesale millinery trade. The church division was 130 strong, with representatives from the Protestant, Catholic, and Jewish sects. The clergy wore their collars and patriotic decorations. As the clergy marched along Fifth Avenue, someone from the crowd shouted, "Hurrah for the Church Militant!" and the enthusiastic onlookers responded with cheers.[78]

To the north of the city, within days of the preparedness parade, the Smileys' guests at Lake Mohonk assembled once again to discuss their plans for peace. Devoted "pacifists" representing a range of opinions on preparedness met for what would be the last of a score of peace conferences at Lake Mohonk. Former president William Howard Taft presided that year, and guests included Charles Macfarland and Frederick Lynch, Charles Jefferson and William Jennings Bryan, as well as Lyman Abbott. Abbott made his usual plea for national readiness and warned that "disarmament never has produced peace." He charged that the United States

was obligated to defend itself—a position few at Mohonk argued with—
but more than that, America had to foster an "international patriotism"
and champion "the rights of man everywhere over this world."[79] The following day, Rear Admiral Austin M. Knight, president of the Naval War
College, called for an enlarged navy—not a navy launched merely for
national defense, but rather a navy for international service. He proposed
"that the United States be made great in physical power in order that its
moral power may be effective beyond its borders," for "without power it
is assuredly not possible to be helpful." While "selfish" nations insisted on
arming, "righteous" nations had to counter evil ambitions until righteousness prevailed. Besides, as a great military power, the United States would
be able to "have almost a controlling voice" at the eventual postwar peace
conference.[80]

The final Mohonk conference nearly coincided with the first anniversary of the sinking of the *Lusitania*. A Carnegie Hall service on May 19
memorialized the tragedy and promoted national preparedness. In his
address to the meeting, Washington, D.C., pastor Randolph McKim was
far from ambivalent about the significance of the sinking. To McKim, the
treachery of the German attack had only grown in the intervening year:
"So horrible was this deed of wholesale murder, executed by the willing
slaves of a remorseless master, that the very fabric of the moral world
seemed to tremble under the shock." Not the slightest doubt remained in
McKim's mind about Germany's immorality or the necessity for an American response. Sounding more like Abraham Lincoln than was his custom,
he resolved that the United States had to see to it that the dead of the
Lusitania had "not died in vain." Furthermore, the American people had to
"demand that this act be punished as well as repudiated." Despite George
Washington's warning against European alliances, he continued, the United
States was obligated to act. In a phrase alien to that Founder's thinking,
McKim, who so often invoked the name of the Republic, claimed that
America could not "avoid responsibility for the interests and destinies of
mankind." No choice remained. "The time has gone when this Republic
can say, 'Am I my brother's keeper?' We belong to the family of nations,
and we have duties to fulfill as a member of the family."[81]

Within a month of the commemoration at Carnegie Hall, civic leaders back in McKim's Washington organized their own preparedness parade for Flag Day, June 14, two years to the day since President Wilson had promised to make the Stars and Stripes the banner of all humanity. While not carried out on quite the scale of Manhattan's spectacle, the Washington parade nevertheless attracted more than sixty thousand participants. A straw-hatted President Wilson marched at the head of the parade, joined by senators, representatives, Supreme Court justices, and those members of the president's cabinet who were not at the Democratic National Convention in St. Louis securing their chief's renomination. The marchers convened at the Peace Monument on Capitol Hill, a marble statue honoring the Navy's Civil War dead and depicting a grieving America weeping on the shoulder of History. From here, the organized ranks proceeded along Pennsylvania Avenue to the White House, and on to a decorated Washington Monument, where Wilson sermonized on loyalty, duty, and the "glory and honor of the United States." Behind the president in the parade marched fraternal orders, suffragists, school teachers and their pupils, volunteer military organizations, the District's National Guard, and Civil War and Spanish-American War veterans. Also in the ranks followed representatives of the National Security League and the Navy League, a contingent of Washington newspapermen, and the Navy Department's Franklin D. Roosevelt. Joining these were the Red Cross, Boy Scouts, Camp Fire Girls, elaborate floats, the Marine band, and countless government employees who had been given the day off to show their strictly "nonpartisan" enthusiasm for defense. Even a small group of the Knights of the White Camellias joined in. In the fifth division came the various churches and the YWCA, with members of Randolph McKim's Church of the Epiphany leading the way.[82]

A year before the presidential election, the editors of the *Christian Century* predicted that preparedness would be the central theme of the 1916 campaign. But while the *Christian Century* feared the "clean-cut departure from our national traditions" that preparedness would signify,[83] the *Outlook*'s editors so strongly opposed continued neutrality that they questioned Wilson's right to lead the nation at such a critical moment. Although they might support his economic policies, they could not endorse his bid for reelection. The country had been founded on inalienable natural rights, and on "the duty of Americans to maintain that right and to attempt to overthrow governments that denied the right." How the current leader of that nation could be neutral when such absolute and universal principles were at stake went beyond the *Outlook*'s comprehension. Wilson was no Abraham Lincoln; of that they were certain. "Instead of rising to a great occasion, instead of touching the consciences of the people and arousing them to their duties," they charged, "Mr. Wilson appears to us to have devoted himself to 'playing safe.' Such a spirit in such a crisis of civilization as the world is now facing repels our sympathy and confidence."[84]

But at St. Louis in June 1916, the Democratic Convention enthusiastically renominated Wilson to face the Republican choice, Supreme Court justice Charles Evans Hughes. At the Democratic convention an exuberant Senator Ollie James of Kentucky, chairman of the convention, gave God's imprimatur to Wilson's presidency: "I can see the accusing picture of Christ on the battlefield, with the dead and dying all around him, with the screams of shrapnel and the roll of cannon, and I can hear the Master say to Woodrow Wilson, 'Blessed are the peace-makers, for they shall be called the children of God.'"[85] Campaigning in the months ahead under the slogan "He Kept Us Out of War," Wilson secured a narrow victory in November. The next few months would show whether Wilson would remain among the Master's blessed peacemakers.

On December 18, 1916, one month after his reelection, Wilson sent a note to the belligerent European nations asking them to state their war aims. In so doing, Wilson hoped to find an opening for peace negotiations, but he succeeded in exasperating the British with what they perceived to be a betrayal by a sympathetic and cooperative neutral.[86] In the United States his note stirred animosity as well. Although Wilson claimed he sought peace—the long-stated objective of church "pacifists" of every variety—a number of prominent clergy severely criticized his gesture. More than sixty eminent church leaders issued a joint statement rebuking Wilson for his diplomacy. Signers of the document included Plymouth Church's Newell Dwight Hillis, Boston pastor George A. Gordon, Lyman Abbott, Princeton's president John Grier Hibben, novelist Winston Churchill, Henry Churchill King, Harry Emerson Fosdick, Gifford Pinchot, and evangelist Billy Sunday, the latter a misfit for his theology but not for his war enthusiasm.[87] Anti-interventionists must have wondered at the spectacle of professed pacifists complaining that the war was going to end too soon, that immediate peace was going to get in the way of permanent peace.

These clergymen warned that Wilson's desire for peace had distracted him from higher priorities. "We are apt to forget," they cautioned, "that there are conditions under which the mere stopping of warfare may bring a curse instead of a blessing. We need to be reminded that peace is the triumph of righteousness and not the mere sheathing of the sword." Wilson's diplomacy would ultimately "sow disaster," they predicted. To end the war at this point meant stopping short of righteousness, leaving Belgium dishonored, the *Lusitania* "murder" unavenged, and the "violation of the laws of God" unanswered. The necessary course was obvious: "The just God, who withheld not his own Son from the cross, would not look with favor upon a people who put their fear of pain and death, their dread of suffering and loss, their concern for comfort and ease, above the holy claims of righteousness and justice and freedom and mercy and truth." Apotheosizing the war to a place in the sacred history of Christ's church, they appealed to "the memory of all the saints and martyrs [that] cries out against such backsliding of mankind."[88] What had been an implicit part of the logic of progressive Protestantism was now plainly spelled out: the distinction between the world and the church was now gone. Secular history had become sacred history, and those who opposed the quest for earthly righteousness were "backsliders" from the faith.

Even the members of the once-pacifist and anti-preparedness Church Peace Union questioned the wisdom of Wilson's call for terms. The *Independent* asked several of the organization's trustees to comment on the president's note. Shailer Mathews welcomed Wilson's overture, but was also concerned that justice might thereby be sacrificed. However wellintentioned, he cautioned, "a hasty peace might prove a colossal danger to the future of civilization. The issues the world faces are vastly more extensive than the military or other interests of the belligerent powers." Likewise, Charles Macfarland stressed that peace had to be concluded "upon righteousness and not on the basis of military advantage." For his part, William H. P. Faunce pleaded for the integrity of a moral universe: "I

cannot pretend to be neutral. If any deity approved the violation of Belgium, he is not my God, and his worship is not my religion."[89]

Faunce's religion was not in jeopardy, however, for in the winter and
spring of 1917 the United States abandoned its already compromised neutrality and moved toward intervention. In January, Wilson renewed his
assurances that the United States was not going to war. But within days,
the Zimmermann telegram was intercepted, proposing an alliance between Germany and Mexico in the event America entered the European
War, and promising to return the lands of the Mexican Cession surrendered in the 1840s. Then, on February 1, Germany resumed unrestricted
submarine warfare, making American vessels targets and intending to sink
enough additional tonnage to force England to negotiate. But this desperate move almost guaranteed American intervention. Indeed, the policy
change soon claimed American lives and goods. On February 3, President
Wilson broke off diplomatic relations with Germany.[90]

America would now demonstrate that God did indeed disapprove of
"the violation of Belgium." As relations between the United States and
Germany crumbled, the war enthusiasm of some of the clergy was extraordinary. The president of Hamilton College, E. W. McDiarmid, claimed
in February in the *Christian Century* that not only was it proper for a Christian to fight, it was "not right for anyone else to go to war!" In a remarkably volatile statement for the pages of the traditionally peace-loving *Christian Century,* McDiarmid proposed that "a Christian nation is the only nation that ought ever to go to war," since only it could understand its instrumentality as a tool in God's hand. Moreover, "unless a nation goes to
war in the spirit of Cromwell and his psalm-singing soldiers or the spirit
of Woodrow Wilson" it could not consider itself a fit servant of God for
the disciplining of the world.[91] By this time in the debate over American
entry into the war, the *Christian Century,* which had been rather hopefully
pacifist, published poetry that urged the nation into battle, and soon its
editorials reflected the spirit of the "holy war."[92]

Also in February, the Reverend Ernest Stires, rector of St. Thomas's
Church on Fifth Avenue where the New York preparedness parade had
passed the previous May, warned his congregation against national disunity in the impending crisis. Any American who did not support the

administration, he charged, simply did not understand the breadth of the issues involved. He feared that half the country failed to understand America's duty—people "who must have forgotten Lincoln's description of the nation [as]. . . conceived in liberty, and dedicated to justice and humanity, and who do not feel that we have been consecrated to keep and extend those principles." Either autocracy or democracy would win the war. To stand aloof was immoral. He pointed to the precedent of the Span-ish-American War, in which "our American ideals led us to war for oth-ers." Now that the nation faced another, greater vicarious war, apathy was inexcusable.[93]

On March 1, the Wilson administration released the Zimmermann telegram to the press, increasing the clamor for war. Three days later, on the first Sunday in March, the Reverend Stires explained to his congrega-tion the absolute issue of the war: "to make a choice for darkness or light, for tyranny or freedom, for treason or justice, for cruelty or pity." The nation's participation was a matter of "destiny" and "duty." Impelled to action, the American people were about to wage war, not for the sake of their own interests, but for Germany's own good and for the good of all humanity. The duty of brotherhood called: "It is moral necessity rooted in our sense of world-relationship which awakens and arms America." Clos-ing the Sunday service, Stires invited his listeners to pray a prayer of con-secration and answer God's clear call to service: "If Christ so loves the world that He bids us bear the sword of Justice to save it, tell Him to-day He will find us ready; that before this Altar we dedicate our country and ourselves to the Christ who died to save men."[94]

On the following day, Secretary of War Newton D. Baker received a telegram from Methodist minister Worth M. Tippy, the executive secre-tary of the Federal Council of Churches' Commission on the Church and Social Service. In a note to the president, Baker identified Tippy as "a kind of interdenominational bishop, organizing the church activities of about twenty-two thousand churches." Tippy asked for nothing less than a dec-laration of war against Germany: "I regret to urge war but I think [the] time has come to go in with all our power. . . . The President needs to go ahead and lead resolutely." Baker passed the telegram on to Wilson with a note that Tippy's view was significant because he, Baker, had "always believed him to be almost a non-resistant," and certainly of "conservative character." Evidently Baker thought Wilson would discern something of the mood of the country, or at least of the church, in the telegram. However, Baker did concede that Tippy had perhaps "been affected by [the] New York atmosphere," a reference to that city's pronounced enthusiasm for war.[95]

For the remainder of March, the Reverend Stires continued to prepare his congregation for war. His sermons amounted almost to weekly updates on world events. On March 18, he praised the revolution that had shaken the Russian empire since his last sermon, and he welcomed another democracy into the family of redeemed nations. Considering as well Germany's promises of democratic reforms that week, it seemed to Stires that Lincoln's "new birth of freedom" was at last spreading worldwide. Drawing a direct line from the Gettysburg Address to the book of Revelation, Stires proclaimed that "the kingdoms of this world are becoming related in the unity of a greater Kingdom. O men and women to whom God hath for a little while entrusted mighty power, use it nobly! Lead the way, that America may lead."[96]

On March 21, a German submarine torpedoed an American tanker off the coast of Holland, killing another twenty Americans.[97] The following Sunday, Stires urged the nation to recognize its role as the world's messiah. As Christ bore His cross to Calvary, so America had to take up hers. By this act of obedience, Stires promised, "America will be found faithful to her high ideal, bearing her cross, cost what it will. She will stand in the noble company of those [nations in the war] whose millions of heroes are loving, serving, dying, that human justice and happiness may live on this earth."[98] The *New York Times* observed that sermons throughout the city on this last Sunday in March were filled with "denunciations of Germany and calls for war," and also claimed that from no church "was a pacifist utterance reported." By way of example, the *Times* reported that Plymouth Church's Newell Dwight Hillis had said that he would forgive the Germans "just as soon as they were all shot" and that he would be pleased to see the Kaiser "hanging by a rope." "If we forgive Germany after the war," Hillis reportedly charged, "the moral universe will have gone wrong." Hillis disputed the accuracy of these quotations and informed the newspaper that he had actually said that "the Kaiser does not dare to die—he is afraid of meeting a million of Jesus' little ones whom he has murdered."[99]

While Hillis was beating the drum for intervention, other clergy lamented the prospect of war. J. Gresham Machen had never claimed to be an idealist or a pacifist, and over the past two years had spoken against American subservience to British policy. In 1915 he advocated genuine international pluralism over the British ambition to impose the "English mind" around the world. In 1916, he mourned America's submission to British foreign policy, lamenting that "the spirit of '76 seems to be dead at last." And now on the eve of intervention, he warned privately that the United States was heading toward bondage and statism, that is, toward

> a permanent alliance with Great Britain, which will inevitably mean a continuance of the present vassalage, and a permanent policy of compulsory military service with all the brutal interference of the state in individual and family life which that entails, and which has caused the misery of Germany and France. Princeton is a hot-bed of patriotic enthusiasm and military ardor,—which makes me feel like a man without a country.[100]

In a similar vein, House majority leader, North Carolina congressman Claude Kitchin, vehemently opposed American entry into the war. Significantly, he blamed the rush for intervention in part on the collusion of big business, the newspapers, and the elite pulpits, reserving special contempt for the interventionist clergy. Offering to speak for the "great silent masses" whose voice was not heard in the metropolitan press and churches, Congressman Kitchin charged that

> The prayers of millions of common people are not likely to avail much against the prayers of the big rich preachers, whose petitions for more bloodshed are given the widest possible publicity by a war-mad press. Allied with these war advocates of the pulpit, weak numerically but strong in the circles bent upon war, are many captains of our great corporations, who are wont in times of trouble to exploit foreign governments as well as their own countrymen with a deadly impartiality. The big predatory interests . . . can always count upon plenty of support from both pulpit and press. . . . [101]

On April 1, 1917, churches across America celebrated Palm Sunday, beginning the traditional observance of Holy Week by marking Jesus' triumphal entry into Jerusalem. But many congregations seemed eager to celebrate the United States' impending entry into the Great War. In a sermon entitled "America Summoned to a Holy War," a crusading Randolph McKim in Washington proclaimed America's duty: "I have no hesitation . . . in saying that the voice of a just God summons us to this War and that it is in the highest sense of the word a Holy War." While armor-clad knights in the Middle Ages may have marched forth nobly at God's call, these earlier "crusades shrink into insignificance compared with the crusade to which we are summoned at the present moment."[102]

That same day, in an extraordinary act, Plymouth Church in Brooklyn, the former pulpit of Henry Ward Beecher and Lyman Abbott, prepared a resolution demanding war with Germany. Beecher's own son presented the document, which rejected a mere "affirmation that a state of war exists," preferring rather "an out-and-out declaration." Plymouth sent the resolution to Washington, and the *New York Times* reported "that the men of the church will at once organize a regiment."[103] Anticipating President Wilson's war message to Congress by more than a day, the progressive clergy declared war on Germany.

6

A RIGHTEOUS PEOPLE IN A RIGHTEOUS CAUSE

THE PROGRESSIVE CLERGY AND

AMERICAN INTERVENTION, 1917–1918

AT PRESIDENT WILSON'S REQUEST, THE United States Senate and House convened in extraordinary session on Monday, April 2, 1917. After more than two years of debate and delay, the president and Congress were about to lead America into the Great War. At noon Vice President Thomas R. Marshall called the Senate to order, and a Washington pastor opened the session with prayer. Linking military intervention to the extension of God's millennial kingdom, he asked God to grant the senators "wisdom and grace to defend the truth and to advocate the cause of righteousness . . . and seek the accomplishment of Thy purpose and the enlargement of Thy kingdom in the earth." On the other side of the Capitol, the House chaplain interceded on behalf of the representatives with as little doubt about the meaning of the war and America's duty. He petitioned God to "guide us in a just and righteous cause; for Thine is the kingdom and the power and the glory, forever. Amen."[1]

With the help of Washington's clergy, the tone had been set for the day's proceedings. After the two chambers organized themselves for business, Wilson delivered his famous war message at 8:40 that evening, an address remembered mostly for its summons to America to "make the world safe for democracy." In his extended remarks, the president blamed Germany for forcing the United States into the war by recklessly resuming unrestricted submarine warfare. Germany had "put aside all restraints of law or of humanity" and waged nothing less than "warfare against mankind." Unsought, war had been "thrust upon" the United States, and the time had come to act. "Our object," Wilson declared, "is to vindicate the principles of peace and justice in the life of the world as against selfish and autocratic power." Autocratic Germany had violated the progressive prohibition against selfishness. Arguing from the principles of international relations long advocated by the social gospel movement, the president held Germany accountable to the precepts of individual Christian ethics. "The same standards of conduct and of responsibility for wrong done," he charged, "shall be observed among nations and their governments that are observed among the individual citizens of civilized states." In essence, this was a war for "peace" and "liberation," a war to free Germany itself. It was a vicarious war, waged on behalf of others and "without selfish object," destined to make "the world itself at last free."[2] Wilson's war message captured the progressive spirit.

The following day, Wilson's son-in-law and secretary of the treasury, William Gibbs McAdoo, congratulated the president on his speech. "You have done a great thing nobly!" he wrote the president. "I firmly believe that it is God's will that America should do this transcendent service for humanity throughout the world and that you are his chosen instrument." McAdoo, whether aware of the similarity in language or not, echoed the progressive clergy's consistent characterization of the war as a "transcendent service for humanity" performed by God's "chosen instrument."[3] With a similar sense of divine commissioning, Wilson confidant Raymond Fosdick recalled some forty years later that the president's inspiring war message had united the country to fulfill America's destiny as a nation: "it seemed as if our generation by some divine providence had been specifically chosen for great and determining events."[4]

While McAdoo and Fosdick were certain that the United States was a chosen nation, the Congress was divided over the president's declaration of war. Some members, even from Wilson's own Democratic Party, vigorously opposed intervention. But by April the majority of the House and Senate clearly favored war. Debate seemed almost pointless. Even Senator Henry Cabot Lodge, one of Wilson's staunchest political adversaries, rallied to the president's call to arms. His choice of words revealed the breadth of the progressive consensus. He clothed the war as a fight "to preserve human freedom, democracy, and modern civilization." To Lodge, Germany's behavior was a throwback to "barbarism," and the United States had to resist this atavistic nation's "effort to thrust mankind back to forms of government, to political creeds and methods of conquest which we had hoped had disappeared forever from the world."[5] Quite simply, Germany impeded humanity's progress—a familiar bit of progressive logic.

Other senators supported the war in equally unequivocal terms. Senator Henry L. Myers of Montana cried for war not merely for the vindication of American rights, but also because "the democracy, the civilization, the Christianization of the world are at stake." LeBaron B. Colt of Rhode Island shared these sentiments and identified Germany as the sworn enemy of "liberty, civilization, Christianity, and all that we hold dear as an enlightened people." "Prussian militarism," he continued, echoing Lodge, "is the system of the Middle Ages."[6]

Senator Ollie M. James of Kentucky—the Democratic Convention chairman who the previous June had pictured Christ on the battlefield blessing Wilson the "peacemaker"—entered into the record a telegram from the Newark, New Jersey, convention of the Methodist Episcopal Church supporting the president's decision. After congratulating the nation for its "patience unexampled," the church convention called for unwavering national unity and resolve, and pointed out as justification for war that "even the patient Christ, whose ambassadors we are, in time of extremity, when pacific measures had failed, said, 'He that hath no sword, let him sell his garment and buy one.'" Another conference of more than three hundred Methodist clergy met in the flag-draped sanctuary of New York's Washington Square Church. As the *New York Times* reported, the German flag "was snatched from its conspicuous place . . . [and] replaced by a large French flag." The Methodist ministers then sang "The Battle Hymn of the Republic."[7]

Not every senator joined in the clamor for war. The Senate's most persistent opponent of intervention was Wisconsin's Robert M. La Follette, who claimed to have received from forty-four states fifteen thousand letters and telegrams condemning the war. In an impassioned speech he pointed to Britain's violations of international law and its policy of systematic starvation of central Europe. Moreover, he scorned Wilson's pledge to "spend the whole force of the Nation" if necessary, and appealed to Thomas Jefferson's neutrality policy. If Wilson truly had been neutral all along, he charged, "we would not be called on to-day to declare war on any of the belligerents."[8] An offended Senator John Sharp Williams of Mississippi responded that La Follette's speech should have been delivered in the German Parliament instead.[9]

Near midnight on Wednesday, April 4, after two days of debate and over the objections of only six members, the Senate passed the resolution for war.[10] The House, however, debated two more days. In these debates, Christian idealism was again conspicuous, and, as in the Senate exchanges, Jesus' teachings were used to justify either intervention or nonintervention.

At least one representative found the war contrary to genuinely pacifist Christianity. Congressman William E. Mason of Illinois implored his colleagues not to repeat the errors of Europe. "I say to you, gentlemen," he warned them in a plea for compassion, "before you go to war, before you say, 'We love the German people, but we want to kill them because we do not like the Kaiser,' pity them, then, if you do not like the Kaiser." He was especially concerned that the United States was about to enter the war during Holy Week. "Let us not declare war in the hour they crucified the Prince of Peace," he admonished the House. Conversely, John Jacob Rogers of Massachusetts justified the war by appealing to the same Prince of Peace. Congress, he proposed, had the opportunity to wage "a war for Christianity itself. God grant that . . . our entrance into war to-day may aid in the wiping of wars for all time from the face of the earth." The House applauded.[11]

Frustrated by such enthusiasm from the floor, Representative Isaac R. Sherwood of Ohio entered into the record a series of letters from antiwar ministers. He also chose a sarcastic letter from a layman who ridiculed the possibility of spreading Christianity with an army:

> We heard a minister state with vehemence "that we should all be willing to take up our cross and follow Jesus," that the great question to-day is "Christ or Prussianism." His idea was that we should shoot Christianity into the Germans with machine guns and cannon. Just how much Christianity he could cram

into a 10 or 12 inch cannon he did not say. But I imagine that a cannon full of this so-called Christianity directed by an accurate gunner into the anatomy of some European heathen would yield forth fruit to an hundredfold.[12]

The majority of the House, though, favored war. Sounding like several of the prowar senators, Representative Henry T. Rainey of Illinois justified the war as a fight for progress against barbarism: "The darkness, the murder, and the bloodshed of the Middle Ages . . . has no place in this new century." The United States had to enter the war to restrain "the world from slipping back into the darkness of the Middle Ages."[13] Other congressmen repeated the call for the salvation of Christian civilization. As Thursday night's debate dragged on into the early hours of Good Friday, one congressman could not resist the inevitable analogy between Christ's atoning sacrifice for the sin of the world and America's own divine mission. Likewise, Representative Murray Hulbert of New York took inspiration from the fact that "Christ gave his life upon the cross that mankind might gain the Kingdom of Heaven, while to-night we shall solemnly decree the sublimest sacrifice ever made by a nation for the salvation of humanity, the institution of world-wide liberty and freedom."[14] On Good Friday, April 6, by a vote of 373 to 50 with 9 abstentions, the House approved Wilson's declaration of war.

One essayist for the *Atlantic Monthly* found the same spiritual significance in the day America had chosen to go to war, noting that Easter's promise of renewal would not come without Good Friday's agony. As Christ's resurrection had followed only after the pain "of Gethsemane, Golgotha, and the Crucifixion," she wrote, so the world's rebirth would require self-denial and even misery. To be worthy of the privilege of bearing the iniquity of mankind, America had to embrace the spirit of sacrifice, put aside every selfish motive, and demonstrate its compassion. Having done so, America then could be confident that "the King of Glory may come in for the refreshment, the re-creation, the salvation of all humanity."[15] This analogy between the United States at war and Christ on the cross served the progressive church well throughout the war. A few months later, Baptist minister Harry Emerson Fosdick prayed that Christ, now "crucified afresh by the sin of the world," would "after this Calvary, grant us . . . an Easter Day and a triumphant Christ."[16]

Comments from the pulpits on the actual Easter Sunday turned to these same metaphors. The Reverend Ernest Stires, rector of St. Thomas's Church on Fifth Avenue, New York, told his congregation that he saw God's hand in all of the previous week's proceedings. America's duty had never been clearer; God's "call summons us to the service of mercy and truth, of righteousness and honest peace. To-day our Easter faith goes into action." He believed that America's ideals would triumph through the war. The principles of the Declaration of Independence and the power of human reason would now govern the world. He, too, noted that America had gone to war on Good Friday, the day of sacrifice, a linking of events that seemed to him "something more than coincidence."[17]

Back in the Senate on Monday the messianic images continued. One senator read a poem entitled "Armageddon." Like the first Messiah, the United States, too, had waited for "the fullness of God's time." Despite the present chaos, God was at work: "For from the beginning 'twas decreed that God shall lead/ Humanity e'er onward, upward, 'til beneath/ Blest Eden's tree of life all men shall brethren be/ In brotherhood of mutual love and trust and peace." The poem captured the progressive faith in an immanent God, a divinely guaranteed process, and America's redemptive role. The senator thought the entire poem "worthy to be a sort of battle hymn of this Republic as we enter into this unknown and unknowable conflict."[18]

WHILE THE WAR's immediate consequences might have been "unknown and unknowable," the forces behind America's entry seemed obvious enough, especially to those who were eager to take credit for propelling a reluctant people into war. Shortly after the vote in Congress, the *New Republic* proudly credited America's entry into the Great War to the political leadership of a new class, the "intellectuals." Though consciously working contrary to the public's instinct against involvement, the *New Republic* conceded, this intellectual elite of journalists, college professors, lawyers, and clergy had wrought "the effective and decisive work on behalf of war." Ruled at last by ideas rather than material interests, the United States had intervened "under the influence of a moral verdict reached after the utmost deliberation by the more thoughtful members of the community." To justify the war, the *New Republic,* which otherwise prided itself on hard-headed realism and practicality, even resorted to the same inflated, religious language used by the progressive clergy and some members of Congress. Picking up the accepted metaphors, the *New Republic* referred to Belgium as a "crucified" nation and to "the righteousness of the Allied cause."[19]

The *New Republic*'s description of the rising intellectual class included the progressive clergy, and they had indeed done their part in bringing America into the war, particularly in creating a more receptive public mind. Although the Protestant denominations contributed to the war effort in some very practical and visible ways—through relief work and various ministries to the soldiers at home and abroad[20]—their farthest-reaching contribution was to the ideology behind the war.

In an editorial written soon after American intervention, Lyman Abbott developed three themes that were indispensable to the progressive clergy in their war for righteousness. These images were not original to Abbott, but he gave them particular clarity. He presented a righteous America, a pagan Germany, and a war inseparable from God's millennia-long redemptive history. True to his expansive progressivism, he argued first that America, as a Christian nation, was obligated to serve the other nations. God intended that the spirit of self-sacrifice among His redeemed peoples stand in bold contrast to the selfishness of the lost. Relying on his usual theological interpretation of political and social institutions, Abbott observed that "in paganism the poor serve the rich, the weak serve the strong, the ignorant serve the wise. In the Kingdom of God the rich serve the poor, the strong serve the weak, the wise serve the ignorant. This is the divine order; and the Son of God himself illustrates this order by his own life and death." Any society not so ordered was pagan and stood as a threat to God's kingdom. America, representing "organized Christianity," understood God's system, while Germany, representing "organized paganism," ignored it. In the midst of this conflict, the church was not to work for some future kingdom in heaven, but rather was "to build a kingdom of heaven upon the earth."[21]

Abbott argued that the church had the added task of inspiring the nation, of motivating men "to transform a pagan world . . . into a kingdom of God." To achieve that rebirth, America required "a thousand voices eloquent with a divine passion for righteousness, pressing home upon the people their responsibility." Drawing an analogy to the Old Testament account of the liberated people of Israel hesitating at the verge of the Red Sea, he claimed that "there are times when faith in God forbids us to stand still, when it summons us to subdue kingdoms and wax valiant in fight." The logic of the war was quite simple: Germany occupied the Promised Land of God's universal New Israel and had to be driven out. The United States possessed the strength, and therefore the obligation, to act. Appealing to the combined spirit of Christ and Abraham Lincoln, Abbott admonished the church to "lead Christ's followers forth, his cross on their hearts, his sword in their hands, with malice toward none and with charity for all, to fight, to suffer, and, if need be, to die for their oppressed and stricken fellow-men."[22]

In this way, the progressive clergy disseminated from the pulpit and the printing press, the unconstrained, metaphorical, abstract thought necessary for total war. And it was this mentality of total war, as historian Herbert Butterfield later recognized, that made modern warfare so destructive. Not technology and industrialization and armaments, but a way of thinking about war, a way of defining one's enemy, one's self, and one's goals. This attitude, Butterfield wrote, "is the clue to the deadliest features of modern war—the hatred, the viciousness, the refusal to compromise."[23] In every respect, the Great War was waged as a "war for righteousness," a war transcendentalized out of all normal mental categories. And not just by the United States. As the *Nation* perceived as early as October 1914, every side in the struggle claimed to be fighting for righteousness: "Each nation believes earnestly that it is in the right; that the war was forced upon it; that it is battling for righteousness and for civilization itself."[24] But in the case of the United States, the progressive clergy helped furnish the emotional and intellectual elements necessary for its side of this "war for righteousness." The danger was not the progressives' claim that God had a purpose in allowing the European War, but their special insight into God's intentions. Knowing that God has a purpose in calamity is very different from knowing what that purpose is. The progressive clergy claimed to be able to read and to reveal what God was doing and why he was doing it. Moreover, they claimed to be the tool to carry out that divine purpose. This attitude created a single-minded passion, with, as Butterfield said, no room for compromise, or limited aims, or dissent. They transported the war out of the sordid but understandable realm of national ambition, rivalry, and interests—where policies and goals can be debated and defined—into the rarified world of ideals, abstractions, and politicized theology, where dissent and limitations are moral failures or even heresies. Thus, drawing upon the metaphors already habitual in the social gospel vocabulary of applied Christianity—crusades, suffering Christ-nation, vicarious wars of service, and so on—the progressive clergy consciously and deliberately provided the images of the United States, of Germany, and of the war's ultimate meaning that were indispensable in waging total war.

Long before 1917, the clergy had envisioned America as the suffering servant among nations, and this image only intensified once the war's actual suffering became part of the American experience. President Wilson helped create and sustain this image of a righteous, redemptive America. On June 5, the day of national registration for the draft—significantly termed "selective service"—Wilson spoke to a Confederate veteran reunion about the nation's task in the present war. He proposed that God had preserved the union through the Civil War to achieve His transcendent purposes, so that the nation might be "an instrument in the hands of God to see that liberty is made secure for mankind." The United States had been saved for this moment in the divine plan. The United States was prepared, he assured the Southern veterans, to devote its wealth and its sons "for the service of mankind."[25] Two weeks later, he received at the White House a delegation from the Northern Presbyterian Church, Wilson's own denomination. The body offered Wilson its services for the war effort and promised "to get our people into line with the splendid idealism" that the president had defined "as the great purpose and ideal of America."[26] Wilson readily acknowledged the awkwardness of church and state cooperation, but he reconciled the purposes of the two institutions by repeating the theme of national purity from his war message two months before, seasoned now with the words of St. Paul: "this is a war which any great spiritual body can support, because I believe if ever a nation purged its heart of improper motives in a war, this nation has purged its heart, and that, if there ever was a war which was meant to supply new foundations for what is righteous and true and of good report, it is this war."[27] The church could devote itself to national service with a clear conscience, for this was a war waged for spiritual goals.

During this first summer of American participation in the war, as the ill-prepared nation mobilized its troops and resources, the editors of the *Biblical World* carried the ideal of service further, claiming that the United States had "a right to exist only as it ministers to universal human weal."[28] In a later issue of this magazine published by the University of Chicago's Divinity School, Samuel McCrea Cavert, assistant secretary of the Federal Council of Churches' War-Time Commission, justified American participation in the war as an act of service to God that would help the world move closer to God's will. The war, he claimed, making the same point as Lyman Abbott, "has now developed into a conflict between forces that make for the coming of the Kingdom of God and forces that oppose it." He concluded with lines from the ever-present "Battle Hymn of the Republic," discerning Christ in the campfires of this war as well.[29]

The clergy explained America's role in this war by relying on the same metaphors as those circulated by George Creel of the government's war-time propaganda office, the Committee of Public Information (CPI). The Creel committee consistently referred to the war as a crusade, explaining that this was a fight "not merely to re-win the tomb of Christ, but to bring back to earth the rule of right, the peace, goodwill to men and gentleness he taught." One government-produced film was entitled *Pershing's Crusaders,* while CPI posters, poetry, and leaflets also played up this powerful metaphor.[30] But of course the progressive clergy had for years described their reform movement as a "new crusade," and from 1914 to 1917 defined the fight for peace in the same way. So clergy like the Reverend Randolph McKim naturally returned to this image, telling his congregation on Thanksgiving Day 1917, in the Church of the Epiphany's flag-filled sanctuary, that the Great War was a "Crusade. The greatest in history— the holiest." The soldiers at the front were engaged in no ordinary mortal combat, but rather were "marching to their Calvary," ready to meet "the armies of Antichrist" and rescue civilization, humanity, and Christianity.[31]

In the three years since his address at the "Peace Cross" on Mount St. Albans in Washington, he had converted from peace to war, but both causes were idealist crusades in the name of perpetual peace.

The progressive clergy not only portrayed the United States as a righteous nation engaged in a modern crusade to liberate the worldwide "Holy Land," but also identified the war as the collective reenactment of Christ's crucifixion on Calvary. Employing the same analogy used by some congressmen when they voted for war on Good Friday, the clergy continued to picture the European conflict as a new atoning sacrifice effecting humanity's final, collective redemption. One essayist for the *Christian Century* claimed that the same fear that prompted Caesar to try to rid the world of Christ motivated Germany to disrupt the efforts of Christian internationalism, plunging the world into chaos. Like ancient Rome, pagan Germany attempted "to eliminate Jesus, to excise the Christ." Caesar and his conspirators had crucified Jesus, and now again, nineteen centuries later, "the Son of man is stretched upon the cross of Calvary." His two metaphorical hands, Belgium and Poland, were "nailed to the cross," while Serbia and Armenia were "his feet streaming with blood."[32] Writing for the *Survey,* the Federal Council's Charles Macfarland promised that the churches would "help transform the world's Golgotha and its Calvary into the resurrection on the third day." United in service, the churches would build international unity and be ready "to roll the stone away" at the world's triumphant resurrection.[33]

Ultimately, the church moved beyond metaphors of crusades, holy wars, and a twentieth-century Calvary, and explicitly identified the United States as the modern messiah. The progressives were not shy about this identification. In fact, Frederick Lynch had called America the "Christ-Nation to the other nations of the world" even before U.S. entry. Yale Divinity School dean and former Mohonk speaker Charles Reynolds Brown wondered in the midst of the war why America should hesitate to picture itself as an international messiah. After all, America served the world with high motives, not in a spirit of vengeance, but for "moral idealism." "May we not believe," he asked, "that this country, strong and brave, generous and hopeful, is called of God to be in its own way a Messianic nation," a redemptive nation through which all the world "may be blessed?"[34]

Speaking to the National Convention of the League to Enforce Peace in 1918, Lyman Abbott applied to the United States a messianic prophecy from the Book of Genesis. After the Fall in Eden, God promised Eve that one day her offspring would defeat Satan, and Abbott identified America as the inheritor of that Messianic mission, the one who would crush Satan's head. Abbott extended the Genesis prophecy to messianic America and satanic Germany: "'The serpent shall bruise man's heel; man's heel shall bruise the head of the serpent.' Now the head of the serpent is erect, it is running out its forked tongue, its eyes are red with wrath; its very breath is poison. We have a difficult task to get our heel on its head, but when we do, we will grind it to powder."[35]

As apocalyptic as their language was, however, the liberal clergy tended to picture the United States more as the suffering servant of Christ's first advent than as the triumphant king of His second. They most typically portrayed America as the "servant nation," much the way President Wilson did. As the Reverend Charles Jefferson described America's duty in 1918, "If any country would be great it must become the servant of all. That is what our Republic is just now trying to be—the servant of all." Although he was a fairly reluctant warrior, Jefferson found it possible to support a war waged by a humble servant for high ideals, and even accepted the suffering, death, and damage that such service entailed because this was the last war. America's "work of destruction is only preparing the way for building up a world federation by which a recurrence of the present heart-breaking catastrophe may be forever avoided, and all the nations may live in peace and mutual helpfulness forevermore."[36]

The messianic image of America also pervaded the patriotic rhetoric of those outside church leadership. After the March Revolution in Russia in 1917, Wilson sent former Secretary of State Elihu Root to the new republic as head of a special diplomatic mission that included the YMCA's John R. Mott. On a lecture tour across the United States after his return from Russia, Root referred in speech after speech to America's destiny. In Seattle he told his audience that the United States had been founded to lead "the upward progress of humanity along the pathway of civilization to a true Christian life." Sounding rather Wilsonian for an old Republican, Root promised that America would emerge from the war "competent to perform its divine mission of carrying liberty and justice throughout the earth."[37] At City Hall in New York, Root welcomed the flood of democracy sweeping away autocracy and identified these momentous political changes as the accomplishment of God's "eternal purpose." He pictured America, moreover, as poised "to do its mighty work in that regeneration of mankind."[38]

Examples of this kind of language in wartime speeches, sermons, and articles are endless. The point is that progressive clergy and politicians alike infused the war with religious imagery and sacralized America's participation in the Great War into the accomplishment of a prophetic, atoning work. Back in 1915, Sidney Gulick had emphasized that Christ's atonement was lived out in "suffering love," through which Christians would help redeem the temporal world. Now America's divinely appointed role in the world's salvation was clear: the nation was nothing less than the twentieth-century messiah, who obediently gave its life for humanity. The new messiah had come boldly through the Gethsemane of indecision, had drunk the cup of God's will, and now bore its cross along modern history's Via Dolorosa to Calvary in full anticipation of the Resurrection.

CRUSADING AMERICA COULD be portrayed in sharpest contrast against a diabolized Germany, the second essential image in the war for righteousness. The irrepressible conflict was usually framed in the starkest terms: While America was pure, sacrificial, and the bringer of worldwide redemption, Germany was corrupt, selfish, and pagan, variously pictured as blood-soaked barbarian, helmeted gorilla, war-mad exporter of Kultur, and the Antichrist hell-bent on world domination. Among the most extreme of all the progressive clergy in his denunciations of Germany was Plymouth Church's own Newell Dwight Hillis. Although his claims often bordered on the absurd, his campaign against Germany from his own pulpit and on national lecture tours received extensive coverage in the *New York Times,* keeping his words before the public.

Shortly after American entry, Hillis embarked on a three-week tour for the American Bankers' Association, promoting Liberty Bonds as a sound investment. In July 1917, the bankers sent him to France and England for six weeks to gather impressions of those war-torn countries that might be useful for the next Liberty Loan drive. Upon his return from Europe, he began a six-part series of sermons at Plymouth Church discussing conditions abroad. His principal concern was German atrocities, and he assured his congregation that the worst they had heard was true. The Germans had "reduced savagery to a science," and consequently, "this great war for peace must go on until the German cancer is cut clean out of the body." He claimed to have documented ten thousand atrocities. [39]

Continuing his diatribe against Germany, Hillis admonished his church on a later Sunday in September to be loyal to the United States and her allies fighting the Huns. Criticism of one nation was disloyalty to all. Warming to his subject, he identified the central question of the war: "Shall this foul creature that is in the German saddle, with hoofs of fire, trample down all the sweet growths in the garden of God [?]" By November Hillis had abandoned any caution in diabolizing Germany and its allies. In a personal attack, he accused violinist Fritz Kreisler of sending the proceeds from his concerts back to Austria to buy guns to kill Americans. Kreisler had indeed served in the Austrian army, but he called Hillis's charge "a baseless and malicious lie" and waited for Hillis "to retract his misstatement publicly and without delay." [40]

Even the one-time pacifist *Christian Century* gave Hillis a forum for his accusations. In October he recounted for that magazine's readers Germany's supposedly well-laid plans, from Bismarck down to the present war, for world domination. According to Hillis, the Huns craved the "Germanization of the whole world." He colored his story with lurid and tantalizing details of a baby "skewered on a bayonet," of wholesale rape, and of "old men and women murdered in ways that only devils could conceive." Picking up the common America-as-schoolmaster metaphor, Hillis exclaimed that the American troops were "*going out to war against a mad dog let loose in the world's schoolroom.*" [41] Hillis's indictment of Germany reached a wide audience. The chairman of one of the State Councils of Defense thanked a New York friend for sending an article by Hillis, writing, "I will use it to advantage." [42]

Hillis's wrath reached the point where he refused to compromise with Germany at all. When in November 1917, British cabinet member Lord Lansdowne admitted that the war had drawn to a stalemate and proposed a peace conference, Hillis became indignant. He wanted nothing to do with forgiveness as long as Germany refused to repent. After all, Germany at that moment was "at the height of his brigandage." Hillis rejected the sentiment for peace because it put "too much stress on human life." "What is human life?" he asked. "All the great things of the world have been done through martyrdom." Considering millions had already died, Hillis must have expected the war to yield great things indeed.[43] True to its character, the unlimited war for righteousness would exact any price.

OCCUPYING THE POLARITIES of the historical continuum from paganism to righteousness, Germany and America waged war within the context of the progressive clergy's already well-defined moral universe. The progressives had been at work since 1914 to reconcile this war with God's goodness and with his progressive plan for humanity. So far, they had accommodated the war into their worldview, and, as might be expected, they had to renew their effort now that America—the Christ-nation—was directly involved. In 1917 the progressive clergy still wrestled with the problem of how God could be benevolent and compassionate and yet allow such a grotesque contradiction to His progressive universe. As one minister noted, "serious minds" groped for answers to their dilemma and looked "for signs of an intelligent and beneficent Force."[44] American participation meant that the war dead would now include American boys, and provided a new and more immediate context in which to ponder this ageless question.

In their search for answers, the Protestant clergy turned to an unlikely source—British author and radical socialist H. G. Wells, who contributed much to the liberal clergy's wartime efforts to understand God's purposes. Even before the war, Wells's novels and essays had found a warm welcome among Protestant liberals. New York pastor John Haynes Holmes predicted in 1916 that one day historians would need to know Wells's work in order "to understand this age."[45] To a remarkable extent, Wells did indeed sound like his social gospel admirers in America, who quoted his works frequently. In an article for the *Independent,* for instance, Wells identified "the world kingdom of God" as the "only true method of human service" and even decreed that all of mankind had to work for the advent of "righteousness."[46] In a two-part essay for the *New Republic* in 1916, moreover, Wells recognized the religious questioning stirred by the war and called on the church to address these moral issues. While the church tended to occupy itself with trivial matters, he warned, a vast spiritual revival was already sweeping Europe and directing a "number of minds in England and France alike towards the realization of the kingdom of God," which to Wells meant the coming of a socialist world state.[47]

Wells's goal of a new world order, and the language he used to describe this vision, paralleled that of the religious progressives. In *Italy, France and Britain at War,* Wells explained "that only through a complete simplification of religion to its fundamental idea, to a world-wide realisation of God as the king in the heart of all mankind, setting aside monarchy and national egotism altogether, can mankind come to any certain happiness and security."[48] Hamilton Holt's *Independent* expressed these same sentiments when America entered the war: "Christian leaders must emphasize the universal elements of religion, and keep internationalism beside patriotism as the inspiration to sacrifice."[49]

Wells's most important contribution to the discussion of the presence of evil in God's meliorist universe came in May 1917, within weeks of American entry. In *God the Invisible King,* Wells worked out in nonfiction form the ideas he had presented earlier in his best-selling autobiographical novel *Mr. Britling Sees It Through.*[50] Wells solved the dilemma of God's goodness versus His omnipotence by denying God His infinite power and thereby preserving His ethical character. Wells had been an agnostic before the war, and he continued to consider "God the Creator" remote and unknowable. But for the more personal "God the Redeemer," the God of the heart, Wells tried to fashion a theology. This progressive, benevolent God worked within creation to achieve righteousness. He was a time-bound God who, alongside mankind, was "struggling and taking a part against evil."[51]

A struggling God was not a weak God, according to Wells, who, without apology and missing the irony, portrayed his God as an imperialist conqueror, intent on establishing His earthly dominion, a kingdom where Caesar's reign would end at last:

> God faces the blackness of the Unknown and the blind joys and confusion and
> cruelties of Life, as one who leads mankind through a dark jungle to a great

conquest. He brings mankind not rest but a sword. It is plain that he can admit no divided control of the world he claims. He concedes nothing to Caesar. . . . The new conceptions do not tolerate either kings or aristocracies or democracies. Its implicit command to all its adherents is to make plain the way to world theocracy.[52]

In the meantime, every soldier of God had to dedicate himself to the eradication of evil from the world. Enlisted in God's service, he had to "take sides against injustice, disorder, and against all those temporal kings, emperors, princes, landlords, and owners, who set themselves up against God's rule and worship." Like the prophets of the social gospel in America, Wells combined his visions of national and international reform into one hope for "world theocracy." And though at times he seemed to use theology merely to clothe his Fabian socialist vision, he also, like the social gospel clergy, claimed that "the kingdom of God on earth is not a metaphor, not a mere spiritual state, not a dream, not an uncertain project; it is the close and inevitable destiny of mankind."[53]

The only complaint the *Independent* could manage about Wells's theology was simply that he had archaically referred to God as a king. "We are done with kings; the kings must go," the editors scolded; "the word 'king' has ceased to be an honorific appellation and is rapidly becaming [sic] a byword and an hissing."[54] Finding a bit more to criticize, one reviewer for the *Dial* called Wells's latest book "the cheekiest buncombe I have read since I read a report of a sermon by the Reverend Billy Sunday."[55] Similarly, John Dewey thought Wells had lost his senses. The American philosopher was startled by the evidence of "the evangelical mind" in the ethical implications of Wells's theology. Dewey correctly prophesied that "from multitudes of evangelical pulpits in the country will issue sermons welcoming Mr. Wells into the fold, accompanied with mild deplorings that he has not yet seen the full light."[56] Dewey's words were fulfilled in part when the Disciples' *Christian Century,* for example, welcomed Wells as an ally and gave considerable attention to his books, especially to *Mr. Britling* and *God the Invisible King*. In fact, *God the Invisible King* was available by mail order through the Disciples Publication Society.[57] Clearly, the progressive clergy quickly and easily incorporated Wells into their understanding of God's purposes in the war.

A variety of liberal writers, theologians, professors, and college presidents contributed to this discussion of the state of God's moral universe that concerned Wells so much. Social gospel author Horatio Dresser, for instance, was optimistic that good would triumph over evil. In his wartime book, *The Victorious Faith* (in which he quoted favorably from Wells), Dresser acknowledged that the war was a severe test of modern Christianity's meliorist faith, but reasoned that God was compelled to allow evil to flourish for a time so that it would finally be exposed for what it is and cast off. Faithful to the progressives' interpretation of God's evolutionary plan, Dresser promised that wars had their place in the world's moral development, fitting into "the whole process through which man struggles out of selfishness into brotherly love." God continued to dwell and work within His creation: "God is with men in war, as in all other evils, to lead men through temptation to spiritual victory." At last mankind was coming to understand "God as immanent in the world," and to realize the truth of Jesus' metaphor of the vine and branches: All humanity is connected to the central life-giving vine of God. Remarkably, Dresser was able to regard the Great War as "an expression of this intimate drawing together among individuals and nations," and to believe that America's entry was inevitable once the "world-forces" drew "the nations toward Social Democracy."[58] Rather than a catastrophe to social gospel ideals, the war was actually a step in the world's divine "drawing together."

Eugene Lyman, professor of the philosophy of religion and Christian ethics at the Oberlin Graduate School of Theology, added nuance to this argument in a series of lectures in the fall of 1917 at Union Seminary in New York. His task was to reconcile the Great War with "the Eternal Creative Good Will." How could a generation of theologians who had embraced evolution as God's method of earthly redemption accept the contradiction of a world war? Although claiming to reject the finer points of Wells's theology, Lyman shared the British author's understanding of man as God's "co-worker" in the world's progress. The war had meaning and value precisely because it stood in the way of brotherhood and therefore forced mankind "into the great cooperative work." Through the war and other struggles it became evident that "the divine reality in its intensest and most poignant meaning is drawing us into fuller relation to itself."

Democracy and the spirit of cooperation would only grow stronger as a result of the war.[59]

Oberlin College president Henry Churchill King was among the progressive theologians who, before American entry, had framed the theodicy question in its starkest terms, seeing no possible reconciliation between God's goodness and omnipotence. Now he linked his own interventionism with his defense of a benevolent God. King had been impatient to get involved in the war and was among those who had signed the ministers' protest to Wilson's peace proposal in 1917. But he professed to hate war as passionately as any pacifist. While calling on Christians to work toward the ultimate triumph of the principles of "permanent peace," he defended war in the meantime as consistent with those principles. As King wrote, *"a righteous people in a righteous cause in the long run tend to be victorious even in the use of physical force.* We could not ultimately keep our faith in God or in the fundamental morality of the universe, if that were not the case." There were only two sides to any battle: those allied with God, and those opposed to Him. Success was guaranteed to God's allies. "Those nations who throw themselves in line with the righteous will of God," he concluded, "must finally prevail, even in the use of physical force."[60] God's moral universe, a universe of sowing and reaping, was in perfect working order.

Another academic, Edward S. Drown, a professor at the Episcopal Theological School in Cambridge, Massachusetts, wrestled with the question in a book titled *God's Responsibility for the War*. At stake, Drown feared, was man's ability to believe in God at all. And the only good God compatible with an evil war was a God of limited liability. The question of why God allowed evil to prosper arose in the first place, Drown argued, only because people erroneously thought of God as both benevolent and freely omnipotent. To say that His goodness and power were somehow mysteriously reconciled, as Calvin had, simply would not satisfy the modern mind. Drown wanted to know how this reconciliation was possible. He conceded that Wells's theology of a finite God was one possible answer, but he chose rather to believe in what he called "conditional omnipotence," which deprived God of His autonomy while allowing Him his goodness and omnipotence. To Drown, this God was a "higher Being" who freely chose to work with free people. God suffered along with His creation, moving toward the progressive realization of His will. The kingdom of God, therefore, would not appear through "divine fiat," but with humanity's cooperation.[61]

Yale Divinity School professor E. Hershey Sneath summarized the liberal Protestant view of the war's place in God's moral universe when he charged Christians to accept "an ethical view of God—that He is a righteous being, that He deals justly with all men and all nations, that He cannot be used by any individual or nation for unrighteous ends, that He is the father of us all, and that He co-operates with men in their efforts to bring in the reign of righteousness upon earth."[62] The logic of American participation in the Great War was simple and the duty unavoidable. The universe, governed by God's immutable physical and moral law, was progressing toward His kingdom. The war, however mysteriously, had to be a part of that ultimately benevolent movement toward perfection. Therefore the war had meaning and did not contradict the progressive worldview. In this meliorist process, America served as God's Chosen One, selflessly offering itself to the work of His earthly kingdom. In 1917–1918, Protestant liberals pictured themselves living in a universe in which God's moral law reigned inviolable, in which America prospered as the nearest approximation yet to God's kingdom on earth, and in which Germany struggled vainly as the last great impediment to that kingdom, collapsing under the weight of its own regressive sins. America and the Allied nations cooperated with God to bring the world closer to righteousness, while Germany opposed the progress of humanity. Combined, these elements helped justify the total war for righteousness.

OTHERS AMONG THE church's liberal leadership defended the war as simply an act of national self-defense. Even those, such as Lyman Abbott who waged war in the name of higher ideals, often justified the war in the name of self-interest. But the claim of self-defense could quickly become a rationalization for aggression. From the principle of self-defense, Abbott drew the corollary that the strong can and must defend the weak. As the father protects his child, and the policeman the traveler, so the nation must defend its own citizens "from pirates on the sea and assassins on the land."[63]

It was indeed possible, as Washington Gladden had warned, to define threats to national security in such a way as to justify almost any military action.

At the 1918 meeting of the League to Enforce Peace, Abbott elaborated on his conception of a defensive war. He explained the present war as an international police action directed against a criminal nation. In fact, the Great War had been misnamed, according to Abbott. It was not a war at all, but rather a *"posse comitatus"* called out by the nations representing law and order against "the worst and most efficient brigandry the civilized world has ever seen." And what, after all, was brigandry but "highway robbery by organized gangs"? One of Abbott's favorite epithets for Germany was "the predatory Potsdam gang."[64]

But it was hardly possible to launch a true humanitarian crusade with such a conventional, nonideological motivation as national defense. As the Great War drew to a close in the autumn of 1918, Lyman Abbott published a lengthy summary of his view of the war. Significantly entitled *The Twentieth Century Crusade,* his book explained once again why the war was a crusade "more Christian" than the crusades of the Middle Ages. He also returned to the metaphor of the crucifixion to describe the conflict. Standing on the first century's Golgotha hill, three crosses bore the bodies of Christ and two criminals, one repentant, the other unrepentant. Similarly, on the twentieth century's Golgotha, three crosses bore the bodies of the redeemer and two groups of criminal nations, the repentant Allies and unrepentant Germany. Departing from the standard messianic image for the moment, Abbott included America among the repentant nations, for although the South was rid of slavery and "the schoolhouse is gradually replacing the wigwam" through progressive redemption, America still had its city slums. Yet earnest Americans were working hard "to banish those crimes against humanity from our civilization."[65] Abbott extended his metaphor by identifying the twentieth-century redeemer. Between the repentant and unrepentant nations on modern Golgotha's third cross hung those men and women from every nation who offered their lives for the sake of the world. The "shedding of blood" for the world's sin continued, "because we live in a world which is a battlefield, in which righteousness and wickedness, truth and error, liberty and despotism, justice and injustice are in perpetual battle one against the other." All those who joined "in the great sacrifice of this world's Golgotha," regardless of their religious faith or lack of it, even if ignorant of the war's spiritual significance, had "taken up their cross" and followed Christ. They had given their lives for their brothers and therefore shared in Christ's never-ending redemptive work.[66]

For Abbott, this one by-product of the war alone justified its place in God's purposes. To the degree that the peoples of the earth sacrificed their own interests, the war meant a "triumph for Christianity such as the world has never before known." Abbott claimed to be weary of attempts to reconcile the presence of evil in the world, content rather to emphasize the good that God had in store for His creation. "God is doing something for us that is much better than stopping the war," this veteran of peace conferences promised; "he is inspiring us with courage to win it." And in the process, America herself benefited by being purged of the last ounce of resistance to God's will. Abbott rejoiced that through the agency of war the American temple would be cleansed of its materialism, redeeming not only the world, but also herself. "Is it not worth all that it costs us," he asked, "to have America changed from a 'money-changers' cave' to a 'great cathedral'?" And God's "divine purpose" also worked through the war to speed the world's progress toward His kingdom. Christ had given America the sword, "and we must not sheathe it until the Predatory Potsdam Gang has perished from the face of the earth."[67]

Over time, even pacifist preacher Charles E. Jefferson came to spiritualize America's war against Germany into an extension of the Christian's fight against Satan and applied biblical metaphors to the Great War. "In fighting against Germany," he wrote in August 1918, "we are wrestling not simply against flesh and blood, but against principalities and powers, against ideas and ideals, against conceptions of the state and of the rights of ruler and people." America fought the war "to assist in the overthrow of this philosophy [of militarism]."[68] In order to rid the world of such barbarism, the progressive clergy embarked on a crusade to expand their nineteenth-century ideal of civilization: an orderly world of Christianity, progress, fraternalism, prosperity, and peace. Germany's greatest crime was that it threatened to plunge the world back into pagan chaos and destroy the progressives' best efforts to build an enlightened and organized world.

ADDING ANOTHER DIMENSION to their crusade, the progressive clergy also interpreted the Great War as the continuation of an earlier quest. While most frequently using biblical imagery and metaphors from *Pilgrim's Progress* to explain the war, these ministers turned nearly as often for inspiration to "The Battle Hymn of the Republic," to the sacred interpretation of the Civil War, and to the speeches of Abraham Lincoln.

The liberal Protestant generation of the 1860s, sounding remarkably like their descendants fighting the Great War, had interpreted the American Civil War as an apocalyptic event, the inauguration of the literal kingdom of God on earth. Long before the Civil War, in fact, a sense of impending crisis and a sincere longing for the Millennium had motivated much of the American reform movement. Henry Ward Beecher's brother Edward interpreted the "agitation of the whole community" in the 1830s as the beginning of a struggle that would intensify until the return of God Himself, "till the last remnant of rebellion has passed away from the earth, and the human race shall repose in peace beneath the authority of Him whose right it is to reign."[69] When the Civil War came, many northern Protestants embraced it as God's battle to achieve national righteousness and to prepare America for the Second Coming.[70] Julia Ward Howe had used more than poetic imagery when she pictured Christ coming with "His terrible swift sword." These earlier progressive Christians who had fought for the Union were among those whom historian George Fredrickson identified as "the optimists, the believers in an ideal American destiny, who rallied to the standard, believing that the war would be a short cut to national perfection."[71]

A young Washington Gladden sat in the congregation at Plymouth Church in November 1860, a few weeks after Lincoln's election, to hear Henry Ward Beecher's Thanksgiving Day sermon. Gladden was captivated by Beecher's proclamation that he would give his own life "cheerfully and easily" for a slave's freedom. Foreshadowing the pulpit rhetoric of nearly sixty years later, Beecher on the eve of the Civil War urged his congregation to sacrifice themselves, claiming that "a heroic deed, in which one yields up his life for others, is his Calvary."[72] Gladden recounted this story at the Plymouth anniversary celebration in 1897, and one member of the church observed that Plymouth had always defended "the right of the church to employ all measures and all instruments which can be consecrated to the service of God and of humanity."[73] Apparently just about anything could be "consecrated to the service of God and of humanity," for this was the church that had sent "Beecher's Bibles" to the Kansas Territory in 1854 and that would declare war on Germany in 1917 ahead of Wilson and the Congress.

This reformist Yankee Puritan spirit of the Civil War lived on in the social gospel[74] and then in the progressive clergy's attitude toward the Great War. The continuity between the two wars, emphasized repeatedly by the liberals themselves, is unmistakable in numerous books, articles, and sermons of the Great War. The progressive clergy appealed endlessly to the ideals of the earlier war. Some liberal preachers, such as Lyman Abbott and Washington Gladden, were old enough to remember the Civil War. But liberal theologians of any generation justified American entry into the European War as the continuation of the church's earlier war for righteousness in the 1860s. The fight for freedom had to be resumed, but this time it was to be carried to the ends of the earth. As the Civil War had been supposed to be a "short cut to national perfection," so the Great War was embraced as a short cut to international perfection.

Retired Dartmouth president William Jewett Tucker called the reemergence of Abraham Lincoln during the Great War "a singular intellectual and moral phenomenon." Tucker noted the "constant quotations from his messages and speeches." Even in England the press referred to Lincoln repeatedly, to the point that the martyred president seemed to Tucker "to be more in evidence than any British statesman." Tucker's explanation for Lincoln's return was "the similarity between the fundamental issues at stake in the present war, and those of the Civil War," as well as Lincoln's own "power of stating moral principles with a finality which holds good for all time."[75]

British statesman David Lloyd George capitalized on the close connection in the American mind between the two wars. On the eve of American entry, the newly appointed prime minister wrote for the *New York*

Times that "the battle which we have been fighting is at bottom the same battle which your countrymen fought under Lincoln's leadership." He identified militarism as the new "slavery" that threatened "freedom and fraternity in all Europe." He deftly fitted the war into the progressives' understanding of America's place in the unfolding history of freedom:

> The American people under Lincoln fought not a war of conquest, but a war of liberation. We today are fighting not a war of conquest, but a war of liberation—a liberation not of ourselves alone, but of all the world, from that body of barbarous doctrine and inhuman practice, which has estranged nations, has held back the unity and progress of the world."

Lloyd George claimed to be removing the impediments to human felicity. He solicited America's aid in this fight by appealing to his trans-Atlantic cousins' powerful impulses of vicarious atoning service, humanitarianism, and unity and progress. He also promised a total war that would yield an unambiguous victory: "In such wars for liberty there can be no compromise."[76]

In the summer of 1917, National Security League member Shailer Mathews offered the same link between the Civil War, Lincoln's rhetoric, and the World War, interpreting the war against Germany as an extension of the earlier crusade. In an article for the *New York Times Magazine*—a piece that was carried by the wire services across the country to towns as remote as Pickens, South Carolina—Mathews confronted the embarrassment of America fighting Germany after having admired her cultural and intellectual achievements for so long, a problem especially acute for the liberal theologians who had embraced German Higher Criticism. He proposed that there were really two Germanys, one of liberalism and progress, the other of autocracy and reaction. It was actually the backward Germany that had made war on democratic institutions and sought world dominion. But by intervening, the United States would open the way "for German liberalism to master the forces which for nearly a century have been its oppression." And then Mathews made the connection with the liberation wrought by Lincoln. "Our Civil war," he wrote, "assured the future of democratic institutions in our united nation." And now this nation joined with others "who have dedicated themselves to the task of seeing that government of the people, by the people, and for the people shall not perish from the earth."[77] The progressives' war for righteousness reached from Gettysburg to the Western Front.

The Reverend Charles E. Jefferson, the New York pastor who had left his pacifism behind and joined the spiritual fight against "principalities and powers," also conceived of the Great War as a renewed battle for the Union, but this time for a much larger union, namely, world federation. As he understood the situation, America had entered the war to save "the United States of the World." The political fragmentation caused in the previous century by states' rights agitation had reemerged in the twentieth century in the form of nationalism, an equally selfish and regressive threat to peace, according to Jefferson. Like the Old South, "Germany claims the right to do as she pleases. She is wedded to a belated ideal." Once cured of its backwardness and petty narrowness, Germany would thank the Allies as the South now thanked the North for its own restored sanity. For "as soon as slavery was destroyed, the South regained its normal mind, and today rejoices that Lee was compelled to surrender his sword to Grant. So it will be with Germany."[78]

So close was the parallel between the two wars in Lyman Abbott's mind that he suggested "The Battle Hymn of the Republic" as an "international battle hymn." Noting that the song did not mention America by name, Abbott thought it easily adapted to the new war for righteousness. "This battle hymn," he wrote in the *Outlook,* "is not merely for our Republic; it is for all republics. . . . It is an international hymn of liberty."[79] Abbott's suggestion was appropriate; the phrase "as He died to make men holy let us die to make men free" described the progressive clergy's interpretation of both the Civil War and the Great War as the political embodiment of Christ's atoning death.

Julia Ward Howe's battle hymn lived on with remarkable vitality in 1917 and 1918. From the pages of Theodore Roosevelt's *Fear God and Take Your Own Part* to countless other books and sermons, the words of "The Battle Hymn of the Republic" served a second time as an emotional explanation and justification of total, redemptive war, with Christ on one side and the Devil on the other, and the fate of God's kingdom in the balance. The Committee on Publicity of the Connecticut State Council of Defense issued a twenty-five page "Outline for Speakers at War Rallies" in which it recommended contrasting the notorious German "Hymn of Hate" to the American "Battle Hymn of the Republic." The sentiment of the Civil War hymn that linked Christ to the war, the committee proposed, "applies to the present crisis even more poignantly than it did to the situation for which it was composed."[80] Likewise, for Oklahoma Senator Robert L. Owen the millennial Battle Hymn provided all the explanation he needed to understand God's purpose. To the persistent question "Where is God?" in the midst of the war, Senator Owen answered that He was "everywhere! With His glorious and beautiful laws working to everlasting perfection, teaching at last by sorrow the weakest and most foolish of His children. Where is God? Let the 'Battle Hymn of the Republic' answer——." All five verses followed.[81] The public heard from many quarters that the Civil War's unfinished redemptive mission was now to be completed in the world at large.

As a crusade and as a modern Calvary, and as an extension of the Civil War, the Great War became for the liberal Protestant clergy a war of ideology with no room for limited objectives or compromise. It was a war for absolutes that combined the armies of heaven and earth into the ultimate battle. In thus uniting heaven and earth, spiritual and temporal forces, Christ and America, the progressive clergy inevitably fused together piety and patriotism into a single devotion. In May 1918, Shailer Mathews lectured at the University of North Carolina on "Patriotism and Religion." Mathews, who had earlier written a book on "the spiritual interpretation of history," rejected any mere economic explanation for the war. Rather, the conflict was a spiritual struggle between the German idea of a "tribal" God and the opposing democratic conception. Mathews directly linked progressive theology with the new democratic faith. Only in "creative religious thinking" was there "the union of the patriotism and the religion of to-morrow." "Monarchical and feudal," Germany stood opposed to the democratic spirit and, by extension, to the modern religious spirit as well.[82]

Since America's success would mean "a better humanity," Mathews continued, anyone who denounced the war effort denied Christianity itself. Dissent was heresy in the war for righteousness. As far as Mathews was concerned, "for an American to refuse to share in the present war, to oppose preparation for war, to induce men to avoid draft, and to attack all forms of military preparation for the purpose of national defense, is not Christian." To defy the American government was to defy God. It was a very simple matter. Both the teachings of Jesus and "the unmistakable tendencies of social evolution" proved that the war was God's war. Furthermore, any faith that prevented "its followers from committing themselves to the support of such patriotism is either too aesthetic for humanity's actual needs, too individualistic to be social, or too disloyal to be tolerated."[83] In other words, everyone had to serve the new order. Tying together the war, the social gospel, and America's expansive messianic self-image, Mathews predicted that from the war would proceed "a patriotism that dares pray and fight for a nation re-dedicated to human welfare, both within and without its borders."[84]

Popular novelist and former minister Harold Bell Wright arrived at the war's ultimate spiritual meaning when he proposed that Jesus Himself had planned this war to liberate humanity from autocracy. Writing for the *American Magazine,* Wright claimed that Christ had "kindled the fire of this world war in those days when he declared for the divine rights of humanity against the assumption of those who falsely claimed a divine right to oppress and enslave humanity." All of history since the Incarnation has been moving toward this moment of consummation, toward the day of universal manumission. America from its founding has been a nation with a mission. Its troops are "the army of the liberty-loving world. Its blood is the blood of humanity, the humanity of Jesus, the humanity for which Jesus lived and died." Wright concluded by plunging into what must stand as the most extreme rhetoric of the war for righteousness:

> A man may give his life for humanity in a bloody trench as truly as upon a bloody cross. The world may be saved somewhere in France as truly as in Palestine. The truths that Jesus gave to the world cost him his life, and those same truths have cost the followers of Jesus millions of lives. The world has always crucified its saviours and always will.

The American soldiers were not merely Christ-like in their acts of service and self-sacrifice; they were giving their lives to save the world as truly as Jesus had given His. Wright brought his essay to the point: "the sword of America is the sword of Jesus."[85] All distinction between the church and the world, the sacred and the secular, the holy and profane had been overwhelmed. Metaphors had finally broken down; they had been transformed into reality, and reality had vanished into illusion.

As ever, the clergy found an ally in the popular press in their effort to remove the distinction between the spiritual and temporal worlds, between Calvary and the Western Front. In 1918 the *New York Morning Telegraph* editorialized on the relationship between Christianity and national service, noting that "loyalty to the flag swiftly is coming to be recognized as of equal or even greater virtue than fidelity to a church, a religious sect, or an ordained priesthood." The newspaper preached an amalgam of sacred and secular ideas that reveals much about the mentality of the war: "Soldiers of Moses, soldiers of Christ, and soldiers of Democracy have become unified in the one Grand Army of Liberty, which is giving the only meaning worth while to . . . 'The Church Militant.'" Soaring even higher, the editors proclaimed that America and the church had become one—"the Bill of Rights and the Bible are being reconciled, the Cross and the colors together top the towers of churches, and one of the high degrees of Holy Orders includes the priesthood of patriotism."[86]

Some politicians as well echoed the clergy's absolute interpretation of the war. Prone to spiritualize America's role in the war, Elihu Root referred to the democratic nations as "God's people." Belgium, England, France, Italy, America, and newly reborn Russia all waged war "in God's name for the principles of His religion" against "the forces of a dark and wicked past" and proceeded in the confidence of "a new day."[87] Similarly, Robert Lansing, Wilson's secretary of state, claimed in a speech at Auburn Theological Seminary that "the new era born in blood and fire on the battlefield of Europe must be a Christian era in reality and not alone in name."[88] The war for righteousness enlisted many evangelists in the cause.

As Henry Churchill King, a man rarely given to understatement, observed, "This is no ordinary war." Indeed. For most of Protestantism's liberal leadership, the war was in some sense a life and death struggle between two mutually exclusive religious, philosophical, and political systems. Compromise was impossible. In March 1918, at the Religious Education Association convention in New York, Union Seminary professor William Adams Brown described the war as unique in human history. It was "a war for the world" in which humanity was divided into two opposing camps: autocracy and democracy. Both sought to unify the world; one through force, the other through mutual agreement. He warned that "between them there can be no compromise; in the end one or the other must conquer."[89]

Throughout the summer of 1918, in the war's closing months, as large numbers of American troops were finally being transported to Europe and at last facing German soldiers in the No Man's Land that had been France, other progressive leaders continued to describe the conflict in the same inflated terms. William H. P. Faunce, at Brown's baccalaureate service in 1918, claimed that the world could not hold both the Central Powers "who believe that government by the people is 'government by the gutter'" and the "twenty nations who believe that the voice of the people is the voice of God."[90] Similarly, in an obituary for Washington Gladden in July 1918, the *Outlook* took the opportunity of his death to note that even this pacifist had come to see the war in its true light. In Gladden's last sermon he had spoken of "the two forces arrayed against each other in deadly conflict, and declared that they could not live together on this planet."[91] The two visions were incompatible and exclusive. The Great War was the final battle of light against darkness, of Christianity against paganism, of democracy against absolutism, and of progress against decay. It was the future arrayed against the past.

As much as the progressive clergy before 1914 had warned of the potential horrors of modern war and the blessings of peace, they failed to see their own role in perpetuating the Great War as a total war, a deadly conflict for abstract and unlimited objectives, a war for righteousness that could never be won. Their millennialist, idealist pacifism had led them into unlimited, uncompromising war. Once they ascribed to America the work of the Redeemer, to Germany the work of the Adversary, and to warfare the work of Calvary, the mentality of total war followed inescapably. Perhaps conceding more than he intended, William H. P. Faunce made this very point in 1918. While of course Christianity had to object to war in principle, he wrote, it called men nonetheless to "resist the devil and all his works, and that resistance may demand the total personality, soul and body, of a man or a nation."[92] The great irony of the war was that, in the very name of perpetual peace, the Protestant liberal clergy rationalized and legitimized the mass destruction of the first total war of the twentieth century, and demanded that it be carried on to a decisive victory.

7

Soldiers of the Cross

The Progressive Clergy's Redemptive War, 1917–1918

Soon after the outbreak of the Great War in August 1914, H. G. Wells declared the conflict to be the "end of an age" and the opportunity for a "new world." Wells challenged his fellow liberals—especially in America—to seize upon the war as a "plastic" moment, a time of social malleability in which to achieve his generation's most cherished goals. The time had come, Wells announced even though the war had hardly begun, to offer practical plans for postwar world federation and for "social reconstruction." Wells summoned his colleagues to act before peace came too quickly and the opportunity slipped from their grasp. The historical moment made rapid and revolutionary change possible. The liberals were to "re-draw the map of Europe boldly, as we mean it to be re-drawn" and to "re-plan society as we mean it to be reconstructed."[1] Thus, Wells combined the twin progressive ambitions of domestic and international reform.

Whether or not the liberal clergy across the Atlantic in America were as directly influenced by this early call to action from Wells as they were by his other wartime essays and novels, clearly they shared his expectation that the war would transform the world.[2] The progressive clergy were convinced that the Great War, though certainly tragic, was nevertheless an opportunity for directed change. As William H. P. Faunce observed in his Bedell Lectures at Kenyon College in 1918, sounding much like Wells, "the whole world is plastic, like clay awaiting the hand of the master-potter." The time had come to remake the world according to the divine plan. Capturing the progressive clergy's attitude toward the war, Faunce declared that "the day of destruction is the day of opportunity."[3]

The clergy promised renewal for the church, the nation, and the world by means of this "day of destruction." Such an expectation in wartime was, of course, not unprecedented in European and American experience. As historian Charles Royster pointed out, the British in the mid-nineteenth century anticipated national moral regeneration to come from the Crimean War, and hopeful observers North and South counted on the American Civil War to purge their peoples of materialism and other vices. Later, philosopher William James, in his celebrated essay from 1910, "The Moral Equivalent of War," accepted warfare's character-building, redemptive benefits and sought ways to preserve the "manly virtues" in a world that otherwise would lose its moral tone once peace reigned universally.[4]

This belief in war's redemptive potential was pronounced in the writings and speeches of the liberal clergy during the Great War. They filtered their experience of the war through a resilient and persistent optimism. No matter what the reform movement, whether a united church, social "uplift," or international peace, the progressives believed that the war would produce extraordinary and rapid results. The war's purgative, accelerative, and atomizing effects would open the way for every ecclesiastical, political, and international reform effort of the past generation. What in August 1914 had been interpreted as a "retrograde step in civilization" became a war of deliverance, achievement, and renewal, a cause for hope rather than fear, a catalyst for fundamental change. As one writer on religion for the *New Republic* noted soon after American entry in 1917, "We are all really optimists, and believe that the new age will see the fulfilment of our wishes."[5] The progressive clergy for decades had heralded an impending religious and social transformation and now announced its arrival as an inevitable consequence of the Great War.

In a variation on this theme, the progressives also claimed that the war marked the dividing line between the regressive, medieval past and the progressive, enlightened future. It was a trial that would purge humanity of almost every imaginable evil, from selfishness to materialism to nationalism to paganism. Edward Scribner Ames, professor in the University of Chicago's Divinity School and among the most radical of the modernist theologians, imagined the war as "an abyss of fire and death between the past and the future." He prophesied that from the perspective of the 1920s the political and social systems of the years before the war would seem as remote and shadowy as the Middle Ages.[6] Much like his fellow theological progressives, Ames dismissed the traditional conception of man's task on earth as represented by John Bunyan's pilgrim in his flight from God's wrath to eternal life. This "simple picture" of salvation, he wrote, had during the war "dissolved into the gigantic struggle of hundreds of millions of men over the whole earth to realize an actual and visible society of righteousness, justice, and love." To Ames, the Great War was humanity's mass effort to win earthly redemption. He did not go so far as to claim, like some theologians, that the war actually supplied the catalyst for such salvation, but he was inspired nonetheless by the willingness of one generation to sacrifice itself for the next. The trenches in France demonstrated the capacity for greatness of people thrust together for an urgent task. While prudently conceding that social progress was not inevitable, Ames nevertheless warned of the consequences of refusing to "believe in progress and in the possibility of improving the world."[7] Though surrounded in 1918 with testimony to humanity's destructive capacity, Ames and other liberals held fast to their prewar optimism.

While seeing the war as a dividing line in time, liberal ministers and editors also pictured the war years as compressed time, an intense moment in which the social evolution normally requiring generations was suddenly transpiring within months. H. G. Wells in 1914 had promised in this regard that "now is the opportunity to do fundamental things that will otherwise not get done for hundreds of years."[8] The liberal church echoed his urgency. As Herbert Willett of the *Christian Century* described his own sense of rapid change at the close of the war, "Objectives that at best could be hoped for only after many years are taken and passed almost in a day."[9] Imagining a war disconnected from precedent and actual historical experience, the progressive clergy concocted an apocalyptic moment of compressed and accelerated time.

Passing through this mystical juncture, the progressives hoped to achieve, or at least advance, their reform agenda. Primary among these objectives was the transformation of the church itself. While concerning themselves with specific ecclesiastical reforms, however, the progressives took pains to note that the war proved decisively that Christianity, despite all the hand-wringing, had not failed. By May 1917 Lyman Abbott could laugh that anyone could have thought Christianity a failure because of the war. Quite to the contrary, it now appeared that Christianity had never been "so great a success." America's entry demonstrated the vitality of Christianity. The crusades of the Middle Ages paled in comparison with the fight now being waged, Abbott contended, returning to a favorite image. In the past, "heroes engaged in a crusade to recover for Christendom the tomb in which the body of Jesus was buried." In the Great War, however, "greater heroes are engaged in a crusade to make a world in which the spirit of Christ may live."[10]

Near the end of the war, Chicago's *Biblical World* could claim that "the Christian point of view" had "gained enormously" through the war. Using what under other circumstances would have been tortured logic, the *Biblical World* reasoned that the very fact that the world was fighting proved the validity of "the Christianity of Jesus." The global struggle was being waged in order "to protect institutions and ideals which in essence are the development of Biblical ethics and religion as they culminate in Jesus."[11] The war did not negate universalized Christian ethics, but rather fulfilled and vindicated them.

Similarly, in reviewing the religious press's opinion on the failure of Christianity, the *Literary Digest* proposed that the criticism once leveled at the church had its "corrective in current events." Those who would condemn the church had to realize that it was "Germany's sin of cruelty" that had instigated the war and had roused the "wrath of the world." This holy indignation proved that Christianity guided the conscience of the world after all. "An age less Christian than ours," the editors reassured their readers, "would not have felt the concern about Belgium." Moreover, "the altruistic and Christian sentiments of Mr. Wilson's program for world peace have been willingly espoused by his countrymen at the sacrifice of, if need be, five millions of men and billions of wealth."[12] Christianity's strength and validity in the modern world had been demonstrated by the national spirit of self-sacrifice.

With confidence in progressive Christianity's integrity and vitality renewed by the experience of war, the liberal clergy promised to make the institutional church, in both its theology and practices, fit for further service in the new era ahead. In April 1918, one essayist in the *Nation* applauded those ministers who had been loosed from "the dead hand" of the past and were therefore prepared to meet "the new social demand." The church had to keep pace with the changing times; its "redemptive mission" had to be understood in the context of "social relations." Consistent with the long-established teachings of the social gospel clergy, the author proposed that "the moral tragedy of the world" had to be understood primarily "as a social fact." The central lesson of the war concerned collective redemption. "We are guilty of each other's sins," he warned, "and the Gospel which is to save us must save us all together."[13] Thus, near the end of the war the modern church, with the aid of some in the national secular press, continued to preach that sin and redemption were fundamentally problems of the external social order, rather than conditions of the internal order of the individual soul.

In the same vein, the *Biblical World* urged the church to "be the social expression" of idealistic, ethical Christianity. Otherwise the church faced the danger of being replaced by more efficient philanthropic organizations such as the YMCA and the Red Cross, which indeed flourished during the war. The *Biblical World* warned the church away from obscurantists who emphasized denominational distinctions, who put theology ahead of "social service," and who separated "religion from devotion to one's fellows." Such atavistic Christians imperiled "the very existence of the churches." While acknowledging the danger of forgetting the essentially spiritual nature of religion, the *Biblical World* proposed nonetheless that in the day of reconstruction "churches will be needed according to the proportion in which they make human fraternity the outward expression of an inward sense of divine sonship."[14]

In 1918 Brown University president William H. P. Faunce delivered the Mendenhall Lectures at DePauw University on "Religion and War" in which he pondered the war's impact on the church. DePauw's president

praised the lectures for giving "a rational and religious basis for true patriotism, world internationalism, and triumphant righteousness."[15] Faunce
chastised the fractured church for not being more unified when the war
began and thereby better prepared for national service. With some exaggeration, he claimed that the church "was so ramified and so split into
fragments that the nations" were not "able to intrust any important war
task into churchly hands." Instead, he lamented, other organizations such
as the YMCA and the Red Cross had filled the humanitarian role that rightfully belonged to the church. Christianity required "new organs of utterance, new channels for action, if the church is to resume its leadership of
men." But Faunce did not despair, for the Great War had opened a path for
service: "The greatest opportunity of two thousand years will come to the
church when the war is over."[16]

Above all, Faunce contended, the church itself had to be a model of
unity to the rest of the world. If Christians refused to overlook their differences, how could the nations be expected to cooperate? In short, he
warned, "Christianity must unite its own forces before it can effectively
urge the nations to unite. It must federate its own sects before it can demand the federation of the world. There must be peace in the church
before there can be peace on earth."[17] Bishop Francis J. McConnell of the
Methodist Episcopal Church agreed, noting that all "the movements toward union have been accelerated by the Great War," and the church's
unified voice, necessary in wartime, needed to be heard just as clearly in
support of the approaching peace conference.[18]

The Federal Council's Samuel McCrea Cavert worried that the church
would not be able to sustain its passion for righteousness once the war
ended. Drawing from philosopher William James, Cavert suggested that
the church needed to find a "moral equivalent of war" in order to carry on
in the noble "spirit of high loyalty and consecrated effort" engendered by
the war. Somehow the church had to continue to live "upon a higher . . .
level of achievement." And the answer, Cavert concluded, lay in perpetuating the wartime spirit through devotion to "the supreme task . . . of
establishing God's kingdom of righteousness and Christlike love in the
whole world." He proposed that "the missionary enterprise," both abroad
and at home, would supply the requisite "moral equivalent of war" that

the church so desperately needed.[19] The progressives longed for, and expected, the war for righteousness to continue after the guns in Europe fell
silent.

The progressive clergy's interpretation of the war as a transforming
event in the life of the church was shared as well by observers outside the
church. Progressive Movement veteran Upton Sinclair, who had risen to
fame in 1906 with his muckraking novel *The Jungle,* turned his attention in
1918 to the church and socialism. In his privately published book, *The
Profits of Religion,* he welcomed the new social consciousness of the church.
Like the liberal clergy, he observed that in the war the church was "confronted by pressing national needs" and compelled "to take notice of a
thousand new problems, to engage in a thousand new activities." As a result of its confrontation with the gritty reality of war, Sinclair predicted,
the church would now be "inspired by things read, not in ancient Hebrew
texts, but in the daily newspapers." And through the individual minister's
baptism in trench warfare, he would be "less the bigot and formalist forever after," having "learned co-operation and social solidarity." In the future, Sinclair predicted, would emerge "the Church redeemed by the spirit
of Brotherhood, the Church which we Socialists will join."[20] This socially
relevant church, of course, had been the goal of the progressive clergy all
along, but with the rise of Bolshevism, the progressive clergy would distance themselves from such socialist dreams. In the meantime, however,
they shared Sinclair's vision of the future and of the benefits of the war.

BEYOND THE GOAL of a redeemed church, the clergy also expected the war
to accomplish, or even accelerate, their domestic reform agenda. They
believed, in fact, that the World War was by definition a war for the social
gospel. They seized upon the war—a global war that seemed to have
shaken the old order to its foundations—as an opportunity to expand the
domain of applied Christianity. Whether in industry, politics, education,
or the economy, the sacrificial spirit of the war would rebuild America's
corrupt institutions. Social solidarity in sin and redemption had been the
guiding premise behind the social gospel movement before the war, and it
continued to color the expectations of progressive Christianity throughout
the conflict. George A. Coe, professor at Union Theological Seminary in

New York and cofounder with John Dewey of the Religious Education Association, repeated the familiar formula soon after America entered the war. "Our generation," he wrote, "has come to see that the redemptive mission of the Christ is nothing less than that of transforming the social order itself into a brotherhood or family itself." Fundamental to that transformation was the understanding that "we are members one of another in our sins, and we are members one of another in the whole process of being saved from sin."[21] The Great War had done nothing to shake the progressive theologians' interpretation of man and society. If anything, at least for the time being, the war inspired the social gospel movement with a greater sense of urgency. If left to its sin, human society seemed sure to perish.

William H. P. Faunce looked with some trepidation at the "universal reorganization" of the social order caused by the war, citing the chaos in Russia. Nevertheless, he remained confident that democracy could not advance too far for Christianity's sake. "A new scale of values" now "permeated civilization" as a result of the war, and the new social solidarity made it impossible ever to "return to the old petty individualism and *laissez-faire*." Consequently, Faunce predicted, "the only welcome man" in the new era would be "the man qualified for team work. 'Me' and 'mine' will be small words in a new world which has learned to say the great word 'our.'"[22]

Of course, the progressives' unifying ambition was to see the present social order transformed into the kingdom of God on earth. The kingdom of righteousness was the central tenet of social gospel theology, and the clergy waged the Great War in the name of that kingdom, fully intending to secure the fruits of victory. Herbert L. Willett, an editor of the *Christian Century* in Chicago, was certain at the close of the war that "the Kingdom of Heaven is at hand." Sounding almost like a premillennialist witnessing the fulfillment of biblical prophecy, Willett observed that anyone "who believes that the tragic events of the time have no revelation of the divine purpose latent in their portentous volume is insensitive indeed to the signs of the times." But he was far more optimistic than the premillennialists. The old order was collapsing all around, pulling down with it all the former "social customs and economic habits." Traditionalism might struggle against its fate, yet across the "redoubts of medievalism, ignorance, and reaction, the forces of progress are sweeping as the lines of the Allies crossed the German trenches."[23] The hastily constructed defenses of reactionary barbarism would not withstand the advance through Europe of God's redemptive army.

Obviously, the progressive clergy were not reticent about their activism, nor about one of the underlying motivations for their support for the war. Oberlin College's Henry Churchill King connected the war for righteousness abroad with the war for righteousness at home. As he said, the reforming spirit of the social gospel knew no geographical bounds; and since expansive, humanitarian love for all men involved "the fight against slavery, the fight against the degradation of women and children, the fight against selfishness and injustice and inhumanity and falseness, . . . [then] there will certainly come times, as in this world-war, when the disciples of Christ cannot be true to the fundamental teaching and example of their Lord without using all the means that God has put within their power against such wrongs."[24]

King could not have been more explicit. The war was the means God put at the disposal of his faithful followers to help rid the world of evil. The war should not be shunned, but embraced. Loyalty to Christ required the Christian to fight for social justice and to wage total war against Germany. King further encouraged the church to pursue "a true social program, by and through the war, as well as after it, to make certain that this world cataclysm shall bear its full fruit in a better civilization than the world has yet seen . . . and more worthy of the name which we give to our civilization—Christian."[25] The idealist, pacifist clergy grasped the war as a key to the kingdom.

The Federal Council of Churches also realized the opportunity the war had brought the activist churches. In a detailed statement published in October 1917, the council listed a series of wartime reforms, including national prohibition as "a first measure of social safety," the end of the "social disease," "child welfare," and national physical fitness. The council then reminded pastors in rural areas to keep "the tone of public opinion in rural communities keyed to national and world duties," lest provincial concerns reemerge after the war. They also proposed that corporate profits be "a reward for service rendered," and that this lofty principle "should be permanently enthroned." Through the war, the world had "taken a big step" toward understanding the community of interests that bound peoples together. The churches sought an end to militarism and the founding of a "world democracy," an end to "competition" and "selfishness" and the building of a "new world order." The churches had the opportunity to build a just and righteous world "in order that God may indeed dwell with men."[26]

Perhaps the most revealing linking of the war to the social gospel came from the editors of the *Christian Century*, a periodical that at one time or another featured the essays of nearly every notable name in progressive Christianity. The editors observed that previously some reformers had despaired that the coming of war meant the end, or at least the setback, of the social gospel's hard-won advances in international law, world unity, and the spirit of social solidarity. But several months after American entry, they could rejoice "how unfounded these forebodings" had been. Across the range of reform efforts, the conflict had "produced results quite opposite to those anticipated at first." The *Christian Century* at first had been reluctant to wear khaki, but by late 1917 it rejoiced that the war had actually "brought the social point of view to even clearer definition in the minds of men than ever before." The editors gloried in the evident "social willingness" of the American people and optimistically predicted that "the right of the State to commandeer its able-bodied citizens for service will survive the war and will be greatly strengthened by it." Military conscription, they anticipated, had set the precedent for continued service to the state. They even hoped to see military training camps become "permanent features of our national life," equipping men not for war but for social service. Through its collective war experience, America at last understood the meaning of social sin and guilt, and was fighting "the social sin of the German nation as a whole." Now that the world accepted the validity of treating Germany as a social problem, it would "be incomparably easier to apply the principle of social sinning to groups and institutions within a single nation and to bring to bear upon them through the social gospel the super-personal forces of condemnation and destruction." The war experience had made it easier to apply the social gospel abroad and at home.[27]

. . . .

IN APPLYING THE social gospel, the progressive clergy relied on the power of a sensitized public opinion. Whatever the cause or reform movement, the liberal clergy still conceived of their role foremost as that of molders of attitudes. Whether opposing alcohol or advocating international peace, activist ministers saw themselves as the source of regenerative ideals, as the motivating impulse behind the reform. They aimed at changing society and the world by changing attitudes, by creating a unified public opinion in support of a particular cause. Some clergy worked only through their own pulpits, while others pooled their efforts into such organizations as the Federal Council of Churches and its affiliated societies. For decades the call had gone out to "Christianize" American society and the world community. In the present physical battle for that end, the progressive church believed that the United States, in Shailer Mathews's phrase, was "in particular need of a Christianized public opinion."[28] In the midst of the liberal church's greatest reform movement ever, the righteousness of the Great War had to be impressed on the American people, especially if the *New Republic* was correct in its assumption that only a minority elite had favored intervention.

On April 15, 1917, less than ten days after Congress passed the war resolution, President Wilson appealed to the nation for sacrificial wartime production of food and industrial goods, and asked editors and advertisers to spread the word. Additionally, Wilson hoped that ministers would not consider his proclamation "an unworthy or inappropriate subject of comment and homily from their pulpits." The *Outlook* complied with the president's request and did its part to get the message "from the President to the people." "The supreme task of the nation has come," the *Outlook* announced. As Wilson had said, "We must all speak, act, and serve together."[29] From the beginning it was evident that everyone would be expected to support the war and equally clear that the progressive church would help mold the single national mind.

The Reverend Randolph McKim, never hesitant about bringing the war into the pulpit, used at least one of his sermons to campaign for the second Liberty Loan. The Episcopal Church's wartime commission asked its clergy to help with the loan drives, and McKim did his part. The commission wanted every member to be reminded of his "*patriotic and moral duty*" in the war for "*Liberty and Righteousness.*" McKim promised that "every $50 invested in a Liberty Bond is another nail driven into the coffin of Prussianism!" He reminded his congregation of the stakes in this war. Their help was essential, for Americans had to fight to the finish "as servants of the Living God, as Soldiers of the Cross, battling to establish righteousness and justice in the world."[30] In a world where the sacred and the secular had already been combined to an extraordinary degree, ministers now passed the collection plate for both God and Caesar.

In 1918 the *Outlook* claimed that the church was essential to the war effort because it helped build faith, efficiency, and courage, all of which were "qualities of mind and heart essential to victory." Pursuing its new task during the war, the church had "to keep uppermost and foremost in the minds of all the people that issue between right and wrong, oppression and liberty, truth and falsehood, unselfishness and self-seeking, the issue between the robber and his victim." In short, the church's responsibility was to see to it that Americans absorbed the progressives' Manichean interpretation of the war. The beauty of the war to the *Outlook* was that it created a national unity of purpose. The editors envisioned all distinctions of class, politics, and theology disintegrating in the heat of war. The *Outlook* hoped that the church would at last find its elusive union through devotion to a single "great cause."[31]

In addition to these general efforts to enlist church members in the war on the home front, the Federal Council of Churches and related organizations took specific steps to direct the course of public opinion. During the war, the Federal Council joined forces with the Church Peace Union, the World Alliance, and the League to Enforce Peace to create the National Committee on the Churches and the Moral Aims of the War. This coordinating agency functioned precisely as its name suggested, that is, as a voice for the "Moral Aims of the War." The committee promoted itself in Wilsonian terms as "absolutely loyal to our Government in its prosecution of the war as a righteous effort to make the world safe for democracy." Sitting on its governing board were Hamilton Holt, Frederick Lynch, Charles Macfarland, and William Howard Taft. And the committee shared more than the Wilson administration's ideals; across the committee's letterhead ran the words "In conjunction with the Speaker's Bureau of the

Committee on Public Information, Washington, D.C."—George Creel's crusading wartime agency. Macfarland later recalled the church committee's work as an "effort to reach the last man in every part of the nation—and also the last woman." The Federal Council's annual report described the committee's mission as an effort to motivate the American people and "clarify their thinking."[32]

George Creel knew that the war effort relied heavily on public opinion and enlisted the churches in the fight. He understood the war primarily as a war of ideas and even described his mission as the spreading of the "gospel of Americanism to every corner of the globe." He unabashedly identified his committee as "a plain publicity proposition, a vast enterprise in salesmanship, the world's greatest adventure in advertising."[33] For its campaign, the Creel committee specifically invited the Church Peace Union to help spread this version of the gospel, and the union was represented on Creel's advisory committee.[34]

The Federal Council, which also worked with Creel, had even stronger ties to the government. The council not only maintained its active Washington Bureau, but also, according to its annual report in 1918, allied its resources and organizations with the Department of Agriculture, the publicity committee for the Liberty Loan, the Department of the Interior, as well as a range of such private groups as the YMCA, the Boy Scouts, and the Red Cross.[35] The council's Charles Stelzle served as the Red Cross's liaison with the churches and other religious organizations. With an enthusiasm typical of the war years, Stelzle exulted that the Red Cross embodied "the moral equivalent of war, satisfying that element which is present in every red-blooded Christian man and woman the world over, who . . . is eager to live the sacrificial life."[36]

The progressive clergy also helped sell the war overseas, especially to Russia, the Allies' most unstable partner. YMCA leader John R. Mott, who not many years before had promised "the evangelization of the world in this generation," had particularly close relations with the Wilson administration. Wilson had referred to him as "one of the most nobly useful men in the world,"[37] and had appointed him as one of the three members of the Mexico Commission in 1916. Once again Wilson called on Mott, this time to go to Russia in 1917 as part of Elihu Root's special diplomatic mission. Together with most Americans, the Protestant liberals hailed Russia's March Revolution as another sign of the coming new age of international democratic brotherhood. A poem in the *Outlook* welcomed "Holy Russia" into the family of redeemed nations, and rejoiced that at last "The world shall be made new/ Since thou hast found thy soul."[38] The problem for Wilson was keeping Russia in the particular family of nations then fighting Germany.

In Russia in June 1917, Mott addressed nationwide meetings of the Orthodox Church. He offered the American progressives' activist blueprint to the Russian people for their own church, urging them in familiar terms to pursue "the fearless and unflinching application of Christ's principles" and to demand that Christianity "be made an adequate transforming power in social and national life and in international relationships."[39] Commission member Charles R. Crane telegraphed Wilson that the Russian church was vital to the democratization of the empire and assured him that Mott had instructed the church in "its relation to the winning of the war." "When Mr. Mott struck the war note," Crane continued, "there was an immediate response and everyone instantly rose and applauded."[40] In a subsequent address in Petrograd to officers of the Cossack armies, Mott urged cooperation between America and Russia in winning the war for liberty.[41]

Upon the mission's return from Russia, Secretary of the Interior Franklin K. Lane discussed the trip with several members, including Mott. With Mott's advice in mind, Lane suggested to Wilson that "the immediate need [in Russia] is a great program of education through moving pictures, speeches, Y.M.C.A.'s, etc. as to what the United States is and why it is in the war."[42]

The progressive clergy played their part in promoting the administration's view of the war both at home and abroad. But their desire for national unity was evident not merely in their positive efforts as agents of public opinion, but also in a negative sense in what they feared and opposed. For example, Frank Mason North, president of the Federal Council from 1916 to 1920 and one of the forces behind the Social Creed of the Churches, became an honorary cochairman of the League for National Unity along with Cardinal James Gibbons of Baltimore. The organization's stated purpose was to counter "dissension" and "sedition." It even opposed an early peace, arguing that "agitation for a premature peace is seditious when its object is to weaken the determination of America to see the war through to a conclusive vindication of the principles for which we have taken arms."[43]

Among the "dissenters" the liberals most vigorously opposed were their old theological enemies, the premillennialists, who formed a large segment of the growing fundamentalist movement. For years the liberal religious press had been careful to note the differences between the fundamentalists and themselves. As the *Outlook* pointed out in a review of the latest installment of the *Fundamentals* in 1914, while the fundamentalists defended the centrality of doctrine, the liberals emphasized Christ's spirit of "love, service, and sacrifice."[44] The social gospel presupposed service and sacrifice, and those who defended an individualist theology were naturally suspect. After 1917 the theological progressives waged war overseas against the regressive German empire as well as at home against the equally atavistic premillennialists.

Shailer Mathews's journal *Biblical World* explicitly linked the two enemies of progress, Germany and the premillennialists. The editors noted that, as anticipated, the theological conservatives blamed the war on Germany's apostasy from orthodox Protestantism and its acceptance of biblical criticism. But many liberals, including Mathews, had received theological training in Germany, and the *Biblical World* pointed to the war as proof instead "of the bankruptcy of orthodoxy as a moral force among nations." Reactionary orthodoxy, it claimed, had "justified every war . . . since the days of Christ." Like the German empire itself, biblical literalism was simply a part of "the Dark Ages."[45]

The attribute of premillennialists most galling to the liberals was that they simply were not progressives. By preaching that the world's transformation required direct divine intervention and that the Great War was much more likely to be the end of the world than the pangs of a new birth, the premillennialists revealed just how far removed they were from the most basic premises of progressive Protestantism. They put no faith in the perfection of man or his institutions, and awaited redemption instead by the personal return of Christ. The premillennialists' interpretation of the

Bible, and their view of human nature and human history, led them to make very dark predictions about the world's immediate future.[46] And yet, the war itself was a "sign of the times" that foretold Christ's bodily Second Coming. As historian Sydney Ahlstrom rightly observed, both liberals and premillennialists interpreted the war as an absolute conflict, believing "that in one sense or another, the war on earth was linked up with a war in heaven."[47] The problem with the premillennialists, William H. P. Faunce concluded, was that they had fallen into "indifference to the human struggle. If one expects that to-morrow the heavens will literally be rolled together as a scroll, he cannot feel overwhelming concern regarding any clouds that now darken the horizon."[48]

Shailer Mathews was alarmed at the wartime surge of interest in the literal Second Coming of Christ and called the hope "naïve." He noted with satisfaction that some premillennialists were "so hostile to the present policies of the government as to have been subject to investigation on the part of the Federal Government." He complained that they "sap the springs of national courage," and—in an odd charge for a professed pacifist—he warned that "with such pacifism intelligent citizens should have no sympathy." Premillennialists were another impediment to the Future; they were "ruining the church and hindering the spread of a genuinely Christian civilization."[49]

Mathews's Chicago colleague Shirley Jackson Case prepared an entire book on the problem of millennialist thinking, attributing this resurgent eschatology, as did Mathews, to the kind of escapism common in wartime. Case called premillennialism, in light of the pressing needs of the day, "especially pernicious." Furthermore, its teachings were antidemocratic and "play[ed] into the hands of all enemies of social and political reform." Premillennialism threatened the "sense of civic duty" as it was applied both to American society and to international conditions. To Case the conflict between premillennialism and his own progressivism could not have struck deeper into the heart of his ideals. The central question was, "shall we still look for God to introduce a new order by catastrophic means or shall we assume the responsibility of bringing about our own millennium . . . ?" In 1918 Case and the progressive clergy at large remained confident in evolution, in humanity, in civilization, and in social betterment.[50] The war's devastation had yet to damage their meliorist worldview.

In May 1918, the *Biblical World* reprinted part of a letter it received suggesting that Germany was funding both the Industrial Workers of the World—the "Wobblies"—and premillennialist propaganda in order to divide the United States.[51] Case repeated a similar charge in July's issue in a frantic warning against the pessimistic, unpatriotic, and even un-Christian premillennialists. To Case, the movement was a little too well-funded, and it spread its message "with a thoroughness suspiciously Teutonic." Supposedly, the movement had the same divisive effect as the radical Wobblies; it was "a missionary of pessimism" and "a pronounced enemy of democracy and a serious menace to the nation's morale in this hour of its need."[52]

Such criticism was not limited to the *Biblical World*. The *Christian Century* also took up the charge, calling premillennialism a "hallucination" and claiming that it was "not only unscriptural and in the deepest sense pessimistic," but also that it was "unpatriotic and subversive of every interest now being urged by the national spirit."[53] One editor, Herbert L. Willett, in his extensive series on millennialism for the *Christian Century,* stigmatized premillennialism as "a theology of denial and despair" that threatened the nation's "loyalty, courage and devotion."[54]

In another issue he claimed that the world emphatically was not approaching its end. The world would not be saved through any abrupt and purely supernatural event, but rather through gradual amelioration. Willett rejected the eschatology of both pre- and postmillennialism because their theologies included the intervention of a literal, physical Second Coming. The return of Christ was not "an episode but a process," he claimed. Christ "comes" incrementally as His will is realized in the social order.[55] Sharing the progressives' concern, social gospel pioneer Walter Rauschenbusch warned in 1917 that the premillennialist system "defeats the Christian imperative of righteousness and salvation" in this present world.[56] The premillennialists, to the contrary, understood themselves as realists and even optimists, for they offered a permanent, supernatural solution to the world's problems.[57] But in 1918 they stood as a troubling contradiction to every assumption of the liberal church, both in theology and politics. The progressive clergy used the opportunity afforded by wartime hysteria to

attack some of its most outspoken theological adversaries and their movement.

DESPITE THE LIBERAL church's determined efforts to build the kingdom of
God some critics actually found the modern church too "otherworldly"
during the Great War. In the lead article for the *Atlantic Monthly* in February
1918, Presbyterian pastor Joseph Odell indicted the American church as
a whole for not backing the war for righteousness soon enough or
passionately enough. He compared the church at the time of world crisis
to Jesus' disciple Peter, who at the moment of Jesus' trial "sat by the fire
warming himself." As Peter had denied his Lord, so the American church
had betrayed Christ by failing to cry out before 1917 in "a passion of
righteous indignation" and with "holy wrath" against Germany.[58]

Odell argued that despite President Wilson's admonition, neutrality
before April 1917 had not been at all binding on the church. Since when,
he wondered, had prophets been bound to surrender their moral judgment and divine calling to the wishes of secular authority? Because the
church raised no voice of protest against Germany, he continued, the task
had been left to others outside the fold, among them novelists Owen Wister
and H. G. Wells.[59] Such secular prophets had to call the church to recognize the truth. Too many in the American church had preached an ascetic
gospel of release from worldly cares, "while millions of individual
Gethsemanes and Calvarys were merging into a real Armageddon." When
ministers in Germany refused to challenge the "blood-sodden Kaiser in
the name of God and Righteousness," the American church should have
assumed the duty. The church had too long followed the anemic Jesus of
the portrait artist and ignored "the bolder features of the conqueror" who
surpassed Oliver Cromwell in "courageous manhood."[60]

Odell had no doubt where this virile Jesus would have stood in August 1914. He never would have been neutral toward Germany's acts of
rape, slaughter, and lawlessness. Defiantly, the Germans had gone about
"the world like a carefully organized band of demented fiends." Although
faced with such self-evident evil, the church had failed to rouse "the soul
of the nation to action." Other organizations, independent of the church,
such as the Red Cross and the YMCA, had been obliged to take up the

church's responsibility. "Though the whole world be in the crucible and every other institution on earth be in the melting pot," the church somehow believed that it could continue in its old ways.[61]

Now, in 1918, Odell concluded, the world was "demanding an immediate and a spiritual interpretation" of the Great War. And people had to be given such an interpretation "or lose both reason and faith." In the face of this need, the church could not return to debates over doctrine, but rather had to supply practical, real-life answers to the world's problems, offering redemption as a fact, not as a theory. In this moment of opportunity, the church could not again fail to lead as it had in 1914. American society had been elevated by the experience of war to the level of unquestioning and unhesitating self-sacrifice. Old reform movements, such as prohibition and women's rights, were now making unprecedented progress, and the American people were ready to examine every institution in the new "pure white light of wisdom." After the war, America would face "cosmic rehabilitation." This was truly a time of opportunity for the church, for "common and even gross men are now willing to think and act upon a lofty plane . . . ; a manumitted mob has crossed the Red Sea and asks the nearest way to the Promised Land."[62]

Considering how active at least a segment of the American Protestant clergy had been before 1917 in promoting the war, Odell's criticism seemed unfounded. Not surprisingly, his article provoked a considerable response from those clergy who had pushed for American entry into the war. One of those responses came from the Reverend Randolph McKim, who early on had considered the European conflict a "holy war." He published a collection of his war sermons in the hope that they would "serve to exonerate the Church from the charge that in the greatest tragedy of human history she was content to sit by the fire warming herself."[63]

The *Outlook,* never a magazine to be accused of warming itself at Peter's fire, responded immediately and forcefully to Odell. It listed the names of several ministers who had spoken out against Germany, among them George A. Gordon, Newell Dwight Hillis, and Harry Emerson Fosdick. Furthermore, it argued, the stars on every church's service flag testified "to the spiritual enthusiasm which has carried their members into this war for humanity." The *Outlook* also pointed to all the seminarians who had eagerly taken up arms as ministers of "the gospel of justice and liberty." In the same way that Germany had obeyed the war-god Odin, America had obeyed Christ, and sought "to make the world's redemption a historic fact." The American church during the Great War was not Peter, the disciple of denial, but rather "that other disciple" who had followed Jesus into His trial on the eve of the world's redemption on Calvary.[64]

Another response to Odell came from essayist George Parkin Atwater writing in the respected *Atlantic Monthly*. Atwater defended the churches' contribution to the war. It was not the worldly minded who had stirred the hearts of the nation's volunteers, he countered, but rather "the churches and the clergy . . . have built the foundation of justice, patriotism, righteousness, and truth into the fabric of rising manhood. The church boys went to war, at the call." But Atwater then rose to greater heights in his defense of the church. The church was in fact embodied in the troops. The United States Army was "the Church militant." It was "the Church in action, transforming the will of the Church into deeds, expressing the moral judgment of the Church in smashing blows." These boys were missionaries. "Our army is preaching the sermon of the American Church to Germany." And that church had been out in front of the American government in recognizing the moral obligation to intervene, he continued. Indeed, "the Church prepared the national mind for the inevitable decision of the government."[65] This was the same point the *New Republic* had made in 1917 in deciding "who willed American participation."

DESPITE THEIR SEEMINGLY unlimited confidence in their task and in themselves, the progressive clergy nevertheless recognized and feared the spiritual battle they knew must be raging within the progressive soul because of the war. They acknowledged the conflict's challenge to the idea of progress. At stake in the redemptive war's outcome was the plausibility of all their claims about the socially transforming power of applied Christianity. If Germany were to succeed, then all their promises would be proven idle, vain, and even deceptive. In writing *The Challenge of the Present Crisis* in 1917, Harry Emerson Fosdick confronted the doubts caused by the war. Everywhere, he noted, people were deciding "whether this war is to leave them social pessimists or not." A moment's doubt would be poison to the progressive movement. "That many are becoming cynical," he continued, "are growing dubious of social possibilities, are surrendering to political skepticism the faith which they never would have surrendered to speculative doubt, is clear to anyone who talks much with men."[66] Progressive Christianity had met the intellectual challenge of the nineteenth century, but would it survive the psychic challenge of the twentieth?

Fosdick pointed to all the reconstructive work to be done after the war and warned of the consequences of failing to continue the reformist fight for progress. Humanity's future depended on it. Yet he did not believe the world was headed toward failure. Quite the contrary: "Education, fraternalized commerce, social idealism, international law, and Christianity—these are not ready for the discard. They are humanity's great hope. This war is not so much an occasion for despair concerning them as it is a challenge to a better understanding and a finer use of them." He remained so optimistic, in fact, that he interpreted the war as evidence "of mankind's increasing interdependence." He claimed that "we are fighting the war on the way up, not on the way down."[67] In his autobiography, Fosdick regretted he ever wrote such things. But at the time the crusading spirit of the war proved irresistible.[68]

William H. P. Faunce agreed that the war need not cause pessimism. In 1918 he pleaded that despite the World War, civilization was not collapsing. But his appeal exposed just how desperate some of the progressives had become to salvage the integrity of their worldview. "We simply wish to point out," he wrote sounding almost satirical, "that the future is not utterly black, the world is not totally irrational, and human civilization is not a foundered ship breaking on the rocks. We wish to show that some good is left when four fifths of the world is at war, and that thoughtful souls need not lose faith in either God or humanity."[69] Even a cataclysm on the scale of the Great War had not shaken his progressive presuppositions.

Joining the defense of progress, Lyman Abbott returned to the old theme of God's superintendence of history. History was not the product of random events, but rather possessed God-given "continuity and coherence." As the progressive theologians had been preaching for decades, Abbott now reasserted that history contained within itself a natural tendency toward higher ideals. The "march of the centuries toward liberty"

could not be stopped by Germany's efforts to return the world to barbarism. Pessimism had no place in the soul of anyone who believed "that God
is in His world, that above all earthly plans and purposes is One who gives
to his children their ideals and inspires them with their courage." True,
the last four years of war might cause doubt, but surely not the history of
the last century. To Abbott it was obvious in "what direction the unseen
forces are carrying the human race."[70]

ONE DIRECTION THESE "unseen forces" were carrying the human race was
toward world brotherhood, the third sphere after the church and society
in the progressives' ever-widening reform efforts. They waged their
redemptive war to remove war itself from the face of the earth. Robert E.
Speer, a friend of John R. Mott and a champion of foreign missions,
defended the resort to war in the "present stage of social and political
development." The war was in fact a "moral obligation" to be waged "until
the international wrong-doing . . . is put down once for all and forever."
This was a punitive war. Speer promised that "there is such a thing as world
progress." One day, war, like polygamy and slavery, would be outgrown
and replaced "with an order of brotherhood and righteousness and unity."[71]
     Similarly, the Reverend Charles Albertson, pastor of the Lafayette
Avenue Presbyterian Church in Brooklyn, saw approaching through the
clouds of war "an epoch of free peoples and of peace no king or chancellor
can ever again molest or break." Heeding Abraham Lincoln's advice,
America had gone forth in charity and without malice "to a war which
. . . shall end war, and with it, end the dream of a world-empire founded
on force." He concluded with an appropriate stanza from "The Battle Hymn
of the Republic," implying that as Christ died to make men holy, so Americans died to make men free.[72]
     In place of a world enslaved by war would arise a world of democracy
and brotherhood. The progressive clergy had always considered democracy to be more than simply a political system, elevating the rule of the
people to a doctrine in their otherwise creedless theology. William H. P.
Faunce claimed he saw little distinction between Christianity and democracy. In 1918 he commented that the great spiritual force "swelling and
rolling round the world" could be called either "democratic Christianity

or Christian democracy," it did not matter which.[73] God Himself had long ago abdicated His monarchical throne and now cooperated with humanity in a manner more compatible with the modern spirit of democracy. Herbert Willett noted at the end of the war that "the conception of God as a monarch, all-powerful, remote, transcendent, and autocratic is no longer suited to the needs or the comprehension of the modern mind."[74] As a result of the war, all the kings of the earth would, like God Himself, yield before the march of democracy.

In a similar fusion of theology with political and social philosophy, missions enthusiast and historian Tyler Dennett pondered the relationship among missionary enterprises, world democracy, and the war. Dennett, later known for his studies of American foreign policy in Asia and for biographies of Theodore Roosevelt and John Hay, was eager to extend to Asia the "democratic fellowship" then embracing the world. He believed that it was in America's "enlightened self-interest" to send out missionaries arm-in-arm with businessmen to bring "backward peoples" into the modern family of nations. He challenged the missionary to see himself no longer simply as an ambassador of the Gospel, but more "as a national representative and as an international agent." The commercial and spiritual "motives can no longer be considered exclusive of or opposed to each other." The proper goal to be set before the missionary was "to develop the latent resources—physical, intellectual, and moral—of backward peoples."[75]

Dennett also recognized the war's boost to the worldwide democratic movement. "Democracy," he declared, "is not merely a catchword of the War; it has become the watchword of the world. The War has accentuated the ideal and accelerated its growth." Dennett then applied to the world situation in 1918 Abraham Lincoln's prediction preceding the American Civil War. The United States, at one time divided itself, now faced a world "half slave and half free," with many millions still in "bondage to illiteracy, ignorance, and superstition." Presumably, all of these ills would be cured by the expansion of democracy, the very ideal that America had entered the war to preserve. Once posit this rationale for war, Dennett reasoned, and the United States was "impelled to continue the task, both now and after the War be over, of underwriting a world democracy with a world

Christianity." To do otherwise, America risked depriving the "backward races" of the fruits of the war.[76] Consistent with their enthusiasm for an "applied Christianity" before the war, liberal Protestants such as Dennett continued to conceive of Christianity as a means to a temporal end, applied in this case to the goal of global democracy.

That democracy was fundamentally Christian the progressive clergy had never doubted. Methodist Episcopal bishop Francis McConnell claimed that democracy was founded on Christ's injunction to "love thy neighbor as thyself." Moreover, it seemed self-evident to him that the war was primarily about the "world-wide advance of democracy." Indeed, "the great war has pretty thoroughly taught that the whole world must come avowedly within the sweep of the democratic movement if there is to be democracy anywhere. Democracy must become world-wide, or the nations must take to armament as never before."[77] He preached a universal political and social system, assuming that the world could be at peace only to the degree that nations were alike. A community of nations would emerge from a homogeneity of political, economic, and religious institutions. As Tyler Dennett proposed, democracy, commerce, and Christianity had to be exported together.

One of the fullest explications of democracy as religion came from Union Seminary professor George Coe, the educator who with John Dewey had founded the Religious Education Association. At the heart of Jesus' teaching about the kingdom of God, Coe found the democratic ideal. He even proposed that the phrase "democracy of God" replace "kingdom of God" as a more precise definition of Jesus' ideal. Coe argued that Jesus' teaching about the "brotherhood of men" led unavoidably "to the ideal of a democratic organization of human society"; it offered mankind the "divine-human democracy as a final social ideal." God Himself was "within human society in the democratic manner of working, helping, sacrificing, persuading, co-operating, achieving." Coe proclaimed that "there is now no separation between human society and divine."[78]

As Coe's comment revealed, underlying the liberals' expectations for democracy and peace was their more fundamental hope for world brotherhood. They had entered the Great War for the sake of international de-

mocracy, to wage a war against war, and also to achieve worldwide cooperation, all goals of progressives both inside and outside the church. Coe's
editorial colleague at *Religious Education,* Henry Cope, reassured his readers that the United States had gone forth in sacrificial service "to secure
peace and righteousness, that world of which the Hebrew prophets sang."[79]
The Old Testament vision of God's kingdom of justice was at last within
reach, to be grasped if the world was willing.

In the winter of 1918, Sidney Gulick, secretary of Andrew Carnegie's
World Alliance for Promoting International Friendship through the
Churches, described the work that lay ahead for the churches in achieving
international righteousness. His points were familiar to his fellow clergy,
who years before the war had advocated an active role for the churches
and the United States in world affairs. "The New Task of American
churches," he wrote with emphasis, "is to Christianize America's international relations." This work fell well within "the range of Christian responsibility." Appealing to the all-too-evident consequences of the lack of
international cooperation, Gulick urged America to seize its "unique opportunity and responsibility for bringing in the new world order." But, he
warned, returning to a constant theme, "permanent world peace can come
only as the fruit and product of international righteousness."[80] First righteousness, then peace, as Teddy Roosevelt would have said.

Gulick's formula for world brotherhood called for the transformation of international sentiments, the substitution of cooperation for competition. As for the church's role in this transformation, Gulick developed
a specific program, including an enlightened public opinion, continued
international service, and social reform. To achieve the "new world order," he urged, "the churches of America should now vigorously promote
nation-wide education in Christian internationalism, unparalleled international benevolence, right domestic legislation, and suitable international
organization." To these ends, every church in America needed to be involved in the movement by studying the issues, by recognizing the Christian duty, by lobbying Congress when necessary, and by operating a local
"Committee on world problems." The success of this plan, Gulick concluded, relied on educating the public and uniting in specific "collective

action." As an example, he offered his own World Alliance, which coordinated its activities with the churches of the Federal Council and eleven other denominations.[81]

Perhaps the single best summary of progressive Christianity's view of the world at the close of the Great War came from the Reverend William P. Merrill, who in his poetry had earlier praised the regenerative task of the state. In *Christian Internationalism,* which he dedicated to Mr. and Mrs. Carnegie, Merrill's fundamental concern was that nations behave "like Christian gentlemen." If they had done so before 1914, he reasoned circularly, the war never would have happened. Internationalist Christians, as citizens of the emerging future society, had to work toward the betterment of mankind. Despite what the traditionalists might preach, "the Christian 'way' is not most of all a way to heaven, but far more a way to fair and happy living for all men here."[82] In a remarkable claim, Merrill explicitly united the modern missions movement, the Great War, and the social gospel into a single theology of the Kingdom:

> The best mark of a "saved" man is not that he wants to go to heaven, but that he is willing to go to China, or to the battle-field in France, or to the slums of the city, or to the last dollar of his resources, or to the limit of his energy, to set forward the Kingdom of God.[83]

In Merrill's expansive ideal there was apparently no distinction between personal redemption, social service, and enlistment in the United States Army.

Merrill's sentimental idealism and theology followed the pattern of prewar progressive thinking, except that now the rhetoric was even more passionate. Merrill ecstatically promised that "the holiest, the most exciting, the most adventurous, the most truly Christian cause is this Christianizing [of] international relations." In fact, he urged, all of the Christian life depended upon the success of internationalism. This was no trivial matter. Merrill insisted that people could not be fully Christian until the world was Christian, because they could not obey "Thou shalt not kill" until the nations stopped fighting. Sanctified Christians could not exist in an unsanctified world. In this environmental approach to the Christian

life, which turned historic Christianity on its head, Merrill placed internationalism at the center of "the whole program and hope of Christian
redemption." As William H. P. Faunce recognized no distinction between
Christianity and democracy, so Merrill declared that "Christianity and
Internationalism are one and the same."[84]

Merrill rejoiced that as a result of its great adventure the United States
had been awakened to its "duty in the world." The anti-imperialists of the
1890s, while right to fear imperialism's threat to democratic institutions,
had been dead wrong about America's involvement abroad. At the time of
the Spanish-American War, he suggested, a noble aspiration "seized the
heart of our nation, to go out and play a worthy part in the common
political life of the world." To satisfy that "worthy impulse" was "honor-
able; to reject it would have been cowardly." Through participation in the
Great War, America had come at last to understand its "world-responsibil-
ity."[85]

Merrill pictured the Great War as the crowning moment of America's
rise to world service, the fulfillment of the nation's clear historical destiny. From the Revolution, to the Monroe Doctrine, to the Civil War, and
then to the culminating Great War, America had defended democracy at
every stage. Thanks to the United States, democracy now would be carried worldwide. The national responsibility that America had assumed at
its founding and had vindicated in the Civil War had to be lived up to for
the sake of "all men everywhere; their right to a free and just life must be
enforced." Reciting a pledge similar to President Wilson's from the summer of 1914, Merrill promised that the American flag, with its stars and
stripes, was to be "a prophecy of the future expansion of world-democ-
racy and world-federation."[86]

Thus, to the extent that the progressive clergy worked to topple monarchs, empires, and every vestige of autocracy, they were intellectual revolutionaries who helped make the United States, under Wilson's leadership, a revolutionary force in world politics, a force to melt the institutions of the nineteenth century in the crucible of war. And yet they never
would have expressed their mission in such stark terms. To them, this was
an accumulative revolution in theology, church structure, politics, social

institutions, and international relations for the sake of world redemption. Having contributed some of the images and metaphors necessary to total war, they also embraced the World War as a redemptive war. The heat of war had opened a moment of accelerated and compressed time in which to achieve the goals of the social gospel movement broadly defined. The Great War would yield a socially conscious, activist, and unified church, a renewed social order, and a fraternal new world order.

8

A NEW WORLD ORDER

THE PROGRESSIVE CLERGY AND THE PEACE, 1918–1920

HEAVY ARTILLERY SHELLING AND FIGHTING on the Western Front continued to the final moments of the Great War. After a month of discussing
terms for an armistice, the Allies offered Germany conditions for an end
to the war. On November 11, 1918, a beleaguered but unbroken Germany
signed an armistice with the Allies. Germany had gambled on one last great
offensive in March 1918 before any meaningful American contribution of
fresh troops could be felt. But after fighting a two-front war for most of the
past four years and now facing a potential socialist revolution at home,
Germany sought to salvage what it could of its empire and honor. The
Kaiser abdicated and fled to Holland, and his generals began the humiliat-
ing process of disarmament on land and sea and withdrawal from all
occupied territory. After four years of virtual stalemate, the Great War
came to an end. President Wilson's emissary to the Supreme War Council,
Colonel Edward House, cabled Wilson from Paris on November 11,
"Autocracy is dead. Long live democracy and its immortal leader."[1]

Within a week, the immortal Wilson issued another Thanksgiving Day
proclamation, this time thanking God for granting peace. Wilson praised
the peace, not "as a mere cessation of arms," but rather "as a great triumph
of right." With a righteous victory came "the confident promise of a new
day . . . in which justice shall replace force and jealous intrigue among the
nations." As Wilson had promised in 1917, America had kept itself pure,

and its success was "not marred or stained by any purpose of selfish aggression." In words that summarized the entire progressive image of the
war, Wilson praised America's soldiers, who "in a righteous cause" had
"won immortal glory" and had "nobly served their nation in serving mankind." But the task was not done. Now, in the "new day," Wilson anticipated "new and greater duties" for the American people.[2]

On the first Sunday following the Armistice, Wilson's emissary to
Russia Elihu Root spoke at the Cathedral of St. John the Divine in uptown
Manhattan. At an afternoon service he shared his vision of America's postwar role, a vision, whether he realized it or not, that embodied every
essential element of the progressive clergy's apocalyptic interpretation of
the war, with all its abstraction, universalism, and sentimentality. He described the recently concluded conflict as "a world struggle for human
freedom" through which America had "learned the lesson of sacrifice."
The war's end meant that a "new era" had arrived and that "modern civilization has not failed." "God Himself was on our side," he continued, "and
so today, thanks to the Lord, Christian civilization triumphs. The old barbarian principle has been laid in the dust."[3]

With barbarism in the dust, one of the most pressing problems facing
American society and the church immediately after the war was that posed
by the returning troops. While the government and local communities
may have been most concerned with integrating the soldiers back into the
economy, the progressive church saw these young men as a potential army
for social reconstruction. The reform-minded clergy intended to see these
men who had experienced "real living" in the trenches arrive home prepared to continue the domestic theater of the war for righteousness. As
Bishop Francis McConnell wrote, while the number of demobilized troops
after the Civil War had been large, the sheer number of returning soldiers
after this war would "affect every corner of our democracy." Moreover,
"definitely radical political and social theories" had lodged in their minds.
McConnell said this not in fear, but in hope.[4]

Baptist minister Harry Emerson Fosdick commented in some detail
on the problem of returning troops. Returning himself from a tour of
several months in France under the auspices of the YMCA and of the British government's Ministry of Information,[5] Fosdick wrote a lengthy ar-

ticle for the *Atlantic Monthly* discussing the spiritual state of the troops and what they would demand from religion and the church at home. He argued that through the experience of war the soldiers had learned the meaning of self-sacrifice, the potential of cooperative action, and the regenerative power of devotion to a higher cause. In short, they had been molded into the very image the progressives desired an activist Christian to be. Anticipating great results from these returning troops, Fosdick warned the churches that they, too, had become "malleable" along with the rest of the world and that the returning soldier would compel them to abandon any lingering reactionary view of society and the church. The troops were "coming home to sway the future of the nation."[6]

Fosdick denied that there had been anything resembling an evangelical revival at the front. Rather, the American soldiers had experienced an even deeper religious awakening; they had "given self to the more-than-self in unstinted dedication." In offering their own lives, they had known "the divine purpose." The church, Fosdick charged, did not understand how much their "boys" had been changed by the war. These soldiers now valued what was truly important and genuine in life. The orthodoxy, cant, and falsehood of the complacent American church would have to give way when these purified souls returned. Indeed, Fosdick warned, "they went out boys; they will come back like the Judgment Day."[7]

To Fosdick the battlefield had become "real," while life at home had become false and shallow. But the returning soldiers would take their spades in hand and dig anew the battlefield trenches across American society, and continue to fight for the cause. The "spirit of the army" and the ideal of "splendid self-sacrifice" had filled them with true religion, the very idealism progressive Christianity needed in order to remake the world. Upon their return, these soldiers would convene their figurative "assizes" and sit in judgment on the churches. They would demand the end of sectarianism and the expulsion of obscurantist orthodoxy and legalism, replacing them with a dedication to social service and to democratic churches. While theologians once had debated whether the church would survive in the modern world by retaining its orthodoxy or by becoming liberal, it was now clear that the church would endure by being "useful," by waging the perpetual war to reform the church and society.[8] Fosdick's profile of the redeemed soldier, of course, seemed only to mirror his own hopes for what a reconstructed Christian should be.

While Fosdick urged the churches to prepare for the returning troops, Oberlin College president Henry Churchill King was concerned with the attitude of the soldiers themselves. Serving in France under the sponsorship of the American Expeditionary Force (AEF) and the YMCA, King distributed to the troops his pocket-sized book, *For a New America in a New World*. In this volume he encouraged the soldiers, as the title made clear, to keep up at home "that same splendid self-devotion which you showed in the war."[9]

King insisted that the blessings of victory should be secured, so that the soldiers' fallen comrades had died for a reason. The world could not be allowed either to drift back into the old days nor slip forward into the wrong kind of new days, such as those offered by Russian Bolshevism. The world stood poised, ready to make "a great forward advance." But progress would not be spontaneous. Rather, the soldiers of the AEF had to dedicate themselves to the struggle for a new world. As Moses on Mt. Sinai had been given the pattern for the Tabernacle—God's earthly dwelling—so mankind at this moment had "to build a new world according to the pattern shown us in our mount of vision." The struggle had not ended with the Armistice, but was "only well begun." Armed with its impressive "moral stamina," the AEF possessed the power to return home and remake America and the world.[10]

King suggested specific domestic and international reforms to complete the divine "pattern." He proposed that America needed a federal department of education, a system of national health care, and public control of both utilities and natural resources. Beyond its borders, America had to work for internationalism, especially for the vital League of Nations. "The time of her isolation is gone," King rejoiced. Echoing Lincoln's Gettysburg Address he called for "a solemn rededication of the living, to the unfulfilled tasks of democracy and of the Kingdom of God." Quoting an army chaplain, he carried the central theme of progressive Christianity over into the postwar era: "There are many signs that the time has come, to make the experiment of *applied Christianity* on a scale as large as the world." The social gospel clergy had championed "applied Christianity" since the 1880s and before, and had interpreted the Great War as an opportunity to apply their Christianity worldwide; and now they were prepared to secure its triumph. King ended his advice to the soldiers with appropriate lines from the "The Battle Hymn of the Republic": "Oh! be swift, my soul, to answer Him! be jubilant my feet! Our God is marching on."[11]

READY TO ENLIST the returning soldiers in the continuing war for righteousness, the progressive clergy renewed their efforts to reform the church, American society, and the world. From the earliest days of the social gospel, liberal Protestants had worked to reconstruct both historic Christianity and the world around them according to the new light of an activist Christianity, to reconcile the City of God and the City of Man into a single righteous metropolis. In the postwar era they continued their war for righteousness at home and abroad. Little had changed in their outlook. Certain that the war had imbued Americans with the necessary humanitarian spirit, the progressive clergy seized the opportunity to build a socially conscious church, an industrial democracy, and an international brotherhood.

In February 1919, three months after the Armistice and well into the peace negotiations, the *Nation*—then under the editorship of the pacifist and internationalist Oswald Garrison Villard, who had never reconciled himself to the war[12]—echoed the theologians in predicting that the tide of postwar reconstruction would engulf the churches as well. Noting that countless ministers had devoted themselves to national service in the YMCA and other organizations, the *Nation* assumed that with their return the emphasis of the church seemed "bound to change." "The trend to what is loosely called 'social service,' already strong before the war," the editors observed, "has been greatly intensified during the war. The church must look to its foundation as well as to its super-structure. It must speak a vital spiritual message."[13] Many clergy agreed that the time had come for the church to reevaluate its primary mission on this earth.

The Reverend C. Arthur Lincoln, pastor of Buffalo's First Congregational Church, thought he knew precisely what this "vital spiritual message" of the church needed to be in the new era. The church's responsibil-

ity, he charged in *Religious Education,* was to build a "Christian Social Order," the "Democracy of Christ." The church had been praying for centuries that God's will would "be done on earth as it is in Heaven." Therefore
the church had to direct its energies "to producing an ever widening circle
of Christian society, a Christian commercial life, a Christian educational
system, a Christian governmental system in the city, the state, the nation
and world society." The church had to "act for the good of all people," an
endeavor that would often "include activity for needed social legislation."
The church's mission was not primarily spiritual, but was in fact decid-
edly temporal; its goal "in the day of world democracy" was "not that men
should become Christian and thus save their souls from hell but that men
should become Christian and work hard to save the world from hell."[14]

In addition to building a socially conscious church, the progressives
advocated a united church as well. Charles E. Jefferson, although he had
been a hesitant belligerent, believed that the war had breathed new life
into the movement toward "Church Unity." Even before the war, he noted,
through the YMCA, the Federal Council, and other interdenominational
organizations, the church had been advancing toward union, but the war
had given "fresh impetus" to these efforts by forcing men who disagreed
theologically into "close and hearty cooperation." Moreover, the war had
taught the church that "the power of organized evil in this world" could
only be challenged successfully by "the organized forces of righteousness."
The stakes were high, for "unless the nations accept the law of Christ, the
world is lost."[15]

Union Theological Seminary president Arthur Cushman McGiffert
shared this vision of a church united for social service. Positing that democracy was the highest good, he encouraged the church to subordinate
itself to that end. As a practical matter, religion was needed "to promote
and sustain democracy." Therefore, he reasoned, it had to dispose of its
"egoistic and other-worldly character." McGiffert threw down the gaunt-
let to the traditionalists, insisting that a religion of individual responsibility and one of social responsibility could not live side by side. "The religion of democracy," he warned, "must cease to minister to selfishness by
promising personal salvation, and must cease to impede human progress
by turning the attention of religious men from the conditions here to

rewards elsewhere."[16] Rather than judge the mundane in the light of the transcendent, McGiffert demanded that his religion fit the spirit of the age and that God Himself conform to the standards set by a progressive world theology.

In the same manner, J. M. Artman, dean of the YMCA College in Chicago, distanced himself from the old theology and the supposedly out-worn view of the role of the church in the world. With some embarrass-ment he conceded that the YMCA had once been afflicted with "abstract theology" and "individualistic salvation," and that some in the organization still held such views. But he observed hopefully that the YMCA's leaders were "gradually freeing themselves from these weaknesses." In place of outmoded ideas, the association was "adopting the socialization of man as the Christian goal." Its focus was not on doctrine, but rather on "the social good of all, that is, society building as over against individual salvation."[17]

Former pastor Henry E. Jackson, who during the war worked for the United States Bureau of Education as an expert in community organiza-tion, had firsthand experience in transforming a church into an agent of community service. He described his effort as a real-life version of Win-ston Churchill's novel *The Inside of the Cup*. Sharing the determination of that novel's main character, Jackson desired the church as a whole "to become a useful social institution." To do so, it needed to abandon its sec-tarianism and to become democratic. As a result of the war, he argued, the American people had become intolerant of autocracy in any form, whether in governments or in the church. Ironically, he continued, "the church, which ought to have led the way to freedom, will now be compelled to follow the example of the state and organize itself democratically."[18]

Repeating a well-worn analogy among progressives, Jackson identi-fied the fundamental division in modern Christianity as that "between the Bunyan conception of Christian, who flees from the wicked city to save himself, and the New Testament conception of Christian, who remains in the city to help save others." Not surprisingly, Jackson desired to remove all distinction between God and Caesar, "between the 'sacred' and the 'secular.'" In the "religion of democracy," he concluded, "politics and reli-gion are inseparable." The task ahead for America was to "put into opera-tion the religion of democracy, as it is expressed in her Declaration of

Independence and in the Sermon on the Mount." The nation's success was guaranteed, for "the story of liberty [was] written in human history by the hand of God."[19]

As was true during the war, the progressive church in the postwar era still conceived of itself foremost as a molder of public opinion.[20] John Marshall Barker, professor of sociology at the Boston University School of Theology, summarized the postwar attitude. "The Church," he wrote in 1919, "is one of the strongest agencies to create and sustain public opinion. Hence the moral and spiritual power of the Church involves responsibility to help fashion the State after the divine ideal. The functions of Church and State differ, but their central purpose should be one and the same." The preacher "strives to bring his hearers to such a standard of civic righteousness that they will become pioneers in a public crusade against specific social wrongs in the community life."[21] But the progressive church was not content to influence national opinion for national reform. The *Christian Century,* for example, suggested that the time had come with the close of the war to build an international public opinion. With the uniting of the world through "wireless" and other means, the wrongs within one nation had become the unavoidable concern of all. The first stirring of this "world conscience" had "wrought the defeat of Germany," and now the church was faced with "the opportunity of moulding and shaping this world opinion."[22]

Some of the secular press shared this desire for a united, socially active church. In the winter of 1919, more than a year after the end of the war, the *Nation* remained confident that the new day still approached. Inspired by the social emphasis of the Catholics and the Protestant denominations, and by the Federal Council's estimate that forty-two million Americans were members of a Catholic, Protestant, or Jewish congregation, the editors claimed that "a vast social force . . . is apparently upon the point of rousing itself." The only obstacle remaining was church disunity. Could the churches, the *Nation* asked, "sink their sectarian rivalries in a common effort for the realization of that kingdom of righteousness among men for whose coming they all regularly pray? If they can, the forces of evil will have a foe to be reckoned with."[23]

Dedicated to denominational cooperation for the sake of the kingdom of democracy, the progressive church set out to reconstruct American society. As the same prewar goals for denominational cooperation persisted into the immediate postwar era, so too the progressive clergy's social gospel objectives for American society thrived after the war. While in no way ignoring international ideals, the liberal church turned its attention immediately to the continuing struggle to "Christianize" American institutions.

Reflecting the spirit of hope that greeted the first Christmas following the war, the *New Republic* urged Christians during the season of peace to "pray for a second coming."The war-ravaged world desperately needed the best efforts of "Christian faith and Christian works," for "the new birth of order and the new birth of freedom hangs dubious and tremulous on the new birth of Christ." But despite this wishing for a wider dissemination of humanitarian ideals, the *New Republic* did add a note of doubt; the editors questioned the ability of "progress" to save either the individual or society. What was missing, they proposed, was "a common sense of sin" and "a willingness to repent."[24]

The *New Republic*'s somber call for a conviction of collective guilt was certainly not new; the social gospel had been demanding such a sense of sin for decades. Instead, the editors' doubt was a fairly typical rejection of the old order and not yet a questioning of the possibility of a new age. They argued that Christians had to devote themselves to meeting actual needs in a suffering world, that at this moment in human history the world needed an activist Christianity; the old pietism offered nothing. The people of the world required "more than consolation and fortitude. They need, above all, deliverance." At Christmas 1918, the editors urged, Christians had to imitate Christ truly in order to free society from its ills, for "the crucifixion of Christ, His resurrection and His assumption of the burden of sin dramatize[d] a process of redemption which should be as salutary for society, as it is for individual men and women." Indeed, "those who imitate Christ place their faith in human perfectibility." Despite its doubts about inevitable progress, the *New Republic* evidently did not doubt the unlimited potential for progress. "Never," it concluded, "have the practices of Christianity enjoyed so good a chance of meeting actual . . . human needs."[25]

The *New Republic*'s attitude late in 1918 indicated just how far the social gospel's premises of man and society had penetrated American thought. The editors accepted the social gospel's contention that Christianity offered human society physical deliverance from its ills and then challenged the church to get on with the effort. Of course the progressive religious press needed no prompting to interpret Christianity's role in postwar America. Looking at the new year ahead, the *Outlook* charged that the most immediate task facing progressives was "to extinguish the flames and rebuild a new social order out of the ruins of the old." In what could have served as a slogan for all of progressive Christianity after the war, the *Outlook* proclaimed that "the war is done but our duty is not done." The war had leveled European society and had "shaken" American institutions as well. But, as always, crisis meant opportunity. Everyone had to work together to achieve "liberty, equality, fraternity" throughout American society: in education, in industry, and in religion.[26]

Contemplating America's role in God's continuing process of redemption as Easter approached in 1919, Lyman Abbott offered to his *Outlook* readers a series of "Lenten Lessons." God was always at work, he wrote; "the world is still on the loom." The World War had removed much of the old "imperfect civilization," but it had "built nothing." The task ahead was to construct God's new world. "The opportunity is afforded us," Abbott rejoiced, repeating his proposal from two months earlier, "to reconstruct our political, our industrial, our educational, and our religious institutions more in conformity with the divine law, more in harmony with the divine spirit." Moreover, "opportunities involve obligations. What we can do we ought to do." To Abbott the Christian's duty could not be more clear: "We are in the world in order to work with God in building the world aright." Quite simply, "it is a command [from God]: he is improving, developing, renovating, reconstructing. This fact is in itself a command to his children to improve, develop, renovate, reconstruct." For Abbott the progressive God was still at work after the war, and the divine mandate to remake the world had not been revoked. With confidence in this holy commission, Abbott exulted that "there is nothing too great for us to undertake with God as our Comrade and our Leader."[27]

As could be expected, Abbott explained this task as an outgrowth of

America's redemptive act of service. The deaths of the soldiers and sailors had been unparalleled atoning works. In April 1919, nearly two years to the day after America's entry into the Great War, Abbott still looked upon the struggle essentially as a spiritual battle. His interpretation of the war had not changed. As he revealingly noted, "During the last four years more men have taken up their cross and followed the Great Leader through Gethsemane to a sacrificial death than in any previous age of the world's history." Though still ashamed that the United States had waited so long to enter the war, Abbott rejoiced that God did "not let us sleep" and that "the enthusiasm of the Cross became too strong to be denied." Fortunately, America "broke the leash" of a "selfish" and "cowardly pacifism." If America had tried to save itself, the world would have been lost. Instead, "we offered ourselves a sacrifice that we might save others." Formerly the focus of the church had been "Salvation," but now "the emphatic word is Service," he rejoiced. "And in Service we are finding Salvation."[28] The war and its aftermath meant service, and service meant redemption. By the spring of 1919, it had yet to occur to Abbott that the cross he had helped hoist upon the shoulders of young Americans might not bring redemption either in this world or the next.

Emerging from the experience of war with the same confidence in the power of Wilsonian mutual service to achieve social regeneration was Methodist minister Worth M. Tippy. Tippy had been active in the prewar social gospel movement,[29] and in 1919 he continued to focus on the coming new era. Like Abbott, he took inspiration from the fact that religion was no longer seen primarily as a personal matter. Organized Christianity now looked toward "world salvation" and realized "that there is no social danger that society is not able to overcome, and no social problem that it is not able to solve." While the individual still had to be reached, Tippy cautioned, there was a "glorious new hope" for humanity, namely, "that society itself is to be rebuilt on the basis of Christ's teachings."[30] In his conception of the new age, Tippy bundled together all of the social gospel's reform efforts, ranging from the individual to world society:

> In the new Christian society, which is coming so rapidly, ignorance, poverty, national hatred, extremes of need and luxury, war and armaments, alcoholism, class struggles, infectious diseases, the evil of burdensome toil, what is

known as industrial slavery, will be brought under control and gradually abol-
ished. The forces of democracy will invade and rebuild every institution of the
world.[31]

In the effort to rebuild the world, it was clear that American liberal
Protestants were ready to lead these invading forces of democracy.

Tippy's Methodist colleague Harry F. Ward advanced an even more
thorough plan for social reconstruction after the war. A decade or so earlier, Ward had been instrumental in formulating the Methodist Social Creed,
which the Federal Council then adopted in 1908 as the Social Creed of the
Churches. In 1919 Ward was a professor of Christian ethics at Union Theological Seminary in New York, and he proposed perhaps the most radical
program to come out of the progressive church for the reformation of
American society. And working with Jane Addams, Oswald Garrison
Villard, John Haynes Holmes, and others, he chaired the American Union
Against Militarism, the committee that organized the American Civil Lib-
erties Union in 1920.[32]

Ward interpreted economic and political history according to a Marxist
stage-theory of development. The world had advanced from slavery and
serfdom to capitalism, and it now approached another fundamental social
reorganization. "The signs are clear," he wrote, "that we have arrived at
one of those conjunctions of economic pressure and idealistic impulse,
which occasion fundamental changes in the organization of life."[33] These
revolutionary changes required new structures for government and other
institutions, including the redefinition of property rights. In order to build
a "new order," the church had to join with economists and social scientists
and provide the necessary "spiritual transformation." Underneath this upheaval moved an indispensable religious renewal that inspired the "collective will." The postwar world was ripe for such a rebirth; the people had
"been taught the effectiveness of mass action" and now anticipated great
changes. Nothing lay beyond the reach of revolution. All "social and governmental institutions" had to be scrutinized. In fact, "so much has been
destroyed and abandoned" as a result of the war that "everything must
justify its right to remain."[34] The era of reconstruction was not a time to
recover what had perished in the storm, but rather a time to build from
new blueprints entirely.

The greatest danger the world faced at this moment of opportunity, Ward continued, was that selfish political leaders would seek to reestablish the old order, "to hold back the new life of the people [rather] than to lead it to fulfillment." He feared that the capitalists were conspiring at the Paris peace conference to build a world amenable to their old habits of exploitation. While praising the United States for embodying "a tremendous missionary force in its democracy," he warned that "more than the political formulae of the past" were needed to solve the world's problems. Ward desired a change in the bedrock economic order; political democracy could only be founded upon economic democracy. Nothing less would do. To achieve that end, Ward's new order would be based on social equality, universal suffrage, industrial efficiency, and the equitable distribution of the fruits of labor. The new age, moreover, would give preeminence to humanity's spiritual aspirations, and work toward world solidarity.[35]

The capitalist system, according to Ward, was irredeemably anti-Christian, and as such Christians had to oppose it. Ward turned to the social gospel's defining and opposing principles of selfishness and service to make his case against capitalism and enlist the church against it. Capitalism was "doomed because its central principle is selfishness, which is the fundamental immorality, and simply will not work." He warned that if "democracy does not make a way for economic change without class war, Western civilization is headed for complete and overwhelming disaster." Fortunately for the future of civilization, he continued, the war had elevated people from their selfish concerns "to the plane of service and sacrifice for a cause." This wartime spirit, Ward urged, had to continue, for "whatever form this new order may take, its vital breath is the sacrificial spirit."[36]

Ward's bold advocacy of socialism, however, tested the limits of any postwar progressive consensus on the goals and essential character of the new era. The fragility of the consensus was revealed when Ward wrote a pamphlet for the Methodist Federation for Social Service in which he defended Bolshevism. Coinciding with the national anxiety stirred by growing labor unrest and the post office's discovery of a number of letter bombs in the spring of 1919, its ill-timed appearance created a storm of controversy. The religious and secular press lined up on either side of the issue, defending or accusing Ward. In the pamphlet Ward equated Bolshevism

with the spirit of Christianity, and its theme indicated how far Christianity had been reconstructed by the progressive church's avant-garde. He
claimed that "the aim of the Bolsheviki is clearly the creation of a state
composed entirely of producers and controlled by producers. This is manifestly a Scriptural aim." The Methodist *Christian Advocate* resented the inevitable impression that Ward's statement was the official position of the
Methodist Church. The socialist *Call,* on the other hand, was delighted to
find an unexpected ally in the church. In spite of the criticism, Ward was
defended by his Union Seminary colleague George Coe, by Chicago Commons founder Graham Taylor, and by Methodist Episcopal bishop Francis
J. McConnell.[37]

Bolshevism, of course, was of immediate concern to the church in the
postwar era. And the new peril replaced the German menace in the minds
of many of the clergy. With Germany defeated, Bolshevism became the
latest embodiment of evil and the preeminent threat to world peace and
security. The call for action against the Bolsheviks revealed the progressives'
inclination to continue their war against any new foe. At the Church of the
Epiphany in Washington, D.C., the Reverend Randolph McKim, who had
so vigorously urged America to assume its duty before 1917, once again
called upon his fellow citizens to rescue the world. In April 1919 he
preached from Ezekiel 33:7: "O Son of man, I have set thee a watchman
unto the House of Israel." The point of McKim's choice of texts was clear:
America, as God's prophet, was appointed to guard the imperiled kingdom. He warned that Bolshevism was "distinctly, definitely and avowedly
our enemy, just as Germany was our enemy for at least two years before
we entered the war." Allied negotiation at Paris with the Bolsheviks was "a
policy of weakness and dishonor." McKim strongly opposed Wilson's appointment of George Herron as a special emissary to Russia. Herron, the
former Grinell professor who had taught "Applied Christianity," had been
admired by the progressives, but his personal morals and political radicalism had long ago cost him his honored place in the social gospel pantheon.
McKim observed that America might "as well send Judas Iscariot to represent Jesus Christ as to send such a man to speak for this great Christian
republic of America."[38]

McKim's answer to Russia's problems was to send not the socialist

Herron but more troops. President Wilson earlier had dispatched four-teen thousand American troops to Russia to protect Allied property and to keep a rail link open, but apparently without any evident intention of unseating the Bolsheviks from power.[39] McKim on the other hand called for outright war against the Bolsheviks, for a "determined and vigorous war, until, with the assistance of our allies, we shall have crushed it to the earth." He called for volunteers for a new "crusade," confident of a swell of American popular support. Surely, McKim concluded, "the people of America will not consent that the results of the war which they have won shall be thrown away by failing to grapple with this new monster, and to throw him to the earth never to rise again."[40]

Russian Bolshevism seemed to endanger the spread of universal de-mocracy and therefore the coming of the kingdom of righteousness. Alva W. Taylor of the *Christian Century*'s editorial staff warned that with Russia run amuck, the world was not yet safe for democracy. He was certain that Russia was "the next big problem for world democracy" and that Bolshe-vism was the world's "most imminent danger." Taylor took it for granted that it was up to the United States to guarantee world democracy.[41] Simi-larly, Frederick Lynch warned that "the menace of Bolshevism and anar-chy" were casting their shadow across Europe, and he urged America to continue to the full its wartime involvement. Holding the United States to its war aims, he reminded the nation that "we went into the war to win democracy for the world. Well, we have not won it yet."[42] Following its undeviating logic, the war for righteousness needed to defeat every "new monster" in its perpetual battle with darkness.

In its official reaction to Bolshevism, the Federal Council of Churches in the summer of 1919 called the dictatorship of the proletariat a "new absolutism." But it moved on to other issues facing an activist church in the postwar world. The Federal Council rejected any Bolshevist-inspired class-based scheme of social reconstruction, choosing instead its own list of reform measures such as the "living wage," public works projects for full employment, sex education, and an end to child labor. It claimed, perhaps with more hope than conviction, that "the value of the churches for national causes" was among "the outstanding discoveries of the war." To continue the advancement of this activist ministry and to address specifi-

cally the problems of American labor, the council proposed the founding
of socially minded urban churches. It envisioned "many hundreds of powerful, highly socialized and democratically organized churches in working
class neighborhoods." These churches would be staffed by ministers trained
especially for the task. Moreover, repeating the promise of its patron John
D. Rockefeller Jr., the Federal Council planned to eliminate wasteful
denominational competition in the cities by dividing the work into
"noncompeting parishes" and by "the closing out of competing churches
and the placing of their financial equities in other noncompeting centers."
At the head of the committee drafting the plan were Henry Churchill
King and Worth M. Tippy.[43]

IN THE MONTHS following November 1918, the progressive clergy not
only addressed the troubles besetting the church and American society in
the postwar era, but also grappled with the urgent task of settling the war
itself through the peace conference and the League of Nations. The
meaning of, and justification for, the war for righteousness hinged on some
sort of world federation, even if imperfect. In December, Woodrow
Wilson took the unprecedented step of traveling to Europe to attend the
peace conference in person as head of the American delegation. The
Church Peace Union cabled words of encouragement to him in Paris,
sending its "heartiest good wishes on the great quest" that he might
"succeed in the noble effort to establish world peace on a righteous basis."[44]
    Before arriving in Paris, Wilson toured England, Italy, and provincial
France. Hailed wherever he went as a conquering hero, his arrival in Europe was heralded as almost the Second Coming of Christ Himself.[45] While
in England, he stopped one Sunday in Carlisle, his mother's birthplace
and where his grandfather, Thomas Woodrow, had been pastor of the
Lowther Street Congregational Church. He visited the church, and after
the sermon addressed the congregation. In his remarks, he paid tribute to
his mother and grandfather and observed how fitting it was that he should
be speaking in a church, for, "after all, what the world now is seeking to do
is to return to the paths of duty, to turn from the savagery of interests to
the dignity of the performance of right." As he faced the peace conference
he took heart, he said, for as the nations had united in "physical force, we

shall now be drawn together in a combination of moral force that is irresistible." Germany had been defeated by that moral force, he continued, and "it is the conscience of the world we now mean to place upon the throne which others tried to usurp."[46]

Wilson unmistakably shared the progressive clergy's spiritual interpretation of the war and of the fight for international peace. Just as clearly, the progressive clergy embraced Wilson as the best representative of their hopes and ideals. Even some in the secular press pictured Wilson as above all a spiritual leader. On the eve of the peace conference, *Current Opinion* thought it appropriate that so religious a goal as world peace—"an entire new world-order of peace, fraternity and mutual helpfulness"—was being championed by a president so deeply rooted in the church. Wilson's desire to see the world ruled by "altruism," the magazine noted, was at heart a Christian impulse: "His revolutionary program is really the application of the principles of Christian missions to the realm of statecraft." This observation was precisely the point the social gospel had been making for decades, and now it seemed that America's president had set out to implement the movement's most cherished ideals. "President Wilson," *Current Opinion* concluded, "has made himself the religious leader of the new era." It was now up to the church to follow this prophet and to be the regenerating spirit behind a renewed world.[47]

Religious progressives supported the formation of a league of nations as a logical and necessary extension of their Christian ideals of service and fraternity, and therefore as another step closer to the kingdom of God on earth. Moreover, a league was essential to justify the war and its suffering, including the battle death or injury of over three hundred thousand Americans. The war against German barbarism, after all, had been waged for peace; the "pacifists" had consistently rationalized it as such. If international cooperation failed, then the dead had died in vain and the church had failed.

It was with some urgency, then, that immediately after the war New York pastor Charles Jefferson called upon his fellow Christians "to insist upon the creation of a League of Nations thru whose tribunals all international disputes shall be brought to the arbitrament of reason."[48] Later he urged America to take up its "cross," to "sacrifice" once again for humanity, "to discard tradition, to depart from precedent." He promised that in the effort to unite the world, "we are moving in the direction the God of history has unmistakably indicated."[49] Similarly, Robert Speer, soon to be elected president of the Federal Council, described the league as "an indispensable and unavoidable implication of all our Christian faith and endeavour in the world."[50] And Harry Emerson Fosdick told his congregation at "Old First" on Fifth Avenue in New York, the site of the 1897 commemoration of the Westminster Confession, that "the endeavor for a League of Nations is the greatest forward step that humanity has dared to take since the abolition of the slave trade." Departing from its accustomed reserve, the congregation applauded Fosdick's challenge.[51]

While the progressives portrayed the league as the necessary extension of Christianity and the inevitable result of the war, they also supported it as a means of perpetuating the war's spirit of service and self-sacrifice. Charles Jefferson summarized the liberals' postwar enthusiasm well when he connected America, the servant nation, to the league:

> If we are true to our high calling, we shall always remain a servant. It is America's high mission among the nations to be the servant of all. We are big and rich and strong, and therefore our service should be constant and generous. There is no permanent happiness for us as a people unless we go up and down the earth doing good. Our foreordained place is in a League of Nations because God created us to serve.[52]

Appealing to an unlikely image, unlikely at least for a Protestant minister who might otherwise have been expected to represent the Atonement as a finished work, Jefferson pictured Christ perpetually suffering on the cross, "dying in order to build a better world." The immanent God suffered with mankind during the war and continued to do so during the peace. The war had taught the need for "great and constant self-sacrifice." Without such ongoing sacrifice, it would be impossible "for humanity to be saved."[53] The progressive clergy's image of America as the suffering servant—as the crucified Messiah—continued undiminished into the postwar era.

Liberal Protestantism's ultimate purpose for international federation was the establishment of the kingdom of God. The social gospel movement considered its great theological achievement to have been the rediscovery of the kingdom idea in the teachings of Jesus. The League of Na-

tions, therefore, as an application of that teaching, was not simply a prag-
matic system for avoiding future conflict, but rather the fulfillment of a
spiritual ideal, the nearer realization of God's righteous rule among the
nations.

On the eve of the Paris peace conference, the Executive Committee
of the Federal Council of Churches discussed the peace and the league.
Sidney Gulick presented a resolution, adopted by the business committee, that praised the league as nothing less than "the political expression"
of the kingdom of God on earth. "What is the Kingdom of God," he asked,
"if it be not the triumph of God's will in the affairs of men . . . ? And what
is this vision of a world-federation of humanity . . . if it be not an international manifestation of the Kingdom of God?"[54] The progressive clergy
had defined the Great War in exaggerated and absolute terms, and they
now transformed the peace process into the same sort of transcendent,
ultimate battle for righteousness. As God's explicit will, the league could
not be opposed; it was, as one church-worker wrote, part of "the perfect
fruition of the Kingdom of God," as inevitable as "the ripening of the har-
vest."[55]

At the Federal Council's meeting, Gulick also presented two resolutions in addition to his statement. The first called for the Federal Council
to collect the signatures of pastors who supported the league and then for
a delegation to be sent to Paris to present these names to Wilson. The
second resolution asked the churches of America to support the league as
"a vital part of the full program of the Kingdom of God."[56]

The Federal Council responded by sending a delegation to Paris in the
hope of meeting with Wilson. In Paris in January, Federal Council president Frank Mason North wrote to the president asking for an interview
to present the council's resolution, which represented, North claimed,
the "undoubted sentiment of the great Protestant citizenship of our country." In his enthusiasm, North told Wilson that he hoped the resolution
"might in some measure strengthen your own position and that of our
American delegates."[57] Wilson responded that he was too busy to receive
the Federal Council's delegation, but asked for a copy of the resolution,
reassuring North that he would give it "careful attention."[58] Several days
later the Church Peace Union's Frederick Lynch, also in Paris with the

Federal Council, wrote to Wilson on behalf of North and the other church leaders present, including Henry Churchill King and Hamilton Holt, the indefatigable champion of world federation. He reminded Wilson of the vigorous support the Federal Council was giving to the league. "They are strong," he wrote, "and they have behind them the whole Protestant body of America. They represent 33,000,000 people."[59]

Wilson needed little reminding of the religious impetus behind his work. On the same day Lynch wrote to him, Wilson had addressed one of the few meetings of all the delegates to the peace conference, pledging himself to continue the battle for righteousness. The American soldiers, he reminded the plenary session, had come to France "as crusaders, not merely to win the war, but to win a cause; and I am responsible to them, for it fell to me to formulate the purposes for which I asked them to fight, and I, like them, must be a crusader for these things whatever it costs."[60] Lynch praised Wilson's speech, believing that it had "ushered in a new era in the history of the world."[61]

Within five months the Allies concluded their negotiations at Versailles and delivered the peace treaty to the Germans on May 7, 1919. That same day, back in the United States, the Federal Council of Churches was in the midst of a special session called to promote the league. They adopted a message to the churches entitled "From World War to World Brother-hood.""The great war for world freedom and righteousness has been fought and won," they declared. Now, in Paris, the victorious powers worked "to apply Christian principles to the dealings of nations with one another" in the form of a League of Nations. It was the clear and present duty of the churches to give "their fullest support to such a League." To the church belonged the opportunity to begin the world over, to "build Christian civilization anew in accordance with the mind of Him whose purpose and passion were the establishment on earth of the Kingdom of God."[62] Sup-posedly, Jesus had striven for such a day as this. The ambition of the social gospel movement and the object of its war for righteousness was to be realized at last.

The unbounded faith of the Federal Council in its divine mission was matched only by that of President Wilson and his administration. Ger-many, faced with the prospect of renewed fighting, signed the Treaty of

Versailles on June 28, 1919, five years to the day since the assassination in Sarajevo of Archduke Franz Ferdinand. Within the week, Wilson's son-in-law, Secretary of the Treasury William G. McAdoo, addressed the Methodist Centenary Celebration in Columbus, Ohio, on the role of the church in the fight for the league. He knew just how to clothe the league for this high-minded audience. He commended Christianity as "the greatest spiritual and moral force in the world," and he warned that the church's influence was desperately needed to secure peace. He admonished the churches to cooperate with each other, claiming that their unity was "essential for the world's salvation." McAdoo seemed to think that Jesus' Great Commission had gotten even larger during the Great War. He called for all the marshaled forces of the "Church militant" to ensure that the gains of the "titanic struggle" would not be lost. He realized that warfare was of course "abhorrent to every Christian instinct and principle," and congratulated the church for condoning "war only when it was convinced that the Christian objective—world peace—could be obtained by no other means." To guarantee that hard-won peace, he asked the church to allow no compromise of the league. America had been founded in a struggle against autocracy, and the war for democracy waged valiantly since 1776 could not be abandoned now.[63]

Soon after McAdoo's speech, President Wilson returned from Paris and faced the Senate, which had to approve the treaty. In his address to the Senate on July 10, Wilson appealed to the authority of God Himself to persuade the body to accept the treaty. "The stage is set, the destiny disclosed," he cautioned them: "It has come about by no plan of our conceiving, but by the hand of God who led us into this way. We cannot turn back. We can only go forward, with lifted eyes and freshened spirit, to follow the vision. It was of this that we dreamed at our birth. America shall in truth show the way."[64] The treaty was God's doing. Wilson and the United States were simply tools in the hand of God to advance His cause, a purpose at work in American history since the Founding. To reject the treaty was to defy both God and destiny, and to spend the years ahead wandering in the wilderness rather than entering the Promised Land.

But Wilson found that he had to part the waters of opposition before he could cross into Canaan. And criticism came from some unexpected sources. Because of several harsh provisions, the Versailles treaty was not popular among some of the progressive clergy. The war had been fought, however vindictively, for the sake of world unity, and the treaty appeared to threaten that overriding concern. It had been a war for righteousness and liberal objectives, and the treaty seemed anything but liberal. Harry Emerson Fosdick wanted a mild peace imposed on Germany in order to see that chastened nation returned as quickly as possible to normal relations with the rest of the world. Like the Germans, he thought the treaty violated Wilson's Fourteen Points, which had been offered as the basis of the Armistice in the first place.[65]

In September 1919, while President Wilson made his exhausting tour through the Midwest to win ratification, the *Christian Century* announced its disapproval of the treaty. It saw the league articles as "the one saving feature of the Treaty," which otherwise was "unjust and vicious," a flat betrayal of a war fought for brotherhood and democracy. The terms of the treaty were "punitive, vindictive, and terrorizing" to Germany. As such, they "are not redemptive, and are therefore not Christian." The progressive clergy had fought the war to extend the power of applied Christianity, and the treaty threatened to undo that work. According to the *Christian Century,* the treaty was a throwback to "the old dispensation," and its provisions doomed internationalism and the "new order." The *Christian Century* had at one time published the wartime ravings of Newell Dwight Hillis and had in its editorials waged a holy crusade, but as deep as its antagonism toward Germany had been, the vengeful treaty seemed only to portend "another Prussia" and another horrible war.[66]

Despite its reservations over the treaty, the *Christian Century* praised the league for what it promised, calling it an "extension" of the kingdom of God. The editors claimed to be at a loss to understand any opposition to it. After all, the league was "the thing all Christians pray for when they say, 'Thy Kingdom Come.'" The *Christian Century,* therefore, had "no sympathy" with the treaty's enemies in the Senate, who perversely objected to the league's idealism. Their views were "opposite" to the *Christian Century*. But a source of further and unexpected discouragement was Wilson himself, who inscrutably refused to amend the league for the sake of salvaging even fragments of a new world order.[67]

According to the progressive clergy, America's role in the history of redemption had been laid out by God. Within His moral universe, to impede the world's salvation was to stand where Germany had dared to interpose itself from 1914 to 1918. But the Senate took that chance and delayed ratification. Some members hoped to add reservations; others hoped to kill the treaty. In September, the Federal Council's Committee on the Moral Aims of the War put all its effort behind ratification. With financial backing from the Church Peace Union and the League to Enforce Peace, the committee mailed background information on the treaty and the League of Nations to eighty thousand ministers. As a result of its appeal, the committee delivered a petition to the Senate in January 1920 bearing the names of some seventeen thousand ministers.[68] The month before, the Federal Council had urged ministers to try to influence the president and the Senate, acknowledging that perhaps some concessions were necessary.[69] But Wilson would not compromise and refused to accept reservations. The treaty went down to final defeat in the Senate on March 19, 1920. Defying both Woodrow Wilson and the will of God, the United States Senate rejected the League of Nations.

9

RIGHTEOUSNESS POSTPONED

THE PROGRESSIVE CLERGY'S ENDURING WORLDVIEW

IN 1924, THE YEAR OF Woodrow Wilson's death, Harvard professor Irving Babbitt noted the passing of America's faith in progress—at least its faith in the nineteenth century's version of progress with its inexorable movement toward "civilization" and its confusion of material and moral improvement. Already recognized as the dividing line of modern history, the Great War in hindsight seemed to separate the attitudes of the 1920s from the lost world of the nineteenth century. The war had intruded upon the earlier era's daydream and challenged its presuppositions. Pondering the timing of this awakening, Babbitt noted that "some persons began to have doubts on this point even before the war, others had their doubts awakened by the war itself, and still others have been made doubtful by the peace." What could "progress" possibly mean in a world that had hurled itself into the abyss of the Great War? Perhaps the idea itself was to blame, Babbitt suggested. Anticipating Christopher Dawson's trenchant critique of progress by more than five years, Babbitt mused that "an age that thought it was progressing toward a 'far-off divine event,' and turned out instead to be progressing toward Armageddon, suffered, one cannot help surmising, from some fundamental confusion in its notion of progress."[1] In his typical Socratic method, Babbitt traced postwar disillusionment to a problem of definition.

Princeton theologian J. Gresham Machen also examined the nature of progress in the modern world. He noted in 1923 that while the world had certainly advanced materially over the generations, "in all other respects it exhibits a lamentable decline." "The improvement appears in the physical conditions of life," he continued, "but in the spiritual realm there is a corresponding loss." His theological adversaries, the prophets of progress, had promised a worldwide spiritual and cultural renewal in the new era following the war, but Machen discerned only decline. From his point of view, the emerging society was sterile, a place devoid of poetry, art, and human freedom, an age that seemed to have nothing but contempt for the achievements of the past.[2]

For realists like Babbitt and Machen, this critique of progress did not amount to disillusionment, for no one could have accused either of these conservatives of having fallen prey to an idyllic imagination. Among progressives, on the other hand, any such heretical doubt in human progress posed a serious threat to their entire worldview and to their theological, social, and foreign policy agenda. Nevertheless, as early as 1917, progressives were in fact reconsidering the kind of progress possible in a world that seemed to have gone so far astray. In what amounted to an obituary for faith in inevitable progress, an essayist for the *New Republic* bade farewell to Victorian optimism in the summer of 1917. Along with men and material, the author suggested, the war had consumed the nineteenth century's "secular deity of progress," a facile faith in inevitable biological and social evolution. Deterministic, predestined progress had died on the battlefields of Europe: "Ten million men have perished to prove that progress is not automatic, not comfortable, and not in any way a law of nature; even more, that there are dark forces that tear at the fabric of civilization as fast as it is woven." Nevertheless, the essay continued, meaningful progress was still possible in a torn and frayed world. Humanity's abrupt awakening was a chance to replace the Victorians' easy reliance on the natural flow of history with the new age's earnest determination to rebuild the world "by unceasing struggle."[3] The war prompted not so much a discussion about the degree of, or potential for, progress, but rather about the inevitability of progress. Among the progressives, only their faith in a certain kind of progress perished in the war.

Confirming Babbitt's conclusion about the timing of doubt in progress, the progressive clergy voiced their own concern about history's inevitable tendency even before the war. As historian William Hutchison noted, introspection and self-examination had actually appeared in liberal Protestantism quite early. While "progressive optimism" continued to dominate their thought, a serious "critique" had emerged that scrutinized some liberal assumptions. Indeed, before the war a handful of progressive theologians had ventured off into pragmatism and radical empiricism.[4] Yet despite this searching critique, their faith persisted in God's immanence, in progress toward the kingdom of God, and in adaptation as the key to the survival of Christianity in the modern world.

Other progressive clergy came to doubt inevitable progress during the war and shared in the general wartime reevaluation of progress. Henry Sloane Coffin, pastor of New York's Madison Avenue Presbyterian Church and professor at Union Theological Seminary, described the world as "tragic" in 1918. In his Lyman Beecher Lecture at Yale University, Coffin conceded that there was some benefit to starting over with "a world that has been 'shivered to atoms,'" but denied that the world contained within itself any natural propensity toward the good. The world was a place of sin that required "judgment and redemption." The war had awakened Coffin to the fact "that we live in a vastly more tragic world than we had supposed, where things that are wrong, if unchecked, get worse and work out to hideous catastrophe." But like the *New Republic,* Coffin thought that this recognition of the world's sinfulness should not cause despair, but instead stimulate greater activity. He urged his Yale audience to fan the fire of the war's crusading spirit, "to keep that holy wrath ablaze, and to direct it to the destruction, both abroad and at home, of those things which mar human brotherhood."[5]

Yale Divinity School president and former Mohonk speaker Charles Reynolds Brown also credited the war with having overturned the idea of inevitable, linear progress. The war, he wrote, marked the end of "Evolution, with a capital E." But Brown did not question the fundamental progressive assumptions about Christianity's duty in the world or its relationship to the war. He believed, in fact, that if there had been "enough Christianity on hand in 1914," the war never would have come. In other words, Christianity had both the mandate and the ability, given the chance, to free the world from war. With some satisfaction he pointed out that it was Germany, after all, the least Christian nation, that had caused the war, and England, the most Christian, that had struggled to avoid it. To Brown, the war provided encouraging evidence of the presence of the spirit of Christian service in the world.[6] So while the war may have ended the idea of inevitable progress, it had done little by the immediate postwar period to shake the progressives' belief in their ability to eradicate evil through institutional reform.

The tragedy of 1914–1918 had raised doubts in the minds of liberal Protestants about the true nature of progress, but it had not prompted anything resembling real disillusionment. Even when they used the word "disillusionment," it denoted a hopeful, productive change in attitude, signifying that the war had caused the world to contemplate its true moral state and to consider its deepest needs. Such disillusionment, like the remorse of the sinner at the mourner's bench, signaled the approach of spiritual rebirth. They hoped that the war would produce the sorrow that leads to repentance, not to despair. As the *Christian Century* had remarked in this connection in 1914, those nations such as the United States which witnessed the catastrophe had been "shocked into a mood of profound meditation, disillusionment and inquiry that is pregnant with new and great impulses toward God and spiritual life." This was not the debilitating doubt looked back upon as an inescapable by-product of so horrible a war, but rather the pangs of conscience necessary for national repentance. Thus, the *Christian Century* could talk in the same breath both of "disillusionment" and of Christ's rebirth in the war-torn world.[7]

A deeper, more authentic reevaluation of liberal assumptions seemed to be indicated by professor John Buckham of the Pacific School of Theology, who criticized the prewar New Theology for being "too optimistic." In 1919 he admitted that the world was much farther from the reign of Christianity than progressive theology had assumed. Nevertheless, Buckham found nothing fundamentally wrong with the theology itself, only with the disappointing extent to which it had been applied to everyday life. The progressive clergy's activist theology had not gone far enough toward reconstructing human thought and action. But now, faced with the war, Christians were compelled to acknowledge the stubborn presence of "the Christless elements and conditions in modern life." The dominant social forces before the war carried humanity "not to that progressive coming of the kingdom which it pictured but straight to the awful cataclysm which befell the world in 1914." This turn of events could not be ignored. Buckham acknowledged that he had been among those who had expected the imminent arrival of "the golden age." Every enthusiasm of the day—social reform, missions, and internationalism—had seemed to indicate that the kingdom of God was very near. Nevertheless, to Buckham the appropriate response to the war's "harsh awakening" was not despair, but rather a "reinforcement of faith," a commitment to a new hope, to "the vision that arises afresh from the ruins of the old order," one that was even "better and larger . . . than that attending the advent of the twentieth century."[8] Righteousness had not been defeated; it had merely been postponed.

Coming closer to a genuine critique of the progressives' war for righteousness, the Reverend William Austin Smith, editor of the Episcopal *Churchman,* had some harsh words for the church's attitude during the war. Speaking before the Congress of the Protestant Episcopal Church in April 1919, Smith criticized his fellow ministers for ever thinking that the war would lead the world to a deeper spiritual life. To promise such results was "an immoral thesis," and religion could only suffer by such a confusion of values. At the heart of the church's embrace of the war, Smith charged, was the perilous idea that the war's "ecstasy and romanticism" were "emotionally identical with the Christian experience of the Cross." Moreover, "the Church appeared to confuse patriotism with religion throughout the war." Smith thought it unconscionable for Christians to rejoice in the presumed spiritual benefits of a war that had cost the lives of millions and had "bathed the world in hate and darkness."[9]

Such a conclusion seemed to indicate that the war experience had prompted deep reflection on first principles and definitions. And, indeed, Smith was embarrassed at his own wartime use of the phrase "a new world." Looking back, he admitted that he did not know what he had meant by the words. He asked his audience to name any evidence in the postwar situation of the presence of the kingdom of God. "If the new world is here," he sighed, "most of us would confess that it isn't so awfully nice after all." And yet like other ministers, despite his obvious despair over the condition of the world, Smith wanted to fulfill his own promises of a new age. Despite being surrounded by a world bathed in "hate and darkness," he did not seem to question the possibility of a new age. He charged that Christianity, finding itself in the midst of "one of the open spaces of history," had the duty to "apply its creed to the wrongs that waste and cramp the lives of men." Although such pessimism seemed to indicate a disjuncture in the thought of postwar Protestantism, the goal had not changed; social reconstruction through an "applied creed" remained the objective of an activist Christianity. If anything, the war had intensified the church's sense of urgency. Ignoring his earlier admonition against confusing piety with mere emotional passion, Smith called for the "romanticists" in the church to forge ahead and "claim the world for Christ." In spite of his own advice not to confuse patriotism and religion, by the end of his lecture he had once again clothed the war in spiritual terms. The war had demonstrated that God was truly at work to make something "superbly beautiful . . . of man's life on earth," and this war of liberty had released a "spirit of freedom" that would transform the world.[10]

Despite the clergy's best efforts to breathe new life into wartime idealism, it was clear to many of them that the mood in America was changing rapidly, and that the new attitude would present them with a problem. Social gospel advocate Charles D. Williams, bishop of the Episcopal Church who had served in France with the Red Cross, identified in 1921 what he believed to be the spirit of the age. "That outstanding characteristic, that dominant note," the Reverend Williams observed, "is disillusionment, with all its natural and spiritually disastrous consequences." He could only hope that this current disposition would be temporary. It had to be, for such despair was "disheartening to all idealists and reformers."[11]

Williams attributed the rise of disillusionment to the betrayal of the war's objectives. The war had stimulated the American people to "high idealism" and they had rightfully expected great results. President Wilson, foremost among the "preachers of righteousness," had led the nation into a war for democracy, peace, and the end of "tyranny." Americans believed that they had waged the "battle of Armageddon" and that the forces of

Christ had triumphed. There had been nothing wrong with the war's ideals, but rather with the fact that those ideals had not been fulfilled. Now in the early 1920s, the League of Nations was in shambles, and Europe seemed to be on the verge of anarchy rather than at the threshold of redemption. Even saintly America was sinking into materialism and national selfishness, Williams charged; it was acting almost like the old pagan Germany. Reactionary forces, evident in the Red Scare and in the suppression of free speech, were emerging, and even the pulpits were turning against the idea of "Christianizing the social order." Significantly, though, Williams considered the postwar period not as a time to reevaluate his ideals, but rather as a time for greater effort in the face of greater need. The church's crusade for the kingdom of God on earth could not retreat.[12] Unlike Babbitt, Machen, and other critics, he was unwilling to question the ideals themselves.

In the immediate postwar years, then, a range of liberal Protestants discounted the inevitability of progress and admitted that the war had not immediately achieved their social gospel objectives as they had promised. Nonetheless, they renewed their crusade to "Christianize" America and the world. At times, this later zeal for a world reborn surpassed even the seemingly boundless enthusiasm of the days before the war. The progressive clergy, in the wake of the war, may have doubted inevitable progress, but did not yet question their competency or their divine commission to remake the world.

In 1920, the Federal Council of Churches held its fourth national conference, and in the report of its activities since its last meeting in 1916, Samuel McCrea Cavert summarized the council's work. True to the spirit of its founding, he reported, the council continued to promote world evangelism, the Christianizing of America, and international brotherhood. But, Cavert warned, blocking the path to the founding of the "Kingdom of Love upon the earth" stood a divisive "cynicism" that cast doubt on world brotherhood as a reasonable goal. Through its own unity, therefore, the church had to be an example for the world to follow by ignoring its differences in devotion to "common tasks." The key question facing the thirty denominations assembled in Boston in 1920, Cavert continued, was how best to infuse the social order, both at home and abroad, with the "Christian spirit," how the churches could "be more efficient in Christianizing America for the service of the world." The continuity within progressive Christianity between its prewar and postwar idealism could not have been clearer. The liberal church still intended to reshape America and the world. Chief among the Federal Council's objectives in 1920 was the "securing of international brotherhood" and a dedication to "the service of Christ that His Kingdom might more fully come upon the earth." Indeed, the council in 1920 believed their organization had come to its "supreme hour of responsibility and opportunity."[13]

That the progressive church renewed its commitment to social service after the war is evident in a striking comment by missionary and evangelist Sherwood Eddy. Eddy, who had spent part of the war working with the American Expeditionary Force in France, claimed in his memoirs that his awakening to the social significance of his Christian faith actually followed his involvement in the war. This was the same Eddy who had toured China before the war in the hope of Westernizing that nation socially and politically through the reconstructive power of Christianity. Despite the fact that his missionary zeal always had been defined by its social implications, he recalled that after the war religion became for him a "*social* experience." In fact, he was certain that he shared this same realization "with thousands of others after the war." The war in his estimation had pushed the progressives further along toward an activist, socialized church. The sequence is instructive. While social gospel ideals had caused many of the progressive clergy to interpret the war in a certain way, for Eddy the war, so he claimed, had caused him to reinterpret the gospel, and not back in the direction of a more conventional, narrow definition of the church's role in the world, but to a much more expansive view. To Eddy, the postwar social gospel meant "economic justice," the end of class and racial division, "clean politics," world peace and fraternity, as well as other temporal reforms. As for Christianity itself, he sought "nothing less than a New Reformation . . . that religion may be thoroughly vitalized, rationalized, moralized, and socialized."[14]

This same observation about a more "socialized" postwar Christianity was made by Shailer Mathews. In 1927 he recounted the recent history of the social gospel and noted the persistent enthusiasm for reform of an era usually remembered as a time of retrenchment, reaction, and isolationism. He observed that while the theoretical groundwork for "social Christianity" had been laid before the war, since that transforming experience, with few exceptions, authors were "more concerned with the discussion of concrete problems" and pastors were "deeply interested in reforms of all sorts." As proof, he cited the growing interest in labor issues and industrial strikes, and recalled with satisfaction that the Federal Council in its activities on behalf of labor had earned the wrath of the Manufacturers' Association in Pittsburgh and of "similar organizations of capital." He also pointed to the growing concern, despite the pessimism of premillennialists and German "crisis" theologians, for world peace and better race relations, the success of Prohibition, and the movement toward church unity. Overall, he claimed, it was evident that the Protestant churches at home and abroad embraced "the social bearing of Christianity as beyond dispute."[15]

Internationalism continued to demonstrate the progressive church's "social bearing," and best illustrated its postwar idealism. The church's supreme objective was still, as Samuel McCrea Cavert pointed out in 1920, the "Christianizing of America for the service of the world." The best opportunity for such world service presented itself soon after the war in the 1921 Washington Armaments Conference. The Federal Council of Churches and other religious groups appealed directly to President Warren G. Harding for an international disarmament conference, flooding him with more than twenty thousand pleas from America's clergy. Responding to pressure from a number of sources, including budget-conscious taxpayers, and no stranger to the idea of America's continuing role as a servant nation, Harding obliged.[16]

Delegates from nine nations convened in Washington on November 11, 1921—Armistice Day. The international body gathered at Arlington Cemetery with President Harding for the burial of the Unknown Soldier. Harding addressed a crowd of one hundred thousand that had come to the tomb to honor the nation's war dead, and his words were carried by radio to countless others. Sounding rather Wilsonian, he reminded his listeners of their country's "unselfishness among nations" and challenged America to give its "influence and strength" to the task of putting "mankind on a little higher plane . . . with war's distressing and depressing tragedies barred from the stage of righteous civilization." The American soldier had "fired his shot for liberation of the captive conscience of the world." Harding thought it appropriate that the remains of a nameless representative soldier should be entombed within sight of the Capitol, the Washington Monument, and the new memorial to Lincoln, "the martyred savior," in Harding's words. He closed by leading the crowd in the Lord's Prayer: ". . . Thy kingdom come, Thy will be done on earth as it is in heaven."[17]

At the Washington conference's opening session, the delegates heard again from President Harding and then from Secretary of State Charles Evans Hughes. The spectators included William Jennings Bryan and H. G. Wells. In a calculated and dramatic moment, Secretary Hughes startled the delegates and the press by proposing real and substantial cuts in naval armaments. Over the next several weeks the major powers, including the United States, Britain, France, Italy, and Japan agreed to halt for ten years the construction of large naval vessels. In a second treaty, four of the powers agreed to arbitrate disputes, and in a third, nine nations promised to honor the Open Door in China.[18]

The Federal Council of Churches' commitment to the success of the Washington Naval Conference was extraordinary. It issued several pamphlets about the international meeting, including two hundred thousand copies of "The Church and a Warless World," one hundred thousand of "Working Towards a Warless World," and nearly a quarter million other various "leaflets." The Federal Council turned once again to the habitual prewar and wartime metaphor of the crusade. One of the Council's pamphlets was entitled "The New Crusade," and by the following September Sidney Gulick had published The Christian Crusade for a Warless World. Aside from this propaganda effort, the council actively lobbied the administration and the Senate to ratify the Washington agreements, and appealed to pastors and church members across America to petition the conference for decisive action. The Advisory Committee of the Washington Conference reported that they received nearly fourteen million letters concerning passage of the disarmament treaties, of which more than twelve and a half million were written "in a manner that showed that they were acting as the result of the campaign among the Churches." The Federal Council proudly announced that the Senate was deluged with "thousands upon thousands of letters and petitions."[19]

It seemed that at last the elusive goal of a world freed from war was close at hand. But the Federal Council's plans for building a fraternal world order were by no means limited to the Washington conference. Consistent with its continuing campaign for a "warless world," the council also lobbied Congress for American participation in the International Court of Justice as well as for closer ties to the League of Nations. Moreover, the Federal Council sent mailings to nearly one hundred thousand churches in order "to arouse public opinion on the necessity for the United States' accepting its full moral responsibility for the protection of the oppressed minorities" in the Near East. Specifically, the council called for the United States to intervene for the "assistance and protection" of the Armenians from the Turks, and in September 1922 it asked President Harding to protect Smyrna, which had been burned in the aftermath of the Turkish-Greek War of 1921–1922. Harding refused to involve the United States directly, but he did send two destroyers to Smyrna for humanitarian aid and to protect American lives and property.[20]

Behind these direct proposals for an activist, interventionist American foreign policy lay the progressive clergy's persistent ideals: the image of America as a messianic nation, a continuing faith in progress, and a powerful crusading spirit. Heralding the advent of the twentieth-century messiah, one of the most astonishing books to emerge from the progressive church in the postwar era appeared in 1922. Samuel Zane Batten, the author who, before the war, had proposed the virtual union of church and state in America for the sake of the social gospel, expanded his vision with *If America Fail,* an impassioned plea for America to fulfill its mission of world redemption. Batten began by reaffirming his faith in God as "a God of history," as one "who calls nations to great historic tasks." He proposed that by its geographic situation alone, linking two oceans, the United States appeared "destined to play a leading role in the world history during the next thousand years and may have much to do with the progress of the kingdom of God." To Batten, America's destiny was the destiny of the kingdom of God. America had to accept its status as "an elect nation" and fulfill its role in "universal history." If it failed, America risked postponing "the redemption of the human race and the progress of the kingdom of God."[21]

In defending America's status as God's elect nation, Batten appealed to such authorities as American historian George Bancroft, English Civil War leader Oliver Cromwell, and transcendentalist Ralph Waldo Emerson, who all, he noted, possessed a strong sense of the presence of God in history. Once posit that God indwells history, Batten claimed, and the conclusion to be drawn from current history was inevitable: "America is indeed a called and chosen nation." In fact, nations were every bit as elect and commissioned as individual Christians. The central premise of the social gospel, the assumption that made an applied Christianity work at all—that institutions, communities, and nations were under the same imperatives, constraints, and blessings of God as were individuals—continued unimpeded into the postwar era. As Batten understood it, "the nation is but the person writ large."[22]

Batten looked back upon the Great War as a blessing to America. At last his country had turned aside from its noninterventionist foreign policy. The war had taught Americans "that we can not stand apart as mere spectators; it has called us out of our isolation and has given us a stake in the world life as an active participant." Confident of America's new role in the world, Batten declared that "from this time forward things will be different with us, and a new national policy is imperative." There would be no retreat into postwar isolation for Batten.[23]

While before the war, Batten had not hesitated to unite the realms of God and Caesar into a single divine social system, he continued in the postwar era to mix prophecy and politics, claiming that in "using the history of Israel as a key we may interpret our own history." To Batten, historical events in the life of America were actually "prophetic events," through which the nation could "read the will of God."[24] The progressive clergy had long taught that God was immanent within His evolving creation and that human history was the progressive revelation of His perfect will, to culminate one day in His righteous kingdom. As the current centerpiece of this divine revelation, America was delegated by God to expand democracy at home and abroad and to *create a Christian civilization.* Such an outcome for the world was God's will, and therefore it had to be achieved. America was *"called to fulfil a Messianic service among the nations."* Indeed, as was true of the individual or the church, "the nation . . . is to live for the same purpose as that which moved Jesus Christ up Calvary."[25]

Rather than exhibiting any doubt or disillusionment, Batten recommitted America—the Christ-nation—to perpetual self-sacrifice for the sins of the world. Americans were "to give our children and our wealth to service and witness for the great principles of the kingdom," that is, for the regenerating ideals of "liberty, equality, and fraternity." America represented the future of humanity; it anticipated and embodied the tendency of the whole world, for "America is a gospel, . . . an interpretation of the kingdom of God, the far-off goal of history." The people of the United States bore "the clear stamp of God" upon them, and they stood "at the very forefront in the march of time." America was the world's best hope for democracy and for civilization, God's chosen instrument, and she could not disappoint the peoples of the earth. Looking toward America as a shining example, Batten continued, "the nations of the earth turn toward us in hope and longing, feeling that the time of their deliverance is at hand."[26] In 1920, Wilson's propagandist George Creel used identical imagery, claiming that during the war "the world, hopeless, despairing, turned to us as the forlorn of Galilee turned to Christ, not knowing, but believing; not asking, but trusting."[27] This imagery pervaded postwar rhetoric inside and outside the church. Virginia Congressman Carter Glass appealed to this symbol in 1921 when he expressed his disappointment over the rejection of Wilson—"the greatest Christian statesman of all time"—and the defeat of the Versailles treaty. The League Covenant, he claimed, "was the consummation, as far as Christian nations could contrive, of the sacrifice on Calvary."[28] For America to fail to bring the redemption it had promised was unthinkable.

While perpetuating their image of America as the international messiah, the progressive clergy also retained their faith in progress, or at least a belief in the possibility of progress. In 1922, Harry Emerson Fosdick delivered the Cole Lectures at Vanderbilt University. He followed in a line of distinguished speakers that included Henry Churchill King, Charles E. Jefferson, William H. P. Faunce, and Robert E. Speer. As part of the Cole series, Fosdick's six lectures were required to be "a defense and advocacy

of the Christian religion," and he chose as his subject the reconciliation of
Christianity with the modern idea of progress. What is so striking about
these lectures is that Fosdick identified "progress" not as the perishing
ideal of a lost world but rather as the "new outlook" dominating philosophical thought in 1922. Echoing progressive Christianity's earlier and
similar efforts to reconcile its faith with Darwinism, Fosdick proposed
that Christianity now had to decide "what her attitude shall be toward this
new and powerful force, the idea of progress, which in every realm is
remaking man's thinking."[29]

Fosdick acknowledged that the nineteenth century's view of progress
had been naïve, and that many of his contemporaries had abandoned their
former faith in inevitable improvement. In light of the fact that sentimental progress now faced ideas of limit and constraint—such as the physical
decay of the universe—mankind required a doctrine more rigorous than
the "soft gospel of inevitable progress." But lest he seem disillusioned,
Fosdick then offered a more scientific idea of progress. Granted, there
were limitations, but through control both of the power of nature and of
"our own mental and moral processes within, we have a machinery for
producing change that opens up exciting prospects before humanity." To
Fosdick, the days ahead still looked brighter than the days behind. "We are
committed to the hope of making progress," he promised, and Christianity needed to come "to intelligent terms with this dominant idea."[30]

No matter how modified Fosdick might have believed his new version
of progress to be, it differed little in any meaningful way from the old. He
even praised H. G. Wells's portrait of God as supplying the best reflection
of what "modern folk" believed in: a God who called "people to a progressive crusade for righteousness." Compatible with that end, the church functioned as "an instrument in God's hands to bring personal and social righteousness upon the earth." While he now questioned the ability of war to
achieve that righteousness, he did not shrink from the fight for national
and international regeneration.[31]

Fosdick warned that Christianity's greatest foe in this new age of
progress was reactionary thinking. As the rest of society embraced "growth
as the universal law" and relied on "controlled change as the hope of man,"
Christianity could not retreat into sublime resignation. By trying to re-

main changeless in a world of change, Christianity "outlawed itself from its own age." Perhaps having the Fundamentalists' counterargument in mind, Fosdick warned that "stagnation, not change, is Christianity's most deadly enemy, for this is a progressive world, and in a progressive world no doom is more certain than that which awaits whatever is belated, obscurantist and reactionary."[32] The progressive clergy had always claimed that they were saving Christianity from destruction at the hands of traditionalists, and they continued to promote adaptation as the best tactic for the survival of Christianity in the postwar world.

Apparently, faith in progress was so strong after the war that Fosdick could actually criticize the American people for being too optimistic, for continuing to hold onto a Victorian notion "of automatic progress toward an earthly paradise." He warned that true progress, an idea grounded in reality, had to take into account the presence of evil in the world and the reality "of personal and social sin."[33] Perhaps Fosdick's call for a new sense of sin had been engendered by the war, but the social gospel had always claimed the same need for a social conviction of sin and responsibility. With the exception of renouncing war as an acceptable Christian policy, which in itself was a significant development in his thought, Fosdick's view of the world in 1922 was not qualitatively different from that preceding the war. Having witnessed the Great War firsthand in France, he could still say in 1922 that "in a world which out of lowly beginnings has climbed so far and seems intended to go on to heights unimagined, God is our hope and in his name we will set up our banners."[34]

But other banners were being unfurled in 1922. Benito Mussolini came to power in Italy, and the world's "heights unimagined" were about to include Adolf Hitler and the Great Depression. Despite his faith in rational, scientific progress, Fosdick recognized the presence of evil in the world and began to reevaluate his acceptance of war as a means of social progress. By the early twenties he identified warfare as the chief of sinners among society's malefactors. The "pacifist" progressive theologians who had accepted war as a means to peace had always claimed that one day humanity would outgrow war, and for Fosdick that time had come. In 1923 he called war "the most colossal and ruinous social sin that afflicts mankind today; . . . it is utterly and irremediably unchristian." Either civilization would awaken to the irrationality of war or be damned. At the root of the world's evil lay the "war system," which rejected Jesus' teachings and which lived on as the most deadly form of atheism. For the future, Fosdick could not picture himself ever "sanctioning or participating in another war."[35]

Fosdick in 1923 reversed the rebuke that Joseph Odell had leveled against the church in 1918, when Odell criticized the church for acting in 1914 like the disciple Peter, who "sat by the fire warming himself" and who denied Jesus at the moment of His trial. The supposedly apathetic church had not entered the war for righteousness soon enough to suit Odell, but Fosdick charged the church of 1914 with a different kind of moral unpreparedness. The church had been "hypnotized by nationalism" and had embraced patriotism without discrimination as to its form. The church had absorbed the values of the world around it:

> In a word, behind the thin disguise of pious hopes for a day of peace and broth-erhood, we had shared those ordinary social attitudes which made war seem at times an imperious call to duty, a summons to self-sacrifice, a solemn chal-lenge to devotion and, if need be, martyrdom.

When the war came, the church was caught up in the spirit of the times. It had defended "the righteousness of war" and could not back out.[36] Despite his criticisms of war, however, in 1923 he still accepted America's global role and mission, and challenged the church to enter the new "crusade," as he called it, for international cooperation and organization.[37]

Although seeming to deal harshly with the church for uniting itself with the spirit of the age, Fosdick had but the year before recommended that Christianity make peace with the reigning idea of scientific progress. Moreover, his explanation for the church's attitude in 1914 rested on the assumption that the church had been blindly swept along by historical currents, when in fact many of the church's liberal leaders, including Fosdick himself, had led the charge into battle. The progressive church was not caught unaware by the war; it was not duped into an unthinking wartime enthusiasm. Rather, it marched forth into the war for righteous-ness, acting on its theology, its politics, its vision of an expansive Ameri-can foreign policy, and its philosophy of history. According to the progres-sive clergy's worldview, an immanent God struggled along with humanity to perfect society and the world; working through the Civil War, the Spanish-American War, and then the Great War, God had prepared the United States to be His Anointed One, ready for its shining moment in the history of redemption. Picturing America also as God's New Israel, the progressive clergy preached—well into the 1920s—that the United States was obligated to establish God's earthly kingdom of righteousness.

Even though often lamenting the consequences of the war, the progressive clergy looked back on their idealism not as dangerous, but as noble, as "magnificent."[38] Newspaper columnist Frank Crane was optimistic enough in 1924 to conclude that "as bad as the world may be today it is vastly better than it ever was before. The sentiment against cruelty, injustice, beastly living and war grows stronger every year"—all achieved through an increasing dependence on the social ideals of Jesus. Indeed, Crane continued, the revolutionary doctrines of the fatherhood of God and the brotherhood of man had "tumbled over the tyrannies and autocracies of the world one after another."[39] Expressing similar optimism, the Federal Council of Churches' president Robert E. Speer surveyed world events in 1924 and claimed that there was no need to "despair of the absolute transformation of the world."[40] Although Europe was falling under the shadow of fascism instead of emerging into the light of the new day, the progressive clergy still relied on humanitarian sentiment and good intentions to liberate the world.

This optimism was not shared by all Americans, however. The literary world of Hemingway, Dos Passos, and Fitzgerald had already surrendered to disillusionment, having "grown up to find all Gods dead, all wars fought, all faiths in man shaken," in F. Scott Fitzgerald's penetrating words.[41] And among both theological and secular thinkers, the progressive clergy and their idealism met aggressive opposition.

From Princeton Theological Seminary in 1923, J. Gresham Machen fired another salvo at Protestant liberalism in his *Christianity and Liberalism,* which Walter Lippmann later called "the best popular argument produced by either side in the current controversy."[42] Machen acknowledged the dramatic changes that had swept the world in the past hundred years, and he agreed with the liberals' assessment of the basic question facing Christianity in the contemporary world, namely, "What is the relation between Christianity and modern culture; may Christianity be maintained in a scientific age?" From this point on, however, he disagreed sharply with the progressive clergy. It was one thing to admit that the world was changing, but quite another to say that Christianity had to change along with it.

Machen proposed that liberalism had not rescued Christianity at all but rather had substituted something alien in its place. Liberalism had constructed an entirely new religion that diverged from the historic faith in every basic doctrine, from the nature of God and man, to the Bible, Christ, salvation, and the church. He rejected liberalism's view of God's immanence, its tendency to identify sin everywhere but within the human heart, and its fondness for statist collectivism. At the root of the problem he found liberalism's penchant for making Christianity a means to another end, for putting "applied Christianity" above more fundamental concerns. He granted the need for Christian influence in the world but lamented that "the liberal believes that applied Christianity is all there is of Christianity, Christianity being merely a way of life." Of its global aspirations, Machen complained that "the missionary of liberalism seeks to spread the blessings of Christian civilization (whatever that may be), and is not particularly interested in leading individuals to relinquish their pagan beliefs."[43] At the heart of the debate was the definition of Christianity's fundamental mission in the world.

In 1924 Irving Babbitt, another relentless critic of the progressives, pointed to the dark side of the "crusading spirit," a temper he considered to be the dominating feature of American life and thought, and which certainly typified the reformist clergy. This national idealism was so strong, he warned, that it was "becoming the dangerous privilege of the United States to display more of the crusading temper than any other country in both its domestic and its foreign policies." He noted how thin the line was that separated the desire of the "uplifters" for "sacrifice" from their desire for control. Prohibition and other reforms, he cautioned, were being driven by the "will to power." Moreover, President Wilson, he recalled, had required enormous power to carry the crusading spirit overseas in the name of "world service."[44] At the root of this imperial spirit lay national pride, the "expansive self" that Babbitt opposed throughout his career. He also warned how "firmly entrenched" the humanitarian spirit continued to be, "especially in academic circles, where it seems to be held more confidently, one is tempted to say more smugly, with each succeeding year."[45]

Although progressive idealism, optimism, and humanitarianism endured with surprising vigor into the postwar era, certain changes in attitude could be detected; although in the 1920s Harry Emerson Fosdick could claim that progress was the dominant idea of the era and Shailer Mathews could call social service the dominant impulse of the church, a reevaluation of the war and America's role in it was under way. In October 1925, the *Christian Century* published the first in a series of articles by noted revisionist historian Harry Elmer Barnes. The series, which asked "Was America Deluded by the War?," suggested that the American people had somehow been duped into participating in the recent conflict. Thus, with the revision of recent history begun, a genuine questioning of the progressives' "crusading spirit" emerged, a doubt especially evident in articles by the brothers H. Richard and Reinhold Niebuhr.[46] But this note of despair can easily be exaggerated, for throughout the twenties the *Christian Century* still talked of "Christianizing" society. In 1925 it advertised a hymnal from its own press that featured songs appropriate for "the new world order" and for "human service and brotherhood," and "democracy" and "world peace."[47] As late as 1928 the periodical was hailing the "outlawry of war" as touted by the Kellogg-Briand Pact.

But that same year Reinhold Niebuhr, a leader of what would be known as "Christian realism," reflected in the *Christian Century* on "What the War Did to My Mind." Claiming that the war had made him "a child of the age of disillusionment," he acknowledged that his generation had been forced to admit that "the war was after all not an anachronism":

> Some of us tried to escape the facts by regarding it as an accident or as the final adventure in the cause of righteousness. . . . [W]e imagined that it would magically purge mankind of its manias of hatred and greed. Those easy faiths were destroyed by the war after the war, the war which is still raging.[48]

Little more than a year after this essay appeared, the United States and the world economy faced the beginning of the Great Depression, and then in 1933 Hitler came to power in Germany, promising his own version of the new world order. Thus, in 1936, with another war on the horizon—in many respects the continuation of the Great War—one young liberal theologian was finally able to write that "our sense of what is possible in history is being revised." Departing from the optimism of the progressive generation he saw "little visible promise of the Christianizing of the social order."[49]

The fact that theologians in the 1930s began to reconsider "what is possible in history" marked an unmistakable change in the mind of the liberal clergy. Since the beginning of their spiritual migration away from traditional Christianity, the progressive clergy had anticipated great good to come from the redemptive hand of history. The God of progress guided His creation toward perfection, and carried humanity from barbarism to civilization. The clergy had promised to transform the world through the power of a social gospel that would reconstruct every corrupt institution that impeded man's progress toward the kingdom of God on earth.

In 1914, when the Great War came, the progressive clergy viewed it as an opportunity to thrust the United States further into world affairs, and thereby advance their quest for international unity, democracy, peace, and social justice while simultaneously furthering America's own domestic political, economic, and social reconstruction. They imagined the war as an absolute struggle that mobilized God and Caesar, the City of God and the City of Man, for their ultimate battle. They pictured America, the Christ-nation, as God's chosen instrument for this moment in divine history, sacrificing itself in Wilsonian service to humanity and leading the armies of righteousness to victory. They announced that the war would at last "Christianize" America and the world.

The immediate failure of the War for Righteousness of 1914–1918 did not quench the progressives' zeal for their social gospel imperatives. With righteousness only postponed, the question remains whether the progressive mind ever truly abandoned its perpetual war.

Epilogue

On a brisk Sunday morning in early February 1924, a solemn crowd waited in front of Woodrow Wilson's home on S Street in Northwest Washington, D.C., to hear word of the failing president's condition. A few admirers distributed cards that testified to their faith in Wilson's ideals: "Peace on earth, good will to men." They then knelt in prayer. At 11:15 on that Sunday morning Wilson died. News of his death spread quickly across the city. At the Church of the Epiphany, where the Reverend Randolph McKim had so often summoned America to its duty, the tower bells tolled Wilson's passing by playing "The Strife Is O'er, the Battle Done."[1]

Harry Emerson Fosdick was preaching at New York's "Old First" when he received word of Wilson's death. He waited until the end of his sermon before sharing the news with his congregation. "I have been preaching under difficulty," he told them. "My heart has been heavy. Ex-President Wilson has fallen to sleep since we began our worship here this morning." The congregation then stood and sang "For All the Saints Who from Their Labors Rest." In hushed tones, the choir sang alone on the verse that includes the phrase "Soon, soon, to faithful warriors cometh rest."[2]

Commenting on Wilson's death, former British prime minister David Lloyd George expressed his understanding of Wilson and of his relationship to the world: "Woodrow Wilson was a very great man, and like all

great men, had his defects, but these will be quickly forgotten in the magnitude of his life work. True[,] he was a failure, but a glorious failure. He
failed as Jesus Christ failed, and, like Christ, sacrificed his life in pursu-
ance of his noble ideal."[3]

Three days later, Wilson's body was laid in the crypt of Bethlehem
Chapel under the towering gothic apse of the unfinished Washington Cathedral, near the spot where, ten years before, in August 1914, Randolph
McKim had prayed at the "Peace Cross." The entrance to the chapel bore
the inscription "The Way to Peace." The Federal Council of Churches released a statement eulogizing the president: "The ideals to which Mr. Wilson gave memorable expression were the ideals of the churches. . . . He
has stirred the soul of America and called us to the path of world service
from which there can be no turning back."[4]

A FEW MONTHS after Wilson's death, a group of tourists led by the
Reverend Charles Macfarland visited the chapel in Staunton, Virginia,
where the wartime president had been baptized as an infant. A veteran of
the Church Peace Union and the Federal Council of Churches, Macfarland
discoursed for the benefit of his pilgrims on the stages of American history.
The United States, he declared, had at last entered into the "fourth and
greatest era" in her history, the age of idealism, in which her light would
"shine across the face of the world of nations." Of course, as the light of the
world, the Christ-nation had required a John the Baptist to prepare the
way. And Macfarland knew who that had been: "I say it advisedly, I say it
reverently—there was a man sent of God whose name was Woodrow
Wilson, to bear witness to that light of the world." Changing metaphors,
he lamented that Wilson, like Moses on Mt. Pisgah, had been allowed by
God to see the Promised Land but not to enter it. Nevertheless, he assured
his listeners, when the world at last crossed the Jordan River into that holy
land, there would be no doubt as to who their Moses had been.[5]

ON THE ARMISTICE Day preceding his death, Wilson had greeted a parade
of veterans and well-wishers that had passed before his Washington home,
some of whom bore League of Nations banners in their hands. Reporter
Mark Sullivan noted the religious atmosphere of the occasion. After

Wilson delivered his prepared remarks, the band began playing "How Firm a Foundation," but the president turned and indicated that he had something further to say. "Just one word more," he began; "I cannot refrain from saying it. I am not one of those that have the least anxiety about the triumph of the principles I have stood for. I have seen fools resist Providence before, and I have seen their destruction. . . . That we shall prevail is as sure as God reigns."[6]

Several weeks later, Raymond Fosdick, brother of the Baptist preacher and chairman of the Commission on Training Camp Activities under Wilson, visited Wilson in his Washington home shortly before the president's death. As the two men talked of the League of Nations and the glimmers of its success, Wilson, "with tears rolling down his face," exclaimed, "You can't fight God!" On the day Wilson died, Fosdick delivered a radio tribute to his fallen hero. Conjuring up "The Battle Hymn of the Republic" once more and capturing the experiences and aspirations of an entire generation, he said, "Woodrow Wilson is dead—but his truth is marching on!"[7]

NOTES

INTRODUCTION

1. William E. Leuchtenburg, "Progressivism and Imperialism: The Progressive Movement and American Foreign Policy, 1898–1916," *Mississippi Valley Historical Review* 39 (December 1952): 483, 500–501. For a dissenting conclusion, see John Milton Cooper Jr., "Progressivism and American Foreign Policy: A Reconsideration," *Mid-America* 51 (October 1969): 260–77. The historiographical debate generated by Leuchtenburg's claim is reviewed in John A. Thompson, *Reformers and War: American Progressive Publicists and the First World War* (Cambridge: Cambridge University Press, 1987), 117–19.

2. Herbert Butterfield, *Christianity, Diplomacy and War* (New York: Abingdon-Cokesbury Press, n.d.), 26–67.

3. Jan Willem Schulte Nordholt, *The Myth of the West: America as the Last Empire,* trans. Herbert H. Rowen (Grand Rapids, Mich.: Wm. B. Eerdmans Publishing Co., 1995), 23 and passim.

4. John Winthrop, "A Modell of Christian Charity," in Conrad Cherry, ed., *God's New Israel: Religious Interpretations of American Destiny,* revised and updated ed. (Chapel Hill, N.C.: University of North Carolina, 1998), 37–41.

5. These images and those in the following paragraphs are a composite from several well-known sources from the 1630s through the 1660s. See primarily Edward Johnson, "Wonder-Working Providence of Sions Saviour," in Perry Miller and Thomas H. Johnson, eds., *The Puritans: A Sourcebook of Their Writings,* vol. 1, revised ed. (New York: Harper Torchbooks, 1963), 148; Thomas Shepard, "A Defence of the Answer," in Miller and Johnson, eds., *The*

Puritans, 119; and Michael Wigglesworth, "God's Controversy with New England," in Cherry, ed., *God's New Israel,* 42–53.

6. Sacvan Bercovitch, *The American Jeremiad* (Madison, Wisc.: The University of Wisconsin Press, 1978), 8–9.

7. Ibid., 9.

8. Ernest Lee Tuveson, *Redeemer Nation: The Idea of America's Millennial Role* (Chicago: University of Chicago Press, 1968), 97.

9. Francis Bacon, *The Advancement of Learning,* edited and with an introduction by G. W. Kitchin (London: Dent, 1965), 79–80.

10. Francis Bacon, *The New Organon,* in Richard Foster Jones, ed., *Essays, Advancement of Learning, New Atlantis, and Other Pieces* (New York: Odyssey Press, 1937), 92.

11. Ibid., 267.

12. Quoted in Bercovitch, *American Jeremiad,* 43.

13. Cotton Mather, *The Great Works of Christ in America,* vol. 1 (Edinburgh: The Banner of Truth Trust, 1979), 45–46 (emphasis in original). Mather's work, originally entitled *Magnalia Christi Americana,* was first published in London in 1702.

14. David Lyle Jeffrey, *The People of the Book: Christian Identity and Literary Culture* (Grand Rapids, Mich.: Wm. B. Eerdmans Publishing Co., 1996), 321.

15. Nathaniel Hawthorne, *The Scarlet Letter,* introduction by Kathryn Harrison (New York: The Modern Library, 2000), 228.

16. Mather, *The Great Works of Christ in America,* 46.

17. Bercovitch, *American Jeremiad,* 90. See also p. 114.

18. Johnson, "Wonder-Working Providence," in Miller and Johnson, eds., *The Puritans,* 159.

19. Bercovitch, *American Jeremiad,* 93–94.

20. Quoted in Tuveson, *Redeemer Nation,* 25.

21. Nathan O. Hatch, *The Sacred Cause of Liberty: Republican Thought and the Millennium in Revolutionary New England* (New Haven, Conn.: Yale University Press, 1977), 22

22. Samuel Sherwood, "The Church's Flight into the Wilderness," in Ellis Sandoz, ed., *Political Sermons of the American Founding Era, 1730–1805* (Indianapolis, Ind.: Liberty Press, 1991), 517–18.

23. Ezra Stiles, "The United States Elevated to Glory and Honour," in Cherry, ed., *God's New Israel,* 82–92.

24. Ibid., 85.

25. Ibid., 90–91.

26. Hatch, *The Sacred Cause of Liberty,* 24.

27. Abraham Keteltas, "God Arising and Pleading His People's Cause," in Sandoz, ed., *Political Sermons of the American Founding Era,* 595–96.

28. Ibid., 598, 603.

29. Ibid., 603–4.

30. Schulte Nordholt, *The Myth of the West,* 111.

31. J. Hector St. John de Crèvecoeur, *Letters from an American Farmer and Sketches of Eighteenth-Century America,* edited and with an introduction by Albert E. Stone (New York: Penguin, 1981), 67–70.

32. Ibid., 70, 82.

33. Ibid., 70.

34. Richard Price, "Discourse on the Love of Our Country," in Sandoz, ed., *Political Sermons of the American Founding Era,* 1027. This oration provoked Edmund Burke to write his *Reflections on the Revolution in France.*

35. Richard Price, "Observations on the Importance of the American Revolution" (1784), in Jack P. Green, ed., *From Colonies to Nation, 1763–1789: A Documentary History of the American Revolution* (New York: W. W. Norton, 1975), 422–25.

36. Ibid., 423, 424 (emphasis in original).

37. Ibid., 425.

38. Arthur S. Link, et al., eds., *The Papers of Woodrow Wilson.* (Princeton, N.J.: Princeton University Press, 1966-1993), 41: 526-27.

39. Nathaniel Hawthorne, *The Blithedale Romance* (Oxford: Oxford University Press, 1991), 62, 117.

40. Herman Melville, *White-Jacket, or The World in a Man-of-War,* ed. Harrison Hayford et al. (Evanston, Ill.: Northwestern University Press, 2000), 150–51.

41. Schulte Nordholt, *The Myth of the West,* 65.

42. Hawthorne, *The Scarlet Letter,* 42.

43. Quoted in Bercovitch, *American Jeremiad,* 171.

44. Robert W. Johannsen, *The Frontier, the Union, and Stephen A. Douglas* (Urbana, Ill.: University of Illinois Press, 1989), 77.

45. John L. O'Sullivan, "The Great Nation of Futurity," *The United States Democratic Review* 6, no. 23 (November 1839): 426–30.

46. Ibid., 426, 427.

47. Ibid., 427, 430.

48. Lyman Beecher, "A Plea for the West," in Cherry, ed., *God's New Israel,* 122–30.

49. Ibid., 123.

50. Ibid., 130.

51. Cited in Tuveson, *Redeemer Nation,* 78.

52. Robert Barnwell Rhett, Speech at Grahamville, S.C., 4 July 1859, in Robert W. Johannsen, ed., *Democracy on Trial: A Documentary History of American Life, 1845–1877,* 2d ed. (Urbana, Ill.: University of Illinois Press, 1988), 144–56.

53. Ibid., 151.

54. Henry Ward Beecher, "The Battle Set in Array," in Cherry, ed., *God's New Israel,* 183.

55. Ibid., 172–75, 182.

56. Henry Ward Beecher, "The Tendencies of American Progress," in Cherry, ed., *God's New Israel,* 235–248.

57. For a fuller treatment of this theme, see my "Savior Nation: Woodrow Wilson and the Gospel of Service," *Humanitas* 14, no. 1 (2001): 4–22.

58. For a critical analysis of the reuse of this language, see David Lyle Jeffrey, *People of the Book: Christian Identity and Literary Culture* (Grand Rapids, Mich.: Wm. B. Eerdmans Publishing Co,, 1996), 327–328.

1 A Vast Spiritual Migration

1. *New York Times,* 9 November 1897; W. A. Hoffecker, "Warfield, Benjamin Breckenridge," in *Dictionary of Christianity in America,* Daniel G. Reid, coordinating ed., (Downers Grove, Ill.: InterVarsity Press, 1990), 1234–35.

2. *New York Times,* 8 November 1897; 12 November 1897.

3. M. G. Toulouse, "Beecher, Henry Ward," in *Dictionary of Christianity in America,* 123.

4. On Bushnell's theology, see the introduction to H. Shelton Smith, ed., *Horace Bushnell* (New York: Oxford University Press, 1965).

5. Washington Gladden, *Recollections* (Boston: Houghton Mifflin and Co., 1909), 167; Charles Howard Hopkins, *The Rise of the Social Gospel in American Protestantism* (New Haven, Conn.: Yale University Press, 1940), 5; M. S. Massa, "Bushnell, Horace," in *Dictionary of Christianity in America,* 202–3; Charles A. Dinsmore, "Bushnell, Horace," in *Dictionary of American Biography,* vol. 3, 350–54.

6. George A. Gordon, *My Education and Religion: An Autobiography* (Boston: Houghton Mifflin Co., 1925), 13, 15, 192–98, 217, 274, 311–12.

7. William Jewett Tucker, *My Generation: An Autobiographical Interpretation* (Boston: Houghton Mifflin Co., 1919), 138.

8. *New York Times,* 12 November 1897.

9. John Maynard Keynes, *The Economic Consequences of the Peace* (New York: Harcourt, Brace and Howe, 1920), 4.

10. Historian William R. Hutchison identified adaptation, the immanence of God, and a faith in progress toward the kingdom of God as the essential principles of theological modernism. Hutchison, *The Modernist Impulse in American Protestantism* (Cambridge, Mass.: Harvard University Press, 1976), 2.

11. *New York Times,* 12 November 1897.

12. Lyman Abbott, "The New Puritanism" in Lyman Abbott et al., *The New Puritanism* (New York: Fords, Howard, and Hulbert, 1898), 26–28, 31.

13. George A. Gordon, "The Theological Problem for To-Day" in Abbott et al., *The New Puritanism,* 143. See also, Gordon, *My Education and Religion,* 118–19.

14. Lyman Abbott, *Reminiscences,* with an introduction by Earnest Hamlin Abbott (Boston: Houghton Mifflin Co., 1915), xxx.

15. Washington Gladden, *Ruling Ideas of the Present Age* (Boston: Houghton, Mifflin and Co., 1895), 16.

16. Abbott, "The New Puritanism," 34–38.

17. Lyman Abbott, *The Evolution of Christianity* (Boston: Houghton, Mifflin and Co., 1892), iv–v, 245.

18. Tucker, *My Generation,* 2, 91.

19. Quoted in Mark Sullivan, *Our Times: The United States, 1900–1925,* vol. 1, *The Turn of the Century* (New York: Charles Scribner's Sons, 1926), 363–64.

20. *Encyclopedia Americana,* 1903 ed., s.v. "Progress."

21. Gladden, *Recollections,* 425.

22. Christopher Dawson, *Progress and Christianity: An Historical Enquiry* (London: Sheed and Ward, 1929; Westport, Conn.: Greenwood Press, 1970), 6–8.

23. Tucker, *My Generation,* 2, 4. For a contemporary summary of the impact of evolutionary thought on theology, see Arthur Cushman McGiffert, *The Rise of Modern Religious Ideas* (New York, 1915), 166–86.

24. Gladden, *Recollections,* 425–26.

25. James R. Moore, *The Post-Darwinian Controversies* (Cambridge: Cambridge University Press, 1979), 71.

26. Moore, *Post-Darwinian Controversies,* 224–27; Martin E. Marty, *Modern American Religion,* vol. 1, *The Irony of It All* (Chicago: The University of Chicago Press, 1986), 35–36.

27. Joseph LeConte, from his *Evolution and Its Relation to Religious Thought* (1888), quoted in Arthur O. Lovejoy, "The Argument for Organic Evolution before *The Origin of Species,* 1830–1858," in *Forerunners of Darwin: 1745–1859,* ed. Bently Glass, Owsei Temkin, and William L. Strauss Jr. (Baltimore, Md.: The Johns Hopkins Press, 1968), 379; Moore, *Post-Darwinian Controversies,* 304.

28. On Augustine's philosophy of history, see Robert A. Nisbet, *Social Change and History: Aspects of the Western Theory of Development* (London: Oxford University Press, 1972), 7–8, 63–97.

29. Shailer Mathews, *The Spiritual Interpretation of History* (Cambridge, Mass.: Harvard University Press, 1916), 20.

30. Ibid., 10, 4, 67.

31. Robert Nisbet, *History of the Idea of Progress* (New York: Basic Books, 1980), 171 and passim.

32. Richard J. Bishirjian, "Croly, Wilson, and the American Civil Religion," *Modern Age* (Winter 1979), 33.

33. Abbott, *Evolution of Christianity,* 247.

34. William Newton Clarke, *An Outline of Christian Theology* (New York: Charles Scribner's Sons, 1898), 444.

35. George Gordon read and evaluated an early draft of this book. Brown also corresponded with Clarke about it. See William Adams Brown, *A Teacher and His Times: A Story of Two Worlds* (New York: Charles Scribner's Sons, 1940), 107.

36. William Adams Brown, *Christian Theology in Outline* (New York: Charles Scribner's Sons, 1906), 197, 416, 419–22.

37. Walter Rauschenbusch, *A Theology for the Social Gospel* (New York: The Macmillan Co., 1917), 30; John Buckham, *Progressive Religious Thought in America: A Survey of the Enlarging Pilgrim Faith* (Boston: Houghton Mifflin, 1919), 310; Hopkins, *The Rise of the Social Gospel,* 322.

38. Tucker, *My Generation,* 6.

39. Sydney E. Ahlstrom, *A Religious History of the American People* (New Haven, Conn.: Yale University Press, 1972), 773.

40. William Newton Clarke, *Sixty Years with the Bible: A Record of Experience* (New York: Charles Scribner's Sons, 1909), 7. It is significant that Clarke built his memoirs around his relationship to the Bible. Coming to terms with the nature of revelation was his life's defining experience. As he explained it, "I began, as a child must begin, with viewing the Bible in the manner of my father's day, but am ending with a view that was never possible

until the large work of the Nineteenth Century upon the Bible had been done. Thus I am entering into the heritage of my generation, which I con*Notes to pages 34–40*sider it both my privilege and my duty to accept" (p. 3).

41. Buckham, *Progressive Religious Thought,* 92.

42. Exponent of the New Theology Theodore Munger nearly embraced pantheism. Munger's close friend George Gordon remarked that "Munger was a good deal of a pantheist," and Munger joked about it in his letters to Gordon. Gordon, *My Education,* 312.

43. Kenneth Cauthen, *The Impact of American Religious Liberalism* (New York: Harper & Row, Publishers, 1962; reprint, Washington, D.C.: University Press of America, 1983), 22. See also McGiffert, *The Rise of Modern Religious Ideas,* 187–221. To McGiffert, God's union with humanity made Christ, man, and nature all divine.

44. Gladden, *Recollections,* 427.

45. Tucker, *My Generation,* 92.

46. A. J. Hoover, *God, Germany, and Britain in the Great War: A Study in Clerical Nationalism* (New York: Praeger, 1989), 96.

47. Eric Voegelin, "The Origin of Totalitarianism," *The Review of Politics* 15 (January 1953), 74.

48. Ralph H. Gabriel, ed., *Christianity and Modern Thought* (New Haven, Conn.: Yale University Press, 1924), vii.

49. Abbott, *Evolution of Christianity,* iii.

50. Ibid., iv, vi.

51. Harry Emerson Fosdick, *The Living of These Days: An Autobiography* (New York: Harper & Brothers, Publishers, 1956), 244, vii, 66.

52. Rauschenbusch, *A Theology for the Social Gospel,* 7.

53. Abbott, *Evolution of Christianity,* iii.

54. J. Gresham Machen, "History and Faith," *Princeton Theological Review* 13 (July 1915), 337–351, in Robert L. Ferm, ed., *Issues in American Protestantism: A Documentary History from the Puritans to the Present* (Garden City, N.Y.: Anchor Books, 1969), 262–276. Machen later made the division between liberalism and orthodoxy more explicit in *Christianity and Liberalism* (New York: The Macmillan Co., 1923; reprint, Grand Rapids, Mich.: Wm. B. Eerdmans Publishing Co., 1987).

55. Machen, "History and Faith," 275–76.

56. Ibid., 276.

57. From the publisher's preface to Abbott et al., *The New Puritanism,* iii, iv–v.

2 APPLIED CHRISTIANITY

1. Gladden, *Recollections,* 297–98. See also *Applied Christianity: Moral Aspects of Social Questions,* 9th ed. (Boston: Houghton, Mifflin and Co., 1896).

2. Hutchison, *Modernist Impulse,* 212–13.

3. For the complete text of Barton's sermon, see Edward Bellamy, *Looking Backward, 2000–1887,* edited and with an introduction by Cecelia Tichi (New York: Viking Penguin, 1982), 195–206.

4. Gordon, *My Education,* 150.

5. Shailer Mathews, *The Church and the Changing Order* (New York: The Macmillan Co., 1907), 107.

6. Tucker, "The Church of the Future," in Abbott et al., *The New Puritanism,* 235.

7. W. H. P. Faunce, "Preparation in College for the Study of Theology," in Gerald Birney Smith, ed., *A Guide to the Study of the Christian Religion* (Chicago: The University of Chicago Press, 1916), 10, 15.

8. Hopkins, *The Rise of the Social Gospel,* 167.

9. Robert T. Handy, *A History of Union Theological Seminary in New York* (New York: Columbia University Press, 1987), 114. Quotation from Henry Sloane Coffin, *A Half Century of Union Theological Seminary, 1896–1945: An Informal History* (New York: Charles Scribner's Sons, 1954), 60. Mrs. Dodge also donated the land for the YMCA's New York headquarters, completed in 1908. C. Howard Hopkins, *History of the Y.M.C.A. in North America* (New York: Association Press, 1951), 413.

10. Coffin, *A Half Century,* 72–73, 96. In 1895 Union took the unusual step for a seminary of admitting its first woman student (p. 97).

11. Brown, *A Teacher,* 163–64; Handy, *History of Union,* 100–101. Brown refers to the settlement as "Union Seminary's Settlement," but Handy points out that it was not actually operated by Union Seminary. In Boston, William Jewett Tucker helped found Andover House. See Rossiter's introduction to Abbott et al., *The New Puritanism,* xvi–xvii.

12. See her two personal views of Hull House, *Twenty Years at Hull-House: With Autobiographical Notes* (New York: The Macmillan Co., 1910) and *The Second Twenty Years at Hull-House, September 1909 to September 1929: With a Record of a Growing World Consciousness* (New York: The Macmillan Co., 1930). For her view of the connection between "organized religion and social amelioration," see her introduction to Graham Taylor, *Religion in Social Action* (New York: Dodd, Mead and Co., 1913).

13. Chicago Commons was founded by Graham Taylor, professor of sociology at the University of Chicago Divinity School. See Addams's introduction to Taylor's *Religion in Social Action.*

14. Brown, *A Teacher*, 157, 159. Brown had visited Toynbee Hall and said of Hull House that "generous spirits from all over the country came to learn the new social gospel and to drink from the fount of Miss Addams' idealism" (p. 159).

15. Shailer Mathews, *New Faith for Old: An Autobiography* (New York: The Macmillan Co., 1936), 134.

16. Charles S. Macfarland, *Across the Years* (New York: The Macmillan Co., 1936), 77.

17. Roland H. Bainton, *Yale and the Ministry* (New York: Harper, 1957), 208. Yale's governing corporation included Theodore T. Munger and President William Howard Taft.

18. Charles W. Eliot, *The Religion of the Future* (Boston: John W. Luce and Co., 1909), 2–3 and passim.

19. "The 'New Religion' Propounded by Dr. Eliot," *Current Opinion* 47 (September 1909), 290–93; "The Religion of the Future," *Outlook* 92 (7 August 1909): 827–29.

20. William R. Miller, ed., *Contemporary American Protestant Thought, 1900–1970* (Indianapolis, Ind.: The Bobbs-Merrill Co., 1973), xxvi–xxvii.

21. Ahlstrom, *A Religious History*, 775.

22. Mathews, *New Faith*, 92. A short-lived magazine called *Christendom*, founded in 1903, was merged with *The World Today*. Richard T. Ely was a contributing editor for *Christendom*, which was intended to be an *Outlook* for the Midwest (pp. 90–91).

23. Walter Rauschenbusch, *Christianizing the Social Order* (New York: The Macmillan Co., 1926 [c. 1912]), 20–21.

24. G. B. Smith, *A Guide*, v.

25. *New York Times*, 15 November 1905; 16 November 1905. For a detailed report of the proceedings by a participant, see Elias B. Sanford, ed., *Church Federation: Inter-Church Conference on Federation, New York, November 15–21, 1905* (New York: Fleming H. Revell Co., 1906).

26. Sanford, *Church Federation*, 10–14.

27. Arthur S. Link et al., eds., *The Papers of Woodrow Wilson* (Princeton, N.J.: Princeton University Press, 1966–1994), 16:227, 228 [hereinafter abbreviated as *PWW*]. Speech preserved in outline form, but parts of it were reported by New York papers. On Wilson's relationship to Mott, see C. Howard Hopkins, *John R. Mott, 1865–1955* (Grand Rapids, Mich.: Wm. B. Eerdmans Publishing Co., 1979), 398–400, 435–38.

28. *New York Times*, 16 November 1905; 18 November 1905; 19 November 1905. For a complete text of the federation plan see Sanford, *Church Federation*, 33–36.

29. *New York Times*, 22 November 1905; Sanford, *Church Federation*, 27. On the 1905 meeting, see also Samuel McCrea Cavert, *The American Churches in the Ecumenical Movement, 1900–1968* (New York: Association Press, 1968), 43–51.

30. Rauschenbusch, *Christianizing the Social Order,* 14–16.

31. Harry F. Ward, *The Social Creed of the Churches* (New York: The Abingdon Press, 1914), 5, 7. The remainder of this book is Ward's point by point explanation of the creed. Each chapter includes a helpful list of "best books." In 1914 Ward was secretary of the Methodist Federation for Social Service and associate secretary of the Federal Council's Commission on the Church and Social Service. In 1919 the YMCA adopted the Social Creed. See Hopkins, *YMCA,* 438.

32. Robert A. Schneider, "Voice of Many Waters: Church Federation in the Twentieth Century," in William R. Hutchison, ed., *Between the Times* (Cambridge: Cambridge University Press, 1988), 113.

33. Macfarland, *Across the Years,* 96.

34. Tucker, "The Church of the Future," 229. Historian Sydney Ahlstrom pointed out that it was possible for the liberal Protestants to talk warmly about Christian union and yet not consider the Catholic Church in their plans. The Reformation had been the work of progress after all, and the Roman church remained the representative of obscurantism and authoritarianism. Ahlstrom, *A Religious History,* 780.

35. Samuel Zane Batten, *The Social Task of Christianity: A Summons to the New Crusade* (New York: Fleming H. Revell Co., 1911), 227. Batten was professor of social science, Des Moines College, Iowa, chairman of the Social Service Commission of the Northern Baptist Convention, and a member of Rauschenbusch's Brotherhood of the Kingdom.

36. Rauschenbusch, *Christianity and the Social Crisis,* (New York: The Macmillan Company, 1907), 355.

37. McGiffert, *The Rise of Modern Religious Ideas,* 79.

38. Schneider, "Voice of Many Waters," 106, 114.

39. Paul Elmer More, "The New Morality," *The Unpopular Review* 1 (January 1914), 56.

40. Study of the social gospel movement has benefited from several histories, among them C. Howard Hopkins, *The Rise of the Social Gospel in American Protestantism, 1865–1915* (New Haven, Conn.: Yale University Press, 1940); Aaron Ignatius Abell, *The Urban Impact on American Protestantism, 1865–1900* (Cambridge, Mass.: Harvard University Press, 1943; London: Humphrey Milford, 1943); Henry F. May, *Protestant Churches and Industrial America* (New York: Harper and Brothers, 1949); Paul A. Carter, *The Decline and Revival of the Social Gospel* (Ithaca, N.Y.: Cornell University Press, 1956); Donald K. Gorrel, *The Age of Social Responsibility: The Social Gospel and the Progressive Era, 1900–1920* (Macon, Ga.: Mercer University Press, 1988); and Susan Curtis, *A Consuming Faith: The Social Gospel and Modern American Culture* (Baltimore, Md.: The Johns Hopkins University Press, 1991).

41. Carter, *The Decline and Revival of the Social Gospel,* 11, 13–14.

42. Curtis, *A Consuming Faith,* 3.

43. For an account of the rural church reform movement and the activities of the Federal Council of Churches, see James H. Madison, "Reformers and the Rural Church, 1900–1950," *Journal of American History* 73 (1986), 645–68.

44. Mathews, *New Faith,* 122.

45. Shailer Mathews, *The Gospel and the Modern Man* (New York: The Macmillan Co., 1910), 36–53, 59. See also Shailer Mathews, *The Social Gospel* (Philadelphia: The Griffith & Rowland Press, 1910), passim, for a succinct discussion of the social gospel by a contemporary.

46. Mathews, *The Gospel and the Modern Man,* 169.

47. Richard Hofstadter, *Social Darwinism in American Thought,* rev. ed. (New York: George Braziller, 1959), 108. A. C. McGiffert believed that evolutionary thought and the social view of man were "closely akin." "Both of them involve unity and continuity. All things are vitally connected with one another." McGiffert, *The Rise of Modern Religious Ideas,* 273.

48. Brown, *Christian Theology in Outline,* 193–94.

49. Mathews, *The Gospel and the Modern Man,* 326. It is important to note that while American Protestantism was beginning to divide into distinct theological camps by 1910 when Mathews made this comment, some theological conservatives, such as William Jennings Bryan and J. Wilber Chapman, supported church federation and a degree of social activism. Of course, this period of "overlap" between modernism and fundamentalism did not last long.

50. Mathews, *The Church and the Changing Order,* 105.

51. Mathews, *The Gospel and the Modern Man,* 6, 305–6.

52. Ibid., 178.

53. Sullivan, *Our Times,* vol. 4, *The War Begins, 1909–1914,* 124.

54. Charles Edward Jefferson, *The New Crusade: Occasional Sermons and Addresses* (New York: Thomas Y. Crowell & Co., 1907), 3–7.

55. Robert M. Crunden, *Ministers of Reform: The Progressive Achievement in American Civilization, 1889–1920* (New York: Basic Books, 1982), 210–19; G. Wallace Chessman, *Theodore Roosevelt and the Politics of Power* (Boston: Little, Brown and Co., 1969), 183–84; Gifford Pinchot, *The Fight for Conservation,* with an introduction by Gerald D. Nash (Seattle: University of Washington Press, 1967), 90–92.

56. Ely, *The Social Law of Service,* quoted in Robert T. Handy, *A Christian America: Protestant Hopes and Historical Realities* (New York: Oxford University Press, 1984), 144–45.

57. Richard T. Ely, *Ground under Our Feet: An Autobiography,* reprint of the 1938 edition (NewYork: Arno Press, 1977), 72, 77, 78, 88–91, 140, 295. Ely also wrote *Social Aspects of Christianity.*

58. Crunden, *Ministers of Reform,* 45, 49–51; Hopkins, *Rise of the Social Gospel,* 184–200.

59. Samuel Zane Batten. *The Christian State:The State, Democracy and Christianity* (Philadelphia:The Griffith & Rowland Press, 1909), 4, 10, 12, 14.

60. Ibid., 165, 288, 291–92, 421, 438.

61. Peter Clark Macfarlane, "Washington Gladden:The First Citizen of Columbus," *Collier's* 49 (29 June 1912), 24.

62. Nisbet, *Idea of Progress,* 276–86.

63. W[illiam] P. Merrill, "The Day of the People Is Dawning," *Christian Century* 34, no. 17 (26 April 1917), 9. Merrill was an ardent internationalist.This poem was included in the Disciple's *Hymns of the United Church,* and used to advertise the hymnal in the *Christian Century* in the 1920s.

64. Batten, *The Social Task,* 8, 228.

65. More, "New Morality," 54.

66. Mathews, *The Church and the Changing Order,* 6–7, 8, 255. See also George A. Gordon, "Reasonable Hopes for American Religion," *Atlantic Monthly* 111 (June 1913), 830, 836.

67. Mathews, *The Gospel and the Modern Man,* 57–58. See also Mathews, *The Spiritual Interpretation of History* (1916), passim, 4, 39.

3 Applied Christianity Abroad

1. See William Hutchison, *Errand to theWorld:American Protestant Thought and Foreign Missions* (Chicago:The University of Chicago Press, 1987), 122–132, and his *Modernist Impulse,* 144. For missionary efforts in the decades preceding the First World War, see especially *Errand,* chapters 4 and 5.

2. William Douglas Mackenzie, *Christianity and the Progress of Man* (Chicago: Fleming H. Revell Co., 1897), 12 and 135–162 passim.

3. Hutchison, *Errand,* 91, 100, 148–50.

4. Paul A.Varg, "Motives in Protestant Missions, 1890–1917," *Church History* 23 (March 1954), 68.

5. Ibid., 72, 77.

6. George Sherwood Eddy, *A Pilgrimage of Ideas, or,The Re-Education of Sherwood Eddy* (New York: Farrar & Rinehart, 1934), 7, 12, 13, 58–59. On his impressions of the Orient, see

Eddy, "Asia Awake and Arising," *World's Work* 28 (August 1914), 401–13. The comment about "physical gospel" is found on p. 409. See also Sherwood Eddy, "An Interview with Yuan Shih-Kai, the First President of the Republic of China," *World's Work* 29 (March 1915), 533–37.

7. Rauschenbusch, *Christianizing the Social Order,* 18.

8. Mathews, *The Social Gospel,* 154–60.

9. Henry Churchill King, *The Moral and Religious Challenge of Our Times* (New York: The Macmillan Co., 1911), 244–45, 309, 312–13.

10. Ibid., 358–64.

11. William H. P. Faunce, *The Social Aspects of Foreign Missions* (New York: Methodist Book Concern, 1914), x, 28, passim.

12. Dorothea R. Muller, "Josiah Strong and American Nationalism: A Reevaluation," *Journal of American History* 53, no. 3 (1966), 490–92, 495, 501.

13. Josiah Strong, *The New Era, or The Coming Kingdom* (New York: The Baker and Taylor Co., 1893), v, 1, 3, 16.

14. From a sermon preached October 11, 1891, and quoted in Jacob Henry Dorn, *Washington Gladden: Prophet of the Social Gospel* (Columbus: Ohio State University Press, 1967), 406.

15. Gladden, *Recollections,* 386–87.

16. Dorn, *Washington Gladden,* 408–14.

17. Gladden, *Recollections,* 388. Gladden presented a very sober view of war and its debilitating moral effects (pp. 221–22).

18. Ira V. Brown, *Lyman Abbott, Christian Evolutionist: A Study in Religious Liberalism* (Cambridge, Mass.: Harvard University Press, 1953), 161–77.

19. Mathews, *The Social Gospel,* 63–69.

20. Herbert Croly, *The Promise of American Life* (New York: The Macmillan Co., 1909), 311–13.

21. Pinchot, *The Fight for Conservation,* 95.

22. David Starr Jordan, "Alsace-Lorraine: A Study in Conquest," *Atlantic Monthly* 113 (May 1914), 688.

23. Frederick Lynch, *The Peace Problem: The Task of the Twentieth Century* (New York: Fleming H. Revell Co., 1911), 9–16, 95, 113.

24. Charles R. Brown, "The Church and the New International Order," Friday evening, 29 May 1914, in Lake Mohonk Conference on International Arbitration, *Report of the Twentieth Annual Lake Mohonk Conference on International Arbitration, May 27th, 28th and 29th*

1914 (Mohonk Lake, N.Y.: The Lake Mohonk Conference on International Arbitration, 1914), 208. Hereafter cited as *Mohonk Report*.

25. Lyman Abbott, in *Mohonk Report, 1896*, 7–11. At an earlier arbitration conference, held in April 1896, in Washington, D.C., Abbott had joined with nearly three hundred members of the American Conference on International Arbitration "to promote," as their report read, "a permanent system of arbitration between the United States and Great Britain," leading eventually to worldwide arbitration. Repeating a familiar theme in internationalism, the conference committee distributed copies of their report to libraries in the hope "that the cause of righteous international peace may thus be promoted." *American Conference on International Arbitration, Washington, D.C., April 22 and 23, 1896* (New York: The Baker & Taylor Co., 1896), preface; the quotation about righteous peace is from a sheet inserted in the front of the report. Josiah Strong and Washington Gladden were also associated with this conference (pp. ix–xiv, 5–7).

26. Abbott, Thursday evening, 4 June 1896, in *Mohonk Report, 1896*, 100, 103.

27. Faunce, Thursday morning, 3 June 1897, in *Mohonk Report, 1897*, 60, 61; Faunce, "Signs of Promise," Wednesday evening, 1 June 1898, in *Mohonk Report, 1898*, 26–27.

28. Strong, "Methods of Promoting Arbitration," Friday morning, 3 June 1898, in *Mohonk Report, 1898*, 73–75. On influencing students see also John R. Mott, Friday morning, 2 June 1905, in *Mohonk Report, 1905*, 137.

29. Abbott, "Christian Forces in Promoting Arbitration," Thursday evening, 1 June 1899, in *Mohonk Report, 1899*, 79–80. Newell Dwight Hillis, speaking at Mohonk in 1906, expressed the same view, saying that of all the kinds of war, wars of self-defense and the defense of the helpless are noble. *Mohonk Report, 1906*, 59.

30. Brown, "The Task of Educating Public Sentiment Difficult but Imperative," Friday morning, 30 May 1902, in *Mohonk Report, 1902*, 98–100.

31. John Milton Cooper, *Pivotal Decades: The United States, 1900–1920* (New York: W. W. Norton, 1990), 104.

32. Abbott, "A Vision of Peace," Wednesday morning, 30 May 1906, in *Mohonk Report, 1906*, 32–33. For attendance, see pp. 167–71.

33. Charles W. Wendte, *Freedom and Fellowship in Religion: Proceedings and Papers of the Fourth International Congress of Religious Liberals, Held at Boston, U.S.A., September 22–27, 1907* (Boston: International Council, 1907), 6–8, 25, 27–28.

34. Ibid., 31. They also sang a new hymn by the elderly Julia Ward Howe.

35. Ibid., 39–42; Charles Royster, *The Destructive War: William Tecumseh Sherman, Stonewall Jackson, and the Americans* (New York: Alfred A. Knopf, 1991; Vintage Books of Random House, 1993), 148–150. For a lively description of Hale in his Boston context, see Arthur

Mann, *Yankee Reformers in the Urban Age: Social Reform in Boston, 1880–1900* (New York: Harper & Row, 1954; New York: Harper Torchbooks, 1966), 11–19.

36. Quoted in Deborah Pickman Clifford, *Mine Eyes Have Seen the Glory: A Biography of Julia Ward Howe* (Boston: Little, Brown and Co., 1979), 270. Ward supported the Spanish-American War as a legitimate war for justice (p. 267).

37. Lynch, "The Church and Internationalism," Thursday morning, 20 May 1909, in *Mohonk Report, 1909*, 77–81. Lynch's critic was H. Hensley Henson, canon of Westminster Abbey. Ibid., 114.

38. Cooper, *Pivotal Decades*, 223.

39. Bryan, Friday morning, 20 May 1910, in *Mohonk Report, 1910*, 165–72.

40. "The Prince of Peace," in Ray Ginger, ed., *William Jennings Bryan: Selections* (Indianapolis, Ind.: The Bobbs-Merrill Co., 1967), 148.

41. *Mohonk Report, 1911*, 4; Bryan, "The Hopeful Outlook for Peace," in *Mohonk Report, 1911*, 46.

42. *Mohonk Report, 1911*, 159.

43. Sanford, "The Federal Council of Churches," Thursday evening, 25 May 1911, in *Mohonk Report, 1911*, 163.

44. Lynch, "A Church Peace League," in *Mohonk Report, 1912*, 197.

45. Charles S. Macfarland, *Pioneers for Peace through Religion* (New York: Fleming H. Revell Co., 1946), 17–23, 28; Sullivan, *Our Times*, vol. 4, *The War Begins*, 161–162. Lynch wrote an admiring biography of Carnegie: *Andrew Carnegie* (New York: Fleming H. Revell Co., 1920).

46. The Federal Council of the Churches of Christ in America, *Annual Reports of the Federal Council of the Churches of Christ in America for the Year 1913* (New York: Federal Council of the Churches of Christ in America, n.d.), 32 [hereafter cited as *FCC Reports*]. *FCC Reports, 1914*, 32–33.

47. Lynch, "The Churches and the Peace Movement," Friday, 29 May 1914, in *Mohonk Report, 1914*, 189.

48. Macfarland, *Pioneers*, 39–40.

49. From Theodore Roosevelt's address before the Progressive Party Convention, Chicago, 6 August 1912, in Arthur M. Schlesinger Jr., ed., *History of American Presidential Elections, 1789–1968*, vol. 3 (New York: Chelsea House Publishers/McGraw-Hill Book Co., 1971), 2226.

50. *FCC Reports, 1913*, 3–4.

51. *PWW*, 30:14.

52. *PWW,* 30:142.

53. *PWW,* 30:186.

54. *PWW,* 30:254.

4 Fit to Serve All Mankind

1. Frederick Lynch, *Through Europe on the Eve of War: A Record of Personal Experiences; Including an Account of the First Conference of the Churches for International Peace* (New York: The Church Peace Union, 1914), 1, 4, 8, 13. Lynch dedicated this book to Andrew Carnegie, "Whose Munificence and Whose Unfailing Certitude that Religion and Goodwill Are One Made Possible The First World Conference of the Churches for International Peace" (from the dedicatory page).

2. For a readable and thorough one-volume history of the Great War, see Martin Gilbert, *The First World War: A Complete History* (New York: Henry Holt and Co., 1994).

3. Lynch, *Through Europe*.

4. Ibid., 7.

5. Ibid., 18.

6. Ibid., 8, 10, 109–12; Charles Chatfield, *The American Peace Movement: Ideals and Activism* (New York: Twayne Publishers, 1992), 21.

7. *FCC Reports, 1914*, 34, 178–79.

8. Lynch, *Through Europe*, 23–25, 36–37.

9. Burton J. Hendrick, *The Life and Letters of Walter H. Page,* 3 vols. (Garden City, N.Y.: Doubleday, Page & Co., 1925), 1:309.

10. Lynch, *Through Europe*, 5–6, 61–62, 100.

11. Ibid., 101, 104–08, 116–17.

12. Macfarland, *Pioneers,* 46–47; Chatfield, *American Peace Movement,* 35–36.

13. "Church Peace Conference Fights War," *Christian Century* 31 (20 August 1914), 799.

14. Lynch, *Through Europe,* 122.

15. Walter Millis, *Road to War: America 1914–1917* (Boston: Houghton Mifflin Co., 1935), 47–48.

16. Quoted in Millis, *Road to War,* 2.

17. Quoted in John R. Nevin, *Irving Babbitt: An Intellectual Study* (Chapel Hill, N.C.: University of North Carolina Press, 1984), 120.

18. William Howard Taft, "A Message to the People of the United States," *Independent* 79 (10 August 1914), 198.

19. Editorial, "Whom the Gods Would Destroy," *Independent* 79 (10 August 1914), 195.

20. Editorial, "Man's Wrath Praising God," *Christian Century* 31 (20 August 1914), 789; Editorial, "Human Progress and the War," *Christian Century* 31 (8 October 1914), 957.

21. Ned B. Stonehouse, *J. Gresham Machen: A Biographical Memoir* (Grand Rapids, Mich.: Wm. B. Eerdmans Publishing Co., 1955), 244.

22. *New York Times,* 21 August 1914.

23. Editorial, "For What Shall We Pray?" *Outlook* 108 (16 September 1914), 119.

24. Editorial, "Prayer and the War," *Christian Century* 31 (24 September 1914), 909.

25. *New York Times,* 5 October 1914.

26. *The (Washington, D.C.) Evening Star,* 5 October 1914.

27. Ibid.

28. *The (Newberry, S.C.) Herald and News,* 6 October 1914.

29. All quotations from "American Opinion on the War," *Outlook* 107 (15 August 1914), 907-08.

30. Randolph S. Bourne, "Theodore Dreiser," *New Republic* (17 April 1915), 7; *Bookman* (January 1914), 463.

31. John Tebbel, *A History of Book Publishing in the United States,* vol. 2, *The Expansion of an Industry, 1865—1919* (New York: R. R. Bowker, 1975), 32.

32. *Everybody's* 32 (April 1915), 450—51.

33. Ibid., 451, 453, 458, 460.

34. Hugh Black, *The New World* (New York: Fleming H. Revell, 1915), 144.

35. Edwin Davies Schoonmaker, "Has the Church Collapsed?" *Century* 89 (February 1915), 481, 483, 488.

36. John Haynes Holmes, *Religion for To-Day: Various Interpretations of the Thought and Practice of the New Religion of Our Times* (Boston: The Beacon Press, 1917), 330, 333.

37. Editorial, "Missions and War," *Outlook* 108 (28 October 1914), 449.

38. Editorial, "Christianity and War," *Outlook* 109 (13 January 1915), 62.

39. Allen R. Dodd, review of *The New World-Religion* by Josiah Strong, in *Bookman* 41 (July 1915), 564.

40. Harry Emerson Fosdick, *The Challenge of the Present Crisis* (New York: Association Press, 1917), 4, 14—20.

41. See James Turner, *Without God, Without Creed: The Origins of Unbelief in America* (Baltimore, Md.: The Johns Hopkins University Press, 1985), 204–07.

42. George A. Gordon, *Immortality and the New Theodicy* (Boston: Houghton, Mifflin and Co., 1897), 87, 88, 90.

43. Henry Churchill King, *Fundamental Questions* (New York: The Macmillan Co., 1917), 2, 4–6, 17.

44. Editorial, "A Mighty Fortress," *Outlook* 107 (15 August 1914), 896.

45. *Outlook* 108 (2 September 1914), 45.

46. Editorial, "The Purpose of the War," *Outlook* 107 (29 August 1914), 1044.

47. Editorial, "God Not on Trial," *Outlook* 108 (30 September 1914), 249–50.

48. Editorial, "Prayer and War," *Outlook* 108 (14 October 1914): 348; Editorial, "Have We Lost Faith?" *Outlook* 108 (25 November 1914), 667.

49. Charles E. Jefferson, *What the War Is Teaching* (New York: Fleming H. Revell Co., 1916), 123–24.

50. Editorial, "God in His World," *Outlook* 111 (1 September 1915), 17–18.

51. Lyman Abbott, "The Last Days of Jesus Christ: VI—Alone on the Cross," *Outlook* 115 (28 March 1917), 559.

5 WITH BATTLE BANNERS FURLED

1. Sidney L. Gulick, *The Fight for Peace: An Aggressive Campaign for American Churches* (New York: Fleming H. Revell Co., 1915), passim, esp. 175–76.

2. Editorial, "Democracy and Military Preparation: The Ideal," *Outlook* 108 (25 November 1914, 664.

3. Ibid.

4. On this point and for a gripping account of the *Lusitania*'s sinking, see Millis, *Road to War,* 154–91.

5. Arthur S. Link, *Wilson: The Struggle for Neutrality, 1914–1915* (Princeton, N.J.: Princeton University Press, 1960), 372; see also Kendrick A. Clements, *Woodrow Wilson: World Statesman* (Boston: Twayne Publishers, 1987), 158–59.

6. *New York Times,* 10 May 1915.

7. Editorial, "The Lusitania Tragedy," *Christian Century* 32 (13 May 1915), 368.

8. *PWW,* 30:147–50.

9. Millis, *Road to War,* 177–178.

10. Charles Seymour, ed., *The Intimate Papers of Colonel House,* 4 vols. (Boston: Houghton Mifflin Co., 1926), 1:439–40.

11. Editorial, *Outlook* 110 (19 May 1915), 103–5; see also Clements, *Woodrow Wilson,* 160.

12. Editorial, *Outlook* 110 (19 May 1915), 117.

13. *New York Times,* 15 May 1915; Frederick L. Paxson, *American Democracy and the World War,* vol. 1, *Pre-War Years, 1913–1917* (Boston: Houghton Mifflin Co., 1936; reprint, New York: Cooper Square Publishers, 1966), 200.

14. Abrams, *Preachers Present Arms: the Role of the American Churches and the Clergy in World Wars I and II, with Some Observations on the War in Vietnam. (*New York: Round Table Press, 1933; reprinted and revised, Scottsdale, Penn.: Herald Press, 1969), 43, 229.

15. McKim, "The National Crisis," in *For God and Country, or The Christian Pulpit in War-Time* (New York: E. P. Dutton & Co., 1918), 1, 4, 5–6, 8, 9.

16. John Grier Hibben, "Preparedness and Peace," Wednesday, 19 May 1915, in *Mohonk Report, 1915,* 86, 88.

17. *New York Times,* 21 May 1915.

18. Harold T. Pulsifer, "The Lusitania," *Outlook* 110 (26 May 1915), 233.

19. Link, *Woodrow Wilson and the Progressive Era, 1910–1917* (New York: Harper & Row, 1963), 177.

20. *New York Times,* 15 June 1915.

21. Randolph H. McKim, "National Opportunity and Responsibility," a sermon preached at the Church of the Epiphany, Washington, D.C., 25 November 1915 (published privately), 3–5.

22. Ibid., 6–9, 11.

23. Annual Message, 5 December 1905, *Works,* 17:347, referenced in Robert E. Osgood, *Ideals and Self-Interest in America's Foreign Relations: The Great Transformation of the Twentieth Century* (Chicago: The University of Chicago Press, 1953), 90.

24. "The Belgian Tragedy," *Outlook* 108 (23 September 1914), 169–78, quoted in Thomas J. Knock, *To End All Wars: Woodrow Wilson and the Quest for a New World Order* (New York: Oxford University Press, 1992), 48; Theodore Roosevelt, "Utopia or Hell," *Independent* 81 (4 January 1915), 13–17.

25. Editorial, "Roosevelt and Righteousness," *New Republic* 9 (13 January 1917), 282.

26. Editorial, *Outlook* 109 (28 April 1915), 950–51.

27. Theodore Roosevelt, *Fear God and Take Your Own Part* (New York: George H. Doran Co., 1916), v.

28. Ibid., 57.

29. Frank Crane, *War and World Government* (New York: John Lane Co., 1915), 34–36, 53–55, 59, 186–90.

30. Frank Crane, "Christianity and War," *Outlook* 109 (3 February 1915), 287.

31. Ibid., 287, 288.

32. *New York Times,* 1 September 1915.

33. "The Peace-Prize Essay," *Literary Digest* 52 (24 June 1916): 1848; Washington Gladden, "The Unescapable Law," *Independent* 88 (13 November 1916), 279.

34. Link, *Woodrow Wilson and the Progressive Era,* 182.

35. Macfarland, *Pioneers,* 18.

36. Charles E. Jefferson, "The Nemesis of Armaments," *Independent* 79 (17 August 1914), 247, 248.

37. Charles Edward Jefferson, *Christianity and International Peace* (New York: Thomas Y. Crowell Co., 1915), 10, 11, 22, 34–35.

38. Ibid., 36, 38.

39. Jefferson, *What the War Is Teaching,* 17.

40. Ibid., 50–51.

41. Ibid., 94, 214, 128.

42. John Whiteclay Chambers II, *The Eagle and the Dove: The American Peace Movement and United States Foreign Policy, 1900–1922,* 2d ed. (Syracuse, N.Y.: Syracuse University Press, 1991), xlviii–xlix, 39.

43. John Haynes Holmes, *New Wars for Old: Being a Statement of Radical Pacifism in Terms of Force versus Non-Resistance, With Special Reference to the Facts and Problems of the Great War,* 5th ed. (New York: Dodd, Mead and Co., 1917), 127, 139. This book was first published in 1916, and its preface is dated November 1, 1915.

44. Ibid., 349.

45. William Jennings Bryan, "Present Peace Problems and the Preparedness Program," 18 May 1916, in *Mohonk Report, 1916,* 144–46, 149.

46. Quoted in Peter Collier and David Horowitz, *The Rockefellers: An American Dynasty* (New York: Holt, Rinehart and Winston, 1976), 151. Rockefeller helped fund the Federal Council of Churches.

47. *New York Times,* 17 December 1914.

48. *FCC Reports, 1915,* 7, 8.

49. *PWW,* 35:329, 330, 333–34. This interpretation of Christianity as primarily a religion

of service rather than of personal redemption was a common theme of Wilson's. See his address to the YMCA celebration, Pittsburgh, Pa., 24 October 1914.

50. *PWW,* 35: 335.

51. *PWW,* 35: 343, 344.

52. Cooper, *The Pivotal Decades,* 235; Clements, *Woodrow Wilson,* 160; Millis, *Road to War,* 187–91, 237–38; William Allen White, *The Autobiography of William Allen White* (New York: The Macmillan Co., 1946), 514; Link, *Woodrow Wilson and the Progressive Era,* 179–80.

53. *New York Times,* 17 December 1915.

54. Gulick, *Fight for Peace,* 7, 8, 9.

55. Ibid., 37, 175, 57, 60.

56. Frederick Lynch, "Religion the Basis of Peace," 21 May 1915, in *Mohonk Report, 1915,* 140.

57. Frederick Lynch, *The Challenge: The Church and the New World Order* (New York: Fleming H. Revell Co., 1916), 20, 33, 187.

58. Address to the Railway Business Association, New York, 27 January 1916, *PWW,* 36:10.

59. Cooper, *Pivotal Decades,* 225–27; Clements, *Woodrow Wilson,* 129–30.

60. *PWW,* 38:79, 83.

61. Robert Freeman Smith, *The United States and Revolutionary Nationalism in Mexico, 1916–1932* (Chicago: The University of Chicago Press, 1972), 54–57.

62. Mott to Wilson, 10 November 1916, *PWW,* 38:631.

63. Quoted in Smith, *The United States and Revolutionary Nationalism in Mexico,* 56.

64. Shailer Mathews, "Ethics for an International Policeman," *Biblical World* 48 (July 1916), 1, 2.

65. Randolph Bourne, "The War and the Intellectuals," in *War and the Intellectuals: Essays by Randolph S. Bourne, 1915–1919,* edited and with an introduction by Carl Resek (New York: Harper Torchbooks, 1964), 8.

66. Chambers, *The Eagle and the Dove,* 74–75.

67. William Howard Taft, "The Challenge of the War," *Christian Century* 33 (29 June 1916), 6. The letter was signed by Mathews, Macfarland, Hamilton Holt, and others.

68. Macfarland, *Pioneers,* 56–57, 59.

69. Knock, *To End All Wars,* 56.

70. *League to Enforce Peace: American Branch* (New York: League to Enforce Peace, 1915), xi–xii; A. Lawrence Lowell, *A League to Enforce Peace,* World Peace Foundation Pamphlet

Series, vol. 5, no. 5, part 1, October 1915 (Boston: World Peace Foundation), back cover.

71. Shailer Mathews, "What the Churches Have at Stake in the Success of the League to Enforce Peace," in League to Enforce Peace, *Enforced Peace: Proceedings of the First Annual National Assemblage of the League to Enforce Peace, Washington, May 26–27, 1916* (New York: League to Enforce Peace, 1916), 168.

72. Editorial, "The Brown University Celebration," *Outlook* 108 (21 October 1914): 403; *New York Times,* 15 June 1915.

73. *New York Times,* 26 April 1916.

74. Knock, *To End All Wars,* 57.

75. John Wright Buckham, "The Principles of Pacifism," *Biblical World* 48 (August 1916), 89.

76. Editorial, *New Republic* 6 (26 February 1916), 101.

77. *PWW,* 33:37–41.

78. *New York Times,* 13 and 14 May 1916.

79. Lyman Abbott, "The Pathway to Peace," 17 May 1916, in *Mohonk Report, 1916,* 36.

80. *New York Times,* 18 May 1916.

81. McKim, "The 'Lusitania' Anniversary," in *For God and Country*, 26–28, 32–33, 36.

82. *The (Washington, D.C.) Evening Star*, 14 June 1916. For the text of Wilson's speech, see *PWW,* 37:221–25.

83. Editorial, "Religion in the Coming Political Campaign," *Christian Century* 32 (25 November 1915), 3.

84. Editorial, "Shall We Vote for Wilson?" *Outlook* 113 (23 August 1916), 941–42.

85. Quoted in Sullivan, *Our Times,* vol. 5, *Over Here, 1914–1918,* 235.

86. Clements, *Woodrow Wilson,* 164.

87. "No False Peace: A Warning by American Religious Leaders," *Outlook* 115 (10 January 1917), 63.88. Ibid. The *Outlook* called this statement "one of the notable documents of the World War."

89. "Is the Time Ripe? Comments on the German Proposal for Discussion of Peace, the President's Note and the Allies' Reply," *Independent* 89 (22 January 1917), 149, 152.

90. Gilbert, *The First World War,* 303–17.

91. E. W. McDiarmid, "On the Eve of Armageddon," *Christian Century* 34 (15 February 1917), 13.

92. For an example of martial poetry, see Thomas Curtis Clark, "The Call," *Christian Century* 34 (15 February 1917), 13.

93. Ernest M. Stires, *The High Call* (New York: E. P. Dutton & Co., 1917), 2–11.

94. Ibid., 15–27.

95. *PWW,* 41:353–54.

96. Stires, *High Call,* 29–40.

97. Gilbert, *The First World War,* 317.

98. Ibid., 59.

99. *New York Times,* 26 and 30 March 1917.

100. Stonehouse, *J. Gresham Machen,* 245, 246, 247.

101. Quoted in Alex Mathews Arnett, *Claude Kitchin and the Wilson War Policies.* (Boston: Little, Brown and Company, 1937), 219-20.

101. McKim, "America Summoned to a Holy War," in *For God and Country,* 92.

102. *Literary Digest* 54 (14 April 1917): 1064; *New York Times,* 2 April 1917.

6 A RIGHTEOUS PEOPLE IN A RIGHTEOUS CAUSE

1. Congress, Senate, J. L. Kibler's prayer to open session, *Congressional Record* (2 April 1917), vol. 55, 101; Congress, House, Henry N. Couden's prayer to open session, *Congressional Record* (2 April 1917), vol. 55, 105.

2. *PWW,* 41:519–27.

3. *PWW,* 41:541.

4. Raymond B. Fosdick, *Chronicle of a Generation: An Autobiography* (New York: Harper and Brothers, 1958), 142. Raymond Fosdick was Harry Emerson Fosdick's brother. He served as chairman of both the secretary of war's Commission on Training Camp Activities and the secretary of the navy's Commission as well. The YMCA's John R. Mott worked under Fosdick for the War Department. See *Survey* 39 (6 October 1917), 4.

5. Congress, Senate, Senator Lodge of Massachusetts, *Congressional Record* (4 April 1917), vol. 55, 208.

6. Congress, Senate, Senator Myers of Montana, *Congressional Record* (4 April 1917), vol. 55, 223; Congress, Senate, Senator Colt of Rhode Island, *Congressional Record* (4 April 1917), vol. 55, 223.

7. Congress, Senate, telegram to Woodrow Wilson from the Methodist Episcopal Church, dated April 3, 1917, *Congressional Record* (4 April 1917), vol. 55, 256; *New York Times,* 6 April 1917.

8. Congress, Senate, Senator La Follette of Wisconsin, *Congressional Record* (4 April 1917), vol. 55, 223–34, 226–27, 230–33.

9. Congress, Senate, Senator Williams of Mississippi, *Congressional Record* (4 April 1917), vol. 55, 235.

10. Congress, Senate, *Congressional Record* (4 April 1917), vol. 55, 261.

11. Congress, House, Representative Mason of Illinois, *Congressional Record* (5 April 1917), vol. 55, 328; Congress, House, Representative Rogers of Massachusetts, *Congressional Record* (5 April 1917), vol. 55, 335.

12. Congress, House, letter from J. L. Hughes, Columbus, Ohio, *Congressional Record* (5 April 1917), vol. 55, 338.

13. Congress, House, Representative Rainey of Illinois, *Congressional Record* (5 April 1917), vol. 55, 388.

14. Congress, House, Representative Hulbert of New York, *Congressional Record* (5 April 1917), vol. 55, 404.

15. Margaret Prescott Montague, "Good Friday, 1917," *Atlantic Monthly* 119 (June 1917), 750, 753, 756.

16. Harry Emerson Fosdick, "A Prayer for World Friendship," *Independent* 93 (5 January 1918), 16. This prayer was provided to the *Independent* by Carnegie's World Alliance for International Friendship through the Churches.

17. Stires, *High Call,* 66–70.

18. Congress, Senate, Charles Pressley Simonton's poem with Williams's comments, *Congressional Record* (9 April 1917), vol. 55, 423.

19. Editorial, "Who Willed American Participation," *New Republic* 10 (14 April 1917), 308–09.

20. See Piper, *The American Churches,* passim.

21. Lyman Abbott, "The Duty of Christ's Church To-Day," *Outlook* 116 (2 May 1917): 13–14.

22. Ibid., 14–15.

23. Butterfield, *Christianity, Diplomacy and War,* 26.

24. Editorial, "Patriotism in War and Peace," *Nation* 99 (8 October 1914), 423.

25. *PWW,* 42:451–53.

26. Remarks by the Reverend Wallace Radcliffe to Wilson at the White House, 19 June 1917, *PWW,* 42:535. Radcliffe was pastor of the New York Avenue Presbyterian Church in Washington, D.C.

27. Wilson's reply to a delegation from the PCUSA, 19 June 1917, *PWW,* 42:537.

28. Editorial, "Christianizing Patriotism," *Biblical World* 50 (July 1917), 2.

29. Samuel McCrea Cavert, "The Missionary Enterprise as the Moral Equivalent of War," *Biblical World* 50 (December 1917), 351, 352.

30. Ronald Schaffer, *America in the Great War: The Rise of the War Welfare State* (New York: Oxford University Press, 1991), 10–11.

31. Randolph H. McKim, "God's Call To America," *For God and Country,* 113, 114, 116, 117, 118, 121, 129.

32. Frank W. Gunsaulus, "The War and the America of Tomorrow," *Christian Century* 34, no. 43 (25 October 1917), 10–11.

33. Charles S. Macfarland, "Spiritual Unity through Sacrificial Suffering," *Survey* 39 (29 December 1917), 358–59.

34. Charles Reynolds Brown, "Moral and Spiritual Forces in the War," in E. Hershey Sneath, ed., *Religion and the War* (New Haven, Conn.: Yale University Press, 1918), 17–19, 20.

35. Lyman Abbott, "Democracy or Autocracy—Which?" in League to Enforce Peace, *Win the War for Permanent Peace: Addresses Made at the National Convention of the League to Enforce Peace, in the City of Philadelphia, May 16th and 17th, 1918* (New York: League to Enforce Peace, 1918), 104.

36. Charles E. Jefferson, "What Are We Fighting For?" *Independent* 95 (24 August 1918), 266.

37. Elihu Root, speech in Seattle, 4 August 1917, in *America's Message to the Russian People: Addresses by the Members of the Special Diplomatic Mission of the United States to Russia in the Year 1917* (Boston: Marshall Jones Co., 1918), 62, 64.

38. Root, speech in New York, 15 August 1917, *America's Message,* 72.

39. *New York Times,* 22 May 1917; 7 July 1917; 17 September 1917.

40. *New York Times,* 24 September 1917; 27 November 1917.

41. Newell Dwight Hillis, "What We Are Fighting Against," *Christian Century* 34, no. 42 (18 October 1917), 10–11.

42. David R. Coker to F. R. Chambers, 17 October 1917, in David R. Coker Papers, South Caroliniana Library, University of South Carolina, Columbia, S.C.

43. *New York Times,* 3 December 1917. Hillis returned to Europe in 1918 with a film company to make a movie version of his book *German Atrocities. Bookman* 48 (October 1918), 260.

44. Charles Carroll Albertson, *The Prophets and the War* (New York: The Meridian Press,

1917), foreword, n.p. Albertson was pastor of the Lafayette Avenue Presbyterian Church, Brooklyn.

45. John Haynes Holmes, "H. G. Wells: Novelist and Prophet," *Bookman* 43 (July 1916), 507.

46. H. G. Wells, "As the World Lives On," *Independent* 89 (8 January 1917), 59.

47. H. G. Wells, "The Religious Revival: I," *New Republic* 9 (23 December 1916), 206; "The Religious Revival: II," *New Republic* 9 (30 December 1916), 234.

48. H. G. Wells, *Italy, France and Britain at War* (New York: The Macmillan Co., 1917), 284.

49. Editorial, "Saving Christianity," *Independent* 90 (14 April 1917), 99.

50. On *Mr. Britling Sees It Through,* see David C. Smith, *H. G. Wells, Desperately Mortal: A Biography* (New Haven, Conn.: Yale University Press, 1986), 222–24.

51. H. G. Wells, *God the Invisible King* (New York: The Macmillan Co., 1917), v, xii, xiv, 5, 6.

52. Ibid., 96, 97.

53. Ibid., 97, 111.

54. Editorial, "God and Mr. Wells," *Independent* 92 (3 November 1917), 207.

55. John Macy, "Mr. Britling Sees Spooks," *Dial* 63 (28 June 1917), 15.

56. John Dewey, "H. G. Wells, Theological Assembler," *Seven Arts* (July 1917), 337–38

57. See Edgar DeWitt Jones, "The Tyranny of Trifles in Religion," *Christian Century* 34, no. 34 (23 August 1917), 9–11.

58. Horatio Dresser, *The Victorious Faith: Moral Ideals in War Time* (New York: Harper & Brothers Publishers, 1917), 124, 129–30, 132, 134, 138–43, 219, 220–21.

59. Eugene William Lyman, *The Experience of God in Modern Life* (New York: Charles Scribner's Sons, 1918), 50, 103–04, 109, 145, 149.

60. Henry Churchill King, *The Way to Life* (New York: The Macmillan Co., 1918), 103, 109. Emphasis in original.

61. Edward S. Drown, *God's Responsibility for the War* (New York: The Macmillan Co., 1919), 1–2, 9, 13–15, 21–27, 33–38, 40–41.

62. E. Hershey Sneath, "The Religious Basis of World Organization," *Religious Education* 13 (June 1918), 192.

63. *New York Times,* 13 May 1917. Abbott's comments are from a statement he wrote for the Vigilantes, "Christianity and the War." The Vigilantes was a preparedness organization formed in March 1917 by writers and artists, including the editor of *McClure's,*

Booth Tarkington, Charles Dana Gibson, Hamlin Garland, Bruce Barton, James Montgomery Flagg, William Allen White, and Henry Churchill King, among others. *New York Times,* 18 March 1917.

64. Abbott, "Democracy or Autocracy—Which?" in League to Enforce Peace, *Win the War for Permanent Peace,* 100.

65. Lyman Abbott, *The Twentieth Century Crusade* (New York: The Macmillan Co., 1918), title page, v–viii.

66. Ibid., ix, xi.

67. Ibid., 37, 51, 54, 86, 90.

68. Jefferson, "What Are We Fighting For?", 250.

69. Edward Beecher, quoted in Timothy L. Smith, *Revivalism and Social Reform in Mid-Nineteenth Century America* (New York: Abingdon Press, 1957), 225.

70. See James H. Moorhead, *American Apocalypse: Yankee Protestants and the Civil War, 1860–1869* (New Haven, Conn.: Yale University Press, 1978). The parallels between the liberal Protestant interpretations of the two wars are remarkable.

71. George M. Fredrickson, *The Inner Civil War: Northern Intellectuals and the Crisis of the Union* (New York: Harper & Row, Publishers, 1968), 2.

72. Washington Gladden, "The Social Problem of the Future," in Abbott et al., *The New Puritanism,* 179.

73. Raymond Rossiter, introduction to Abbott et al., *The New Puritanism,* xxii.

74. Hofstadter, *Social Darwinism,* 105; Timothy L. Smith, *Revivalism and Social Reform,* 225.

75. Tucker, *My Generation,* 10–11.

76. David Lloyd George, "The Case for War for Democracy," *Survey* 37 (17 February 1917), 564–65. Originally published in the *New York Times.*

77. Shailer Mathews, "Why We Fight Germany—In Plain Words," *The Pickens (S.C.) Sentinel,* 30 August 1917.

78. Jefferson, "What Are We Fighting For?", 266.

79. Lyman Abbott, "An International Battle Hymn," *Outlook* 116 (27 June 1917), 321.

80. Box 51, Governor Richard I. Manning Papers, South Carolina Department of Archives and History, Columbia, S.C.

81. Robert Latham Owen, *Where Is God in the European War?* (New York: The Century Co., 1918), 14, 49, 51–52.

82. Mathews, *Patriotism and Religion,* preface, 16, 31–32.

83. Ibid., 76, 100, 115.

84. Ibid., 161.

85. Harold Bell Wright, "The Sword of Jesus," *American Magazine* 85 (February 1918): 7–8, 54, 56–57.

86. Quoted in the *Literary Digest* 47 (13 April 1918), 33.

87. Root, "Sympathy with Russia," Address to the American Bar Association, Saratoga Springs, N.Y., 7 September 1917, in *America's Message*, 103, 104.

88. Robert Lansing, "When Peace Comes," *Christian Century* 35, no. 40 (17 October 1918), 10.

89. William Adams Brown, "The Contribution of the Church to the Democracy of the Future," *Religious Education* 13 (October 1918), 343, 348. One writer for the *Atlantic Monthly* promised in 1918 that the church would not be content with a peace short of "the complete mastery and dissipation of every evil organization or movement of government." No compromise; "better that every vestige of our material civilization should be swept away, than that we should compromise the issue between righteousness and evil." George Parkin Atwater, "Peter Stood and Warmed Himself," *Atlantic Monthly* 121 (April 1918), 525.

90. *New York Times*, 27 May 1918.

91. Obituary for Washington Gladden, *Outlook* 119 (17 July 1918), 442.

92. William H. P. Faunce, *Religion and War* (New York: Abingdon Press, 1918), 68.

7 Soldiers of the Cross

1. From a series of articles published in Britain in August 1914 and collected under the title "The War That Will End War." Excerpted in W. Warren Wagar, ed., *H. G. Wells: Journalism and Prophecy, 1893–1946* (Boston: Houghton Mifflin Co., 1964), 79, 82–84. For Wells's importance to the intellectual history of his time, see W. Warren Wagar, *H. G. Wells and the World State* (New Haven, Conn.: Yale University Press, 1961).

2. In December 1914, the *Christian Century* reprinted an article by Wells defining the war as "the Last War" and the beginning of a new era in human history. H. G. Wells, "The World's Last War," *Christian Century* 31 (3 December 1914): 1453; reprinted from the *Metropolitan*.

3. William H. P. Faunce, *The New Horizon of State and Church* (New York: The Macmillan Co., 1918), 21.

4. James's essay excerpted in Chambers, *The Eagle and the Dove*, 14–17.

5. Kirsopp Lake, "The Future of Religion," *New Republic* 11 (9 June 1917), 155.

6. Edward Scribner Ames, *The New Orthodoxy* (Chicago: The University of Chicago Press, 1918), 2.

7. Ames, *New Orthodoxy*, 4, 19–20, 24–25, 103.

8. Wagar, *H. G. Wells: Journalism and Prophecy,* 84.

9. Herbert L. Willett, "The Nation's New Responsibility," *Christian Century* 35 (14 November 1918), 7.

10. Editorial, "The Spiritual Glory of This Day," *Outlook* 116 (30 May 1917), 185.

11. Quoted in *Literary Digest* 59 (2 November 1918), 30.

12. *Literary Digest* 59 (23 November 1918), 31, 32.

13. William Herbert, "The Pulpit and Reconstruction," *Nation* 106 (25 April 1918), 502.

14. Quoted in *Literary Digest* 59 (2 November 1918), 30.

15. George R. Grose, introduction to Faunce, *Religion and War,* 5.

16. Faunce, *Religion and War,* 126–28, 148.

17. Faunce, *New Horizon,* 40.

18. Francis J. McConnell, *Democratic Christianity: Some Problems of the Church in the Days Just Ahead* (New York: The Macmillan Co., 1919), 37, 38. McConnell noted that he wrote the last chapter in October 1918 (p. 76).

19. Samuel McCrea Cavert, "The Missionary Enterprise as the Moral Equivalent of War," *Biblical World* 50 (December 1917), 348, 349, 350.

20. Upton Sinclair, *The Profits of Religion: An Essay in Economic Interpretation* (Published by the author, Pasadena, Calif., 1918), 293, 299–300.

21. George A. Coe, *A Social Theory of Religious Education* (New York: Charles Scribner's Sons, 1917; reprint, New York: Arno Press and The New York Times, 1969), 6.

22. Faunce, *Religion and War,* 153.

23. Herbert L. Willett, quoted in *Literary Digest* 59 (30 November 1918), 30.

24. King, *Way to Life,* 128.

25. Henry Churchill King, "The Church's Responsibility and Opportunity," *Christian Century* 34, no. 35 (30 August 1917, 11.

26. Special Committee of the Federal Council of the Churches of Christ, "Christian Duties in Conserving the Social, Moral and Spiritual Forces of the Nation," *Christian Century* 34, no. 40 (4 October 1917), 9–12.

27. Editorial, "The War and the Social Gospel," *Christian Century* 34, no. 52 (27 December 1917), 5–7.

28. Shailer Mathews, *Patriotism and Religion* (New York: The Macmillan Co., 1918), 131.

29. *PWW,* 42:71–75; Editorial, "From the President to the People," *Outlook* 115 (25 April 1917), 729.

30. McKim, "The Duty of the Hour," in *For God and Country,* 97, 100, 106.

31. Editorial, "The Church and the War," *Outlook* 118 (24 April 1918), 663, 664.

32. Macfarland, *Pioneers,* 65, 68, 71, 73; *FCC Reports, 1918,* 11–12.

33. George Creel, *How We Advertised America: The First Telling of the Amazing Story of the Committee on Public Information That Carried the Gospel of Americanism to Every Corner of the Globe* (New York: Harper & Brothers Publishers, 1920), 3, 4.

34. Macfarland, *Pioneers,* 56–57.

35. *FCC Reports, 1918,* 8, 9.

36. Ibid., 23-24.

37. Quoted from *Harper's Weekly* in Hopkins, *Mott,* 435.

38. Amelia Josephine Burr, "Holy Russia," *Outlook* 115 (28 March 1917), 544.

39. John R. Mott, speech before the Great Sobor of the Russian Orthodox Church, Moscow, 19 June 1917, in *America's Message,* 109–10. Mott's role in the Root Mission is treated extensively in Hopkins, *Mott,* 476–520.

40. Charles R. Crane to Wilson, telegram, 21 June 1917, *PWW,* 43:13, 14.

41. Hopkins, *Mott,* 498–500.

42. Lane to Wilson, 10 August 1917, *PWW,* 43:424.

43. *PWW,* 44: 325–27.

44. Review of *The Fundamentals, Outlook* (16 September 1914), 123. *The Fundamentals,* financed by California millionaire Lyman Stewart, appeared in twelve installments between 1910 and 1915, which were distributed at no charge. See George M. Marsden, *Fundamentalism and American Culture: The Shaping of Twentieth-Century Evangelicalism, 1870–1925* (Oxford: Oxford University Press, 1980), 118–23.

45. Editorial, "Historical Criticism and the War," *Biblical World* 51 (May 1918): 257, 258.

46. See Richard M. Gamble, "'This Sad World': Premillennialists and International Peace during the First World War," *Proceedings of the South Carolina Historical Association, 1991,* 18-28 passim.

47. Ahlstrom, *A Religious History,* 886.

48. Faunce, *Religion and War,* 106.

49. Mathews, *Patriotism and Religion,* 101, 102, 128.

50. Shirley Jackson Case, *The Millennial Hope: A Phase of War-Time Thinking* (Chicago: The University of Chicago Press, 1918), v, vi, vii, 230, 238.

51. *Biblical World* 51 (May 1918), 272.

52. Shirley Jackson Case, "The Premillennial Menace," *Biblical World* 52 (July 1918): 20, 21, 23. For more on Case and Mathews and the *Biblical World* during the war, see Marsden, *Fundamentalism and American Culture,* 146–48.

53. Editorial, "The Millennial Hallucination," *Christian Century* 35, no. 5 (31 January 1918), 8.

54. Herbert L. Willett, "Activities and Menace of Millennialism," *Christian Century* 35, no. 34 (29 August 1918), 7–8.

55. Herbert L. Willett, "Is Christ Coming Again?" *Christian Century* 53, no. 35 (5 September 1918), 6–7.

56. Rauschenbusch, *A Theology for the Social Gospel,* 211.

57. Gamble, "This Sad World," passim.

58. Joseph H. Odell, "Peter Sat by the Fire Warming Himself," *Atlantic Monthly* 121 (February 1918), 145–46. Odell was pastor of the First Presbyterian Church of Troy, N.Y.

59. Wister wrote a prowar book called *The Pentecost of Calamity*.

60. Odell, "Peter Sat by the Fire," 146, 148, 149.

61. Ibid., 150, 151, 152.

62. Ibid., 153, 154.

63. McKim, *For God and Country,* vi.

64. Editorial, "That Other Disciple," *Outlook* 118 (20 February 1918): 280, 281. Odell's and the *Outlook*'s biblical allusions are from John 18.

65. George Parkin Atwater, "Peter Stood and Warmed Himself," *Atlantic Monthly* 121 (April 1918), 521–25.

66. Harry Emerson Fosdick, *The Challenge of the Present Crisis* (Philadelphia: American Baptist Publishing Society, 1917), 2, 3. Over 200,000 copies of this book were distributed in Britain and America. Robert Moats Miller, *Harry Emerson Fosdick: Preacher, Pastor, Prophet* (New York: Oxford University Press, 1985), 80.

67. Fosdick, *The Challenge,* 7, 12.

68. Fosdick, *The Living of These Days,* 121.

69. Faunce, *Religion and War,* 134.

70. Lyman Abbott, "'Our God Is Marching On,'" *Outlook* 119 (7 August 1918), 547, 549.

71. Robert E. Speer, *The Christian Man, the Church and the War* (New York: The Macmillan Co., 1918), 8, 10, 25, 26, 31.

72. Albertson, *The Prophets,* 61, 78, 80.

73. Faunce, *Religion and War,* 168.

74. Herbert L. Willett, "The War and the Kingdom of God," *Christian Century* 35, no. 48 (12 December 1918), 6. Such a view of God was pervasive in liberal theology. In 1918 Methodist Episcopal bishop Francis McConnell wrote that "we cannot think of God as Absolute in the old sense. . . . It is not a mere coincidence that along with the recent growth of the democratic idea there has gone a tendency to insist upon the need of so thinking as to bring Him closer to the streams of human life." McConnell, *Democratic Christianity,* 2, 3.

75. Tyler Dennett, *The Democratic Movement in Asia* (New York: Association Press, 1918), 9, 10–11.

76. Ibid., 5, 252.

77. McConnell, *Democratic Christianity,* vi, vii, 58.

78. Coe, *Social Theory,* 54, 55.

79. H[enry] F. C[ope], Editorial, *Religious Education* 13 (August 1918), 266.

80. Sidney L. Gulick, "Training in World Brotherhood," *Religious Education* 13 (February 1918), 15.

81. Ibid., 16–17.

82. William Pierson Merrill, *Christian Internationalism* (New York: The Macmillan Co., 1918), 1, 3, 4, 7, 9.

83. Ibid., 10.

84. Ibid., 12–13, 15, 67.

85. Ibid., 81, 82, 83. At war's end, the *Christian Century*'s Herbert Willett similarly exulted that America had "at last, and forever, passed from the category of an insular, separated, cloistered nation to that of a world power, respected and honored, and from this time forth destined to be taken into serious account in all the future of international activities." Willett, "The Nation's New Responsibility," 6–7.

86. Merrill, *Christian Internationalism,* 85–87, 89.

8 A NEW WORLD ORDER

1. Seymour, *Intimate Papers of Colonel House,* 110–43.

2. Wilson's Thanksgiving Proclamation, 16 November 1918, *PWW,* 53:96.

3. *New York Times,* 18 November 1918.

4. McConnell, *Democratic Christianity,* 77.

5. Miller, *Fosdick,* 80; Fosdick, *The Living of These Days,* 122.

6. Harry Emerson Fosdick, "The Trenches and the Church at Home," *Atlantic Monthly* 123 (January 1919), passim, 22. For Fosdick's account of reaction to this article, see Fosdick, *The Living of These Days,* 131–32.

7. Fosdick, "The Trenches," 22–24, 26.

8. Ibid., 24–33.

9. Henry Churchill King, *For a New America in a New World* (Paris: The Young Men's Christian Association, 1919), v.

10. Ibid., 2–3, 5, 7, 21, 51, 52, 57.

11. Ibid., 59–60, 61, 63.

12. On Villard's attitude toward the war, see Oswald Garrison Villard, *Fighting Years: Memoirs of a Liberal Editor* (New York: Harcourt, Brace and Co., 1939), 326–47.

13. Editorial, *Nation* 108 (8 February 1919), 183.

14. C. Arthur Lincoln, "Essentials of the Program of a Church in a Democracy," *Religious Education* 14 (June 1919), 170, 171, 172.

15. Charles Edward Jefferson, "The Coming Union of Churches," *Independent* 99 (9 August 1919), 184.

16. Arthur Cushman McGiffert, "Democracy and Religion," *Religious Education* 14 (June 1919), 158, 160–61.

17. J. M. Artman, "The Function of the Association in Relation to Religious Education in the Community," *Religious Education* 14 (October 1919): 322, 323. For a bristling indictment of the YMCA's efforts at social "uplift" among the AEF, see James H. Powers, "The Y.M.C.A. in France," *New Republic* 18 (8 February 119), 55–57.

18. Henry E. Jackson, *A Community Church: The Story of a Minister's Experience Which Led Him from the Church Militant to the Church Democratic* (Boston: Houghton Mifflin Co., 1918), xii, xvi–xvii, xxiii-xxiv, xxx. The book's subtitle was not an indication of disillusionment with the church's involvement with the war, but rather with the church's militant orthodoxy.

19. Ibid., 324, 326, 351, 352.

20. Horace C. Peterson's and Gilbert C. Fite's contention that the churches supported the war "primarily because their members wanted and expected them to do so" does not fit the clergy's behavior or their image of themselves as molders of public opinion. In war and in peace, the churches were active rather than reactive. See *Opponents of War, 1917–1918* (reprint, Seattle: University of Washington Press, 1968), 113.

21. John Marshall Barker, *The Social Gospel and the New Era* (New York: The Macmillan Co., 1919), 207, 213.

22. Editorial, "The Public Opinion of the World," *Christian Century* 35 (12 December 1918), 3.

23. Editorial, "The Voice of the Church," *Nation* 109 (20 December 1919), 788, 789.

24. Editorial, "The Greatest of These," *New Republic* 17 (21 December 1918), 209, 210.

25. Ibid., 211.

26. Editorial, "1919," *Outlook* 121 (1 January 1919), 11.

27. Lyman Abbott, "Lenten Lessons I," *Outlook* 121 (5 March 1919), 383.

28. Lyman Abbott, "Lenten Lessons VI," *Outlook* 121 (9 April 1919), 599.

29. Tippy's neglected role in the social gospel movement is emphasized in Gorrell, *The Age of Social Responsibility*.

30. Worth M. Tippy and Paul B. Kern, *A Methodist Church and Its Work* (New York; Nashville: The Methodist Book Concern and Smith & Lamar, 1919), 68–69.

31. Ibid., 24.

32. On the ACLU, see Chambers, *The Eagle and the Dove,* 166–68.

33. Harry F. Ward, *The New Social Order: Principles and Programs* (New York: The Macmillan Co., 1919), v.

34. Ibid., v, vi, 4, 5, 6, 21–22.

35. Ibid., 9, 14–15, 21–22, 23, 29–30, 35–159. Like several other progressive theologians, such as George A. Coe, Ward also included the wonders of eugenics in his new order. He believed that "select mating" would ensure that greater "capacity will be spread more and more throughout the whole population." A world with too many differences imperiled democracy (p. 365).

36. Ibid, 368, 377, 382–83, 384.

37. "Bolshevism and the Methodist Church," *Current Opinion* 66 (June 1919): 380.

38. Randolph H. McKim, "The Peril of Bolshevism and the Duty of America," A sermon preached 6 April 1919 (Privately printed), 39. Cooper, *Pivotal Decades,* 316.

40. McKim, "The Peril," 6, 9.

41. Alva W. Taylor, "Soviets and Bolsheviks," *Christian Century* 36 (6 February 1919), 13.

42. Frederick Lynch, "The League as a Bulwark against Bolshevism," *Christian Century* 36 (17 April 1919): 6–7.

43. From the plan prepared by the Committee of Direction of the Commission on the Church and Social Service, quoted in the *New York Times,* 14 July 1919; "The Church and Social Reconstruction," *Survey* 42 (2 August 1919), sec. 2, 685–89.

44. Quoted in the *New York Times,* 14 December 1918. The cable was signed by, among

others, William H. P. Faunce, Hamilton Holt, Charles E. Jefferson, Charles Macfarland, Shailer Mathews, William Merrill, John R. Mott, and Robert Speer.

45. Robert H. Ferrell, *Woodrow Wilson and World War I, 1917–1921* (New York: Harper & Row, 1985), 139–40.

46. Quoted in "The President at Church," *Outlook* 121 (8 January 1919), 45–46.

47. "Religion's Opportunity Now That the War Is Over," *Current Opinion* 66 (January 1919), 45.

48. Charles E. Jefferson, "The Great Peace," *Independent* 96 (23 November 1918), 243.

49. Charles E. Jefferson, "The League of Nations and Religion," *Christian Century* 36 (13 March 1919), 7–8.

50. Robert E. Speer, "The Witness Bearing of the Church to the Nations," *Federal Council Bulletin* 2 (June 1919), 92, quoted in Robert Handy, *A Christian America,* 16.

51. Quoted in Miller, *Fosdick,* 91.

52. Charles Edward Jefferson, *What the War Has Taught Us* (New York: Fleming H. Revell Co., 1919), 70.

53. Ibid., 71, 72, 83.

54. *FCC Reports, 1918,* 72–73.

55. Hugh Robert Orr, "Training in the Democracy of Jesus, in the Church School," *Religious Education* 14 (August 1919): 271. Orr was director of education at the Emory Methodist Church, Pittsburgh.

56. *FCC Reports, 1918,* 73–75.

57. Frank Mason North to Wilson, 11 January 1919, *PWW,* 53:718.

58. Wilson to Frank Mason North, 14 January 1919, *PWW,* 54:56.

59. Frederick Henry Lynch to Wilson, 25 January 1919, *PWW,* 54:277–78.

60. Speech by Wilson to the Plenary Session of the Inter-Allied Conference for the Preliminaries of Peace, 25 January 1919, *PWW,* 54:268.

61. Frederick Henry Lynch to Wilson, 25 January 1919, *PWW,* 54:278.

62. The Federal Council of the Churches of Christ in America, *Report of Special Meeting, Cleveland, Ohio, May 6, 7, 8, 1919* (New York: National Office, 1919), 72, 73–74.

63. W. G. McAdoo, *A League to Prevent War* (New York: League to Enforce Peace, 1919), 3–4.

64. Quoted in Edwin S. Gaustad, *A Religious History of America* (New York: Harper and Row, 1966), 325.

65. Miller, *Fosdick,* 90.

66. Editorial, "The Common Guilt," *Christian Century* 36 (18 September 1919), 6–7.

67. Editorial, "The Dilemma of the Covenanter," *Christian Century* 36 (25 September 1919), 7–8; Editorial, "The President's Will," *Christian Century* 36 (2 October 1919), 6–8.

68. Macfarland, *Pioneers,* 73.

69. *New York Times,* 12 December 1919. For more on the church's struggle for the treaty, see James L. Lancaster, "The Protestant Churches and the Fight for the Ratification of the Versailles Treaty," *Public Opinion Quarterly* 31 (winter 1967–1968): 597–619. Lancaster concluded that most support for the treaty came from those "churches most directly influenced by the theology of the 'social gospel'" (p. 599).

9 Righteousness Postponed

1. Irving Babbitt, *Democracy and Leadership* (Boston: Houghton Mifflin, 1924; reprint, with a foreword by Russell Kirk, Indianapolis, Ind.: Liberty Fund, 1979), 25.

2. Machen, *Christianity and Liberalism,* 9–10.

3. R. L. Duffus, "Progress—1917," *New Republic* 11 (14 July 1917), 298, 299–300.

4. Hutchison, *Modernist Impulse,* 185–225.

5. Henry Sloane Coffin, *In a Day of Social Rebuilding: Lectures on the Ministry of the Church* (New Haven, Conn.: Yale University Press, 1918), 14, 15.

6. Charles Reynolds Brown, "Moral and Spiritual Forces in the War," 12–15.

7. Editorial, "The War and the Future of Religion," *Christian Century* 31 (29 October 1914), 1029.

8. Buckham, *Progressive Religious Thought,* 315–16, 317–18.

9. William Austin Smith, "The War and Religion," *Nation* 108 (10 May 1919), 728.

10. Ibid., 728, 729, 730.

11. Charles D. Williams, *The Prophetic Ministry for Today* (New York: The Macmillan Co., 1921), 157, 158. For a summary of his theology and ministry, see *Dictionary of American Biography,* vol. 20, 251–52.

12. Ibid., 158–64, 166–69, 181.

13. Samuel McCrea Cavert, *The Churches Allied for Common Tasks: Report of the Third Quadrennium of the Federal Council of the Churches of Christ in America, 1916–1920* (New York: Federal Council of the Churches of Christ in America, 1921), 12, 13, 15–16, 17, 58, 113–14.

14. Eddy, *A Pilgrimage,* 63, 65, 66.

15. Shailer Mathews, "The Development of Social Christianity in America," in Gerald Birney Smith, ed., *Religious Thought in the Last Quarter-Century* (1927; reprint, Freeport, N.Y.: Books for Libraries Press, 1970), 228–39.

16. Gaustad, *A Religious History of America,* 326–327; L. Ethan Ellis, *Republican Foreign Policy, 1921–1933* (New Brunswick, N.J.: Rutgers University Press, 1968), 82. For Harding's use of the Wilsonian word "service," see his inaugural address.

17. *New York Times,* 12 November 1922; Robert K. Murray, *The Harding Era: Warren G. Harding and His Administration* (Minneapolis: University of Minnesota Press, 1969), 149–150.

18. Thomas H. Buckley, *The United States and the Washington Conference, 1921–1922* (Knoxville, Tenn.: The University of Tennessee Press, 1970), 69, 70–71; Murray, *The Harding Era,* 151, 153–156.

19. *FCC Reports, 1922,* 11, 23–24, 25, 53, 54, 65–66. In his book on the Washington conference, Buckley interpreted the FCC's support as "in part atonement for support of the World War" (p. 174). But this assumes that they believed there was need for atonement, when in fact they did not see any contradiction between the war and permanent peace. The war and the Washington Naval Conference were part of the same application of Christianity.

20. Ibid., 12, 23–25; Marjorie Housepian, *Smyrna 1922: The Destruction of a City* (London: Faber and Faber, 1972), 112. The Protestant churches had a real stake in Smyrna, which was home to two schools operated by the American Board of Commissioners for Foreign Missions, as well as a very active YMCA and YWCA (Housepian, *Smyrna,* 106). The massacre of Christian Armenians by Moslem Turks especially roused American emotion (Murray, *The Harding Era*), 357.

21. Samuel Zane Batten, *If America Fail: Our National Mission and Our Possible Future* (Philadelphia: The Judson Press, 1922), preface, n.p.

22. Ibid., 3–4.

23. Ibid., 5.

24. Ibid., 7.

25. Ibid., 7, 13–14, 18–19.

26. Ibid., 20, 21, 22-40, 185, 241, 243–60.

27. George Creel, *The War, the World and Wilson* (New York: Harper & Brothers Publishers, 1920), 3.

28. Carter Glass to John Stewart Bryan, 3 November 1921, quoted in George Brown Tindall, *The Emergence of the New South, 1913–1945,* vol. 10 of Wendell Holmes Stephenson

and E. Merton Coulter, eds., *A History of the South* (Baton Rouge, La.: Louisiana State University Press, 1967), 69.

29. Harry Emerson Fosdick, *Christianity and Progress* (New York: Fleming H. Revell Co., 1922), unnumbered pages preceding preface, and 8.

30. Ibid., 31–41.

31. Ibid., 42, 43, 45, 106.

32. Ibid., 128, 132–33, 143, 165.

33. Ibid., 171, 175.

34. Ibid., 247.

35. Harry Emerson Fosdick, introduction to Kirby Page, *War: Its Causes, Consequences and Cure* (New York: George H. Doran Co., 1923), vi, vii.

36. Ibid., vii, viii.

37. Ibid., ix. For a more detailed statement of Fosdick's changed view of war, see Harry Emerson Fosdick, "A Christian Conscience about War," in Frederick C. Hicks, ed., *Famous Speeches by Eminent American Statesmen* (St. Paul, Minn.: West Publishing Co., 1929), 731–41. This sermon was given before the League of Nations in Geneva, 13 September 1925.

38. Ralph H. Gabriel, ed., *Christianity and Modern Thought* (New Haven, Conn.: Yale University Press, 1924), vi.

39. Frank Crane, *Why I Am a Christian* (New York: Wm. H. Wise & Co., 1924).

40. Robert E. Speer, "Christianity and International Relations," in Gabriel, ed., *Christianity and Modern Thought,* 195.

41. F. Scott Fitzgerald, *This Side of Paradise* (New York: Charles Scribner's Sons, 1920; Scribner Classics/Collier Edition, 1986), 282.

42. Walter Lippmann, *A Preface to Morals* (New York, 1929), 31–32, quoted in Marsden, *Fundamentalism,* 191.

43. Machen, *Christianity and Liberalism,* 2–10, 54, 63–65, 150–56.

44. Babbitt, *Democracy and Leadership,* 313–314. Charles Howard Hopkins's conclusion in 1940 that the Great War "brought to an end the era of optimism and progress in which social Christianity had developed" simply does not stand. Hopkins, *The Rise of the Social Gospel,* 327.

45. Babbitt, *Democracy and Leadership,* 340.

46. Harry Elmer Barnes, "Was America Deluded by the War?" *Christian Century* 42 (8 October 1925): 1238–1242. See H. Richard Niebuhr, "Back to Benedict?" *Christian Cen-*

tury 42 (2 July 1925), 860–861, in which he accepts the "old antithesis" of a transcendent God and of a church at war with the world.

47. *Christian Century* 42 (2 July 1925), 875.

48. Reinhold Niebuhr, "What the War Did to My Mind," *Christian Century* 45 (27 September 1928), 1161, 1163.

49. John Coleman Bennett, "The Social Interpretation of Christianity," in Samuel McCrea Cavert and Henry Van Dusen, eds., *The Church through Half a Century: Essays in Honor of William Adams Brown* (New York: Charles Scribner's Sons, 1936), 119, 127.

Epilogue

1. *New York Times,* 4 February 1924; Gene Smith, *When the Cheering Stopped: The Last Years of Woodrow Wilson* (New York: William Morrow and Co., 1964), 245.

2. *New York Times,* 4 February 1924, 9.

3. Ibid., 1.

4. *New York Ttmes,* 5 February 1924, 1, 2, 3.

5. Macfarland, *Across the Years,* 265–66.

6. Smith, *When the Cheering Stopped,* 229–32.

7. Raymond Fosdick, *Chronicle of a Generation,* 44; *New York Times,* 4 February 1924, 8. Fosdick recounted the story of his last meeting with Wilson in his radio address and in his memoirs. The transcript of his radio address carried in the *Times* did not include Wilson's comment about the irresistible will of God.

INDEX

ABOUT THE AUTHOR

Richard M. Gamble is Assistant Professor of History at Palm Beach Atlantic University in West Palm Beach, Florida, where he has taught in the history and honors programs since 1994. His essays and reviews have appeared in a number of scholarly and popular journals, including *Humanitas*, the *Journal of Southern History*, and the *Independent Review*.